OREGON BEACHES

A TRAVELER'S COMPANION

JOHN SHEWEY

All inquiries should be addressed to: Caxton Press, 312 Main Street, Caldwell, Idaho 83605.

ISBN# 978-087004-613-1
Library of Congress Cataloging-in-Publication Data

Names: Shewey, John, author.
Title: Oregon beaches, a traveler's companion / by John Shewey.
Description: Caldwell, Idaho: Caxton Press, [2017] | Includes bibliographical references and index.
Identifiers: LCCN 2017041807 (print) | LCCN 2017041952 (ebook) | ISBN 9780870046186 (E-book) | ISBN 9780870046131 (pbk. : alk. paper)
Subjects: LCSH: Beaches--Oregon--Guidebooks. | Oregon--Guidebooks.
Classification: LCC F874.3 (ebook) | LCC F874.3 .S54 2017 (print) | DDC 917.9504--dc23
LC record available at https://lccn.loc.gov/2017041807
Design: BlondCreative: www.blondcreative.com

Printed and bound in Canada.
Published by:

CAXTON PRESS

Caldwell, Idaho USA
198286

Contents

Introduction | 3

Chapter 1: Oregon Beach Basics | 9

Planning a Visit, Beach Safety, Rules and Regulations

Chapter 2: Oregon Beach Activities | 25

Beachcombing, Tide-pooling, Beach Hiking and Biking, Board Sports and Boating, Driving the Beach, Birdwatching at the Beach, Crabbing and Clamming, Surf Fishing

Chapter 3: North Coast Beaches: Clatsop and Tillamook Counties | 69

Chapter 4: Central Coast Beaches: Douglas, Lane, and Lincoln Counties | 149

Chapter 5: South Coast Beaches: Coos and Curry Counties | 259

Appendix: Oregon Beach Events | 386

Appendix: Key Contacts | 394

Acknowledgments | 396

Agate Beach in Port Orford—one of several Agate Beaches in Oregon. Photo by John Shewey

INTRODUCTION

The fertile North Pacific Ocean carves a remarkably diverse 363-mile-long Oregon coastline that ranges from wide, windswept sand beaches to starkly rugged wave-hammered headlands. The state's beaches take many forms: beautiful swaths of gleaming sand stretch for miles; hidden beaches defy access, tucked into tiny coves carved into sheer basalt headlands by eons of pounding surf; rocky beaches guarded by jagged sea stacks teem with marine life. Many Oregon beaches offer solitude and invite exploration and discovery; others draw ebullient summer crowds, especially to beachside communities such as Seaside, Cannon Beach, and Newport.

Whether you seek fun in the sun on a beach crowded with like-minded souls, or prefer solitude on a little-known beach hidden from the masses, Oregon offers opportunity aplenty. The busiest beaches are situated on the central and north coast, within easy reach of the state's population centers (Portland and the Willamette Valley); the south coast, especially the far south, is almost a world of its own, a coastline of tremendous geological diversity tucked into a sparsely populated far corner of the state. Moreover, Oregon's beach crowds, where they occur, are largely seasonal, with some of the most popular summertime beaches being nearly devoid of visitors come winter, when resolute beach lovers don heavy rain parkas to leave lonely footprints in the sand.

Beaches are dynamic environments, ever changing with the tides, waves, wind, and seasons. You can visit the same beach repeatedly and never cease to make new discoveries and observations. That protean nature of beaches is essential to their allure. Their beauty, too, is mercurial. An Oregon beach can be serene and inviting and then quickly transform to dangerous and punishing, but each personality offers unique splendor.

This guidebook is your portal to Oregon's beaches. Every accessible beach in the state is covered herein, from Crissey Field Beach at the California border to Clatsop Spit at the mouth of the mighty Columbia River. *Oregon Beaches, A Traveler's Companion* provides details about beach access, along with tips on activities and amenities, and offers insights gleaned by the author's years of exploring Oregon's coastline.

Remarkably—uniquely—the state's beaches belong to the public and access is assured by law.

Because of Oregon's rugged coastal topography, development along the state's beaches occurred in fits and starts well after the Willamette Valley was already a major far-west hub, both commercially and culturally. Once railroads reached the coast in the late nineteenth century, the Oregon Lands Board started selling parcels of beach and other tidelands, spurring the development of resorts and hotels along the shore. Almost immediately the selling of Oregon coastlands became a subject of heated controversy, and in 1911, in part on his promise to assure Oregon's beaches remain public property, Oswald West (1873–1960) was elected governor of Oregon.

Some years prior, he had served as a state land agent and famously recovered nearly a million acres of state lands fraudulently claimed by private entities and individuals. He was well acquainted with the controversy over the Oregon coastline, and while he faced stout opposition in the Oregon Legislative Assembly, he successfully argued that public ownership of the beaches was necessitated by transportation concerns: with nothing but local roads available to wagons and early automobiles, the state's many long, flat, sand beaches served as thoroughfares—there was simply no other way to drive up and down the coast. So in 1913, the legislature declared that the entire coastline was in fact a public roadway. That same year, the legislature created the Oregon Highway Commission, tasking it with establishing three major roadways in Oregon, one of them being The Coast Highway.

West served but a single term, opting not to run for re-election in 1915, but his legacy is etched in the rugged coastal headlands and the drifting white sands of the publicly owned Oregon seashore. That legacy came under attack in 1966, when Portlander William Hay, owner of the Surfsand Motel in Cannon Beach, figured he had found a loophole in the law that had declared Oregon's beaches to be public highways. He reasoned that because the law stipulated that the state owned the beach from the low-tide line to the high-tide line, any beachfront above that mark was not public. He thus cordoned off his property all the way down to the high-tide line with large driftwood logs—anyone wanting to stroll or drive the beach past his enclosure had to wait for the tide to recede. Guests at the hotel enjoyed lounging in beach chairs under umbrellas; trespassers were not tolerated.

Complaints rolled in, prompting the Oregon Highway Department to investigate, and sure enough, they recognized the loophole in the original beach access legislation from 1913. With guidance from the Highway Department, the House Highway Committee soon produced House Bill 1601, but coastal legislators kept it bottled up despite the best efforts of committee chair Sydney Bazett of Grants Pass. But Associated Press reporter Matt Kramer took up the cause, naming HB 1601 the "Beach Bill," and publicizing its plight in a series of newspaper stories. The ire of the public came to bear, and Governor Tom McCall joined the fight, even taking scientists, media representatives, and lawmakers to Cannon Beach, touring the beach by helicopter and by foot; McCall was photographed glaring at the logs demarcating the upper beach cordoned off by the Surfsand Motel owner.

The long, sand beach south of Cape Lookout on the north coast. Photo by John Shewey

United States Highway 101, the Coast Highway, runs the length of the Oregon coast. Photo by Doug Kerr/CreativeCommons

McCall's actions on behalf of the Beach Bill finally forced opponents of the measure to back down, and the bill passed on June 7, 1967. McCall signed it into law on July 6, saying, "It is one of the most far-reaching measures of its kind enacted by any legislative body in the nation. This bill guarantees that Oregon's coastline will remain secure for generations to come."

The bill, in part, states that "...it is the public policy of the State of Oregon to forever preserve and maintain the sovereignty of the state heretofore existing over the seashore and ocean beaches of the state from the Columbia River on the North to the Oregon-California line on the South so that the public may have the free and uninterrupted use thereof."

Fittingly, Oswald West State Park, about 10 miles south of Cannon Beach, features a memorial to Kramer, which reads, "The people of Oregon hereby express their gratitude to Matt Kramer of the Associated Press, whose clear and incisive newspaper articles were instrumental in gaining public support for passing of the 1967 Beach Bill. This landmark legislation guarantees forever the public's right to the free and uninterrupted use of one of Oregon's most popular recreation attractions, its ocean beaches."

Over the years, though challenges to the beach law have arisen in various forms, Oregon's beaches remain public and largely accessible. However, the beaches are not necessarily entirely public property, and the accuracy of the assumption that they are depends to some extent on definitions and locations. The public owns the wet-sand beach up to the ordinary high-tide line, but the dry-sand beach usually belongs to the adjoining upland property, whether public or private, and in many places the dry-sand beach is private property. Despite the private ownership of some upper beaches, Oregon law nonetheless ensures that the public enjoys perpetual easement to access the dry-sand beach up to what is called the statutory vegetation line or to the line of established upland shore vegetation, whichever is farther inland. So in essence, Oregonians and visitors enjoy the rare privilege and right to recreate on any of the state's many beaches. In places, private property, such as housing tracts and commercial development, blocks ready access to substantial lengths of coastline, but in most such places, easements, even if widely scattered, provide at least limited access.

United States Highway 101—the Oregon Coast Highway—was conceived and completed in the 1920s and 30s, creating a nearly 400-mile-long route that traces the coastline, coursing inland only long enough to circumvent substantial headlands, wetlands, and other obstacles. Engineer Conde McCullough (1887–1946), planned and oversaw construction of the new highway's innovative bridges that span creeks, rivers, bays, and inlets. His work is celebrated throughout the region, and the 5,305-foot-long North Bend Bridge spanning Coos Bay, opened in 1937, was renamed in his honor as the Conde McCullough Memorial Bridge.

The Coast Highway, more recently dubbed the Oregon Coast Scenic Byway, is the artery that provides ready access to the state's incredible diversity of beaches—public beaches for all to enjoy.

CHAPTER 1

Lighthouse Beach near Charleston. Photo by John Shewey

OREGON BEACH BASICS

Oregon Beaches provide year-round intrigue and widespread opportunity for many forms of recreation, from hiking and beachcombing to natural and cultural history to board sports and social celebrations. From vast, miles-long stretches of sand to rugged, surf-battered rocky expanses, and from tiny hidden pocket beaches to popular tourist favorites, the state's coastline offers something for everyone. Within a few miles and a few minutes, anywhere on the Oregon coast, you can go from bustling, busy, energetic beaches to serene, uncrowded—even deserted—little-known beaches.

And the coastal towns that serve visitors to Oregon's beaches are equally diverse, an assemblage of eclectic communities ranging from both historical and working mill towns and commercial fishing towns, to small villages created for and largely sustained by tourism. Most of Oregon's coastal communities are strung along U.S. Highway 101, which runs 363 miles north to south through Oregon coast, frequently following the coastline, but diverting inland to skirt natural obstacles such as headlands, estuaries, and sand dunes. Where Highway 101 courses away from the beach, secondary routes often take on the duty of reaching the coast, such as along the 30 miles of coastline from Pacific City north to Oceanside and the 35 or so miles of roads departing North Bend/Coos Bay to

reach Charleston and then heading southward toward Bandon. In some places, Highway 101 runs high above the ocean, providing spectacular vistas but no access, owing to sea cliffs and steep mountainsides, while in many stretches, the highway runs for miles mere feet above the level of the beach.

The highway is busiest in summer, but tourism on the Oregon coast is a year-round affair. The beaches themselves change with the seasons and with the tides; each new day and each new tidal exchange from high to low and back again brings rejuvenation and transformation. From summer to winter, many beaches change even more dramatically. Summer wave patterns differ from winter wave patterns in both the average interval between waves and the height and power of those waves. Wintertime waves, larger and more powerful on average than summer waves, with longer intervals, scour sand from beaches, depositing it just offshore. This sand transport reveals the substrate of many sand beaches, often uncovering bedrock, cobble, or scattered boulders, or, in a few places, even the petrified remains of ancient forests. The sand returns in summer, piling back up on the beaches. As with the tides, these seasonal changes paint new and ever-changing faces on the beaches. Beaches are tumultuous, dynamic environments, and their transformative nature creates much of their natural splendor.

○ Planning Your Visit

For most Oregonians, a trip to the beach requires little in the way of planning: jump in the car and drive to the coast. But for visitors from farther away, visiting the coast for more than a daytrip, logistics are more complicated. Paramount to overnight visits is making reservations for lodging, whether hotel, rental house, or campground. Reservations are especially important during the busy summer season, which stretches from Memorial Day weekend through September (and often a week longer on both ends of that timeframe).

The Oregon Coast is universally busy during that prime tourism season, but the extent of the crowds depends largely on location: if a major event is underway, such as the Seaside Beach Volleyball Tournament during the second weekend in August, not a single rental room of any kind—hotel, motel, cottage, beach house, condo—will be available on a drop-in basis anywhere in or near Seaside, and not even if you call a week or two in advance. Some years, the south coast hosts a huge music festival, and annually it throws a big off-road-vehicle bash. On such summer weekends, not only are the motel/hotel rooms completely booked, but so too are all the campgrounds. So in planning your trip to the Oregon coast, be sure to first check on major events that might eliminate any chance of finding lodging, and then by all means reserve your room, house, or campsite well in advance of your trip. The last chapter of this book provides a list of events on the Oregon coast—so that you can plan to participate in them (which can be a wonderful part of the Oregon experience), or plan to avoid them or work around them.

Each coastal community offers excellent resources for trip planning, and of course various travel-related web sites provide myriad reviews for lodging options, as well as restaurants and other businesses. In addition, because so much of the Oregon coast is administered by the Oregon State Parks department, this agency provides copious details about beaches and nearby attractions, as does the Oregon Coast Visitors Association, www.visittheoregoncoast.com. A few locations on the coast are managed by federal agencies—the U.S. Forest Service and the Bureau of Land Management—and they too provide excellent information. The appendix to this book provides a complete list of contacts, and key contacts are also listed for most beaches discussed in chapters 3, 4, and 5.

The summer crowds on the coast are not uniformly distributed. The busiest beaches and the busiest coastal towns and roads are those closest to Oregon's largest population centers in the Willamette Valley (from Portland south to Eugene). So the central and north coast tend to be much more crowded

Seaside, Oregon. Photo by Alex Butterfield/CreativeCommons

Oregon Coast Aquarium in Newport. Photo by Oregon Coast Visitors Association

than the far-away south coast. But in Oregon, crowded is a relative term. Certainly the most popular destinations—places like Cannon Beach, Seaside, Fort Stevens State Park, Newport, and Lincoln City—draw substantial beach crowds during summer. But even the most tourist-laden locations have their quiet times. A sunrise walk on the beach at Seaside or Cannon Beach reveals a surprisingly quiet and lonely scene; a short drive and/or hike to adjoining or nearby but lesser-known beaches is often rewarded with seclusion and solitude. But many visitors revel in the busy summer beach scene, enjoying the social atmosphere among friends and family and new acquaintances.

Once the busy summer season draws to a close, the beaches transform along with the weather. The hustle and bustle of the busiest coastal towns subsides, at least to some extent, and even the most popular beaches enjoy a respite from the throngs. Still, the Oregon coast remains a major tourism draw year-round, so lodging reservations are still advisable in the off-season, and especially so until mid- to late October, anytime near the holidays, and after the end of March.

Winter on Oregon's beaches delivers its own kind of magic. Unless storms are brewing in the Pacific, the Oregon coast enjoys ample sunny days in winter. But those winter storms are part of the intrigue, delivering the most dynamic, dramatic, and wondrous natural scenes along Oregon beaches, and often providing the best opportunity for beachcombing and wildlife watching.

No matter the time of year, visitors to Oregon's beaches need to dress for cool and often wet weather. A sunny, 75-degree summer day often begins as a cold, damp, foggy morning. The wind blows often, and often blows hard. During summer, a layer or two of warm clothes and a light rain jacket at the ready is standard issue; during winter, plan for temperatures between the 30s and the 50s and carry good rain gear. On the other hand, beautiful, sunny, warm weather dominates throughout the summer along the coast, with temperatures typically from the mid-60s to the high 70s.

Highway 101 is the primary route along the Oregon Coast all the way from Astoria to the California border. On the whole, it is a curvy, busy highway, oft laden with RVs (especially in summer). It routes directly through the towns along the entire coast, and in so doing, is slow going through places such as Seaside, Tillamook, Lincoln City, Newport, Coos Bay, and Brookings. And that's all part of the experience because these towns, along with the many small communities on and near Highway 101, imbue the Oregon coast with a palpable charm and eclecticism; they beg exploration as much as the nearby beaches. Take your time; on Highway 101, you won't go anywhere in a hurry, so plan accordingly. The key routes to the Oregon coast mostly arrive from the east—Highway 30, 26, and 6 from the Portland area; Highway 18/22 and its connectors from the Portland and Salem areas; Highways 20 and 34 from the Albany/Corvallis area; Highway 126 from Eugene; Highway 38/138 from Drain and Sutherlin; Highway 42 from Roseburg; and Highway 199, which leads to Northern California from Grants Pass to connect with Highway 101 north of Crescent City. Other than lengthy Highway 199, each of these routes delivers motorists from western Oregon cities to the coast in 60 to 90 minutes under normal traffic conditions.

A few beach-access sites require nominal daily entrance fees. Day passes for state parks can be purchased on site, while annual and 24-month permits are sold online at store.oregonstateparks.org, and at major Oregon State Park offices. A state parks camping receipt serves as a daily permit for each day that you are registered. A federal recreation pass or daily fee provides access to the handful of federally-managed beach sites in Oregon that require an entrance fee—Sand Lake Recreation Area, Yaquina Head Outstanding Natural Area, Cape Perpetua Scenic Area, Sutton Recreation Area, and Oregon Dunes National Recreation Area. The interagency Oregon Pacific Coast Passport is valid at all state and federal fee sites along the coast and is available at all US Forest Service and Oregon State Parks offices (for information and a list of locations to obtain the pass, visit www.fs.usda.gov/Internet/FSE_DOCUMENTS/fsbdev7_007119.pdf).

Photo by John Shewey

○ Beach Safety

The number one rule when visiting Oregon beaches is this: never turn your back on the ocean. The second-most important rule is: never turn your back on the ocean.

If you're sensing a theme here, it's not because the Oregon beaches are particularly dangerous; but these ocean shores absorb a powerful, dynamic, tumultuous, oft-unpredictable surf. Oregon's ocean shores have claimed plenty of lives over the decades, but in almost all cases, such accidents stem from a simple lack of appreciation and proper respect for the power of the Pacific Ocean, whether the root cause is naiveté, good old-fashioned stupidity, lack of awareness, or genuine bad luck.

But the age-old advice has long been an adage on the coast: never turn your back on the ocean. No matter how absorbed you may be in beach activities, keep an eye on that surf. Rogue waves—sneaker waves, as they are known—can occur with little or no warning, and scientists don't fully understand why they occur. Sometimes the surf will provide warning of a large breaker by a brief but pronounced quietude as one wave drains out and an unusually long lull occurs before the next one forms up to roll in, but other times, big breakers seem to come out of nowhere and while most are not the infamous sneaker waves, breakers vary considerably in size and power.

The old mariner's tale that waves travel in groups of seven, with the seventh being the largest actually holds a grain of truth: waves are formed by wind (not by tides), and those wind-formed waves tend to travel in groups. When such wave groups originate at a considerable distance from shore, they have time to coalesce to some extent, with the smaller waves being absorbed into the bigger waves, and the biggest waves tending to travel in the middle of the pack. These wave groups often total 12 to 16 waves, so sure enough, the largest wave is likely to be at the middle—number six, seven, or eight. However, a variety of factors affect the size and number of waves in a set, the most important being how far out at sea the waves formed, and how powerfully they are driven by wind. Massive storms far out in the Pacific can produce huge waves and consequently towering breakers when those waves collide with the beach—the kind of breakers that surfers seek. Near-shore storms and strong winds can produce smaller but more rugged and choppy surf, equally dangerous to the unaware beachgoer who forgets rule number one.

Moreover, wave patterns change with the seasons. During winter, waves within sets of waves tend to be more widely spaced than during summer, but because of frequent winter storms at sea, these winter waves can also average larger than their summer counterparts. Regardless of season, waves work in unison with onshore/near-shore currents to shape beaches, carving out irregularities in what might appear to the casual observer to be even, level, sand beach. But even the gentlest-sloping beaches have contours, including roughly parallel alternating sand bars and troughs running along the shoreline, cuts (channels) running across those bars and troughs at angles, and holes formed at the deepest parts of troughs. The waves and currents that shape beaches range from the most innocuous soft waves rolling onto the sand to dangerous rip currents that flow like rivers against the direction of the incoming breakers.

Dangerous rip currents, unpredictable waves, and rugged surf are three obvious dangers of straying too far into the water—or into it at all—on the Oregon coast. But another danger, and one that comes as a surprise to many visitors, is the cold ocean water, from 49 to 58 degrees. Water temperature peaks during summer, from June through September, and Oregon's north coast averages 2 to 7 degrees warmer than the water of the southernmost beaches. However, even 56-degree water begins to feel cold quickly— hence the reason that Oregon surfers wear thick wetsuits. This ain't Hawaii. Of course Oregon's beaches range from wide open sand to rugged basalt escarpments and bedrock, and the rocky beaches present additional risks. The rocks can be incredibly slippery, especially if coated with any of various

kinds of marine vegetation—so much so that in some cases you simply cannot walk on them. The danger of slipping is magnified at low tide when slippery rock surfaces are exposed. Likewise, many shoreline rocks have jagged edges and others are studded with barnacles—in either case, a fall means you're likely to lose some skin. In many places, rocky shorelines are hammered by the surf, and powerful waves can easily sweep away onlookers who venture too close to the edges. No matter your activity—tide-pooling, fishing, harvesting mussels, birdwatching—stay away from the edges and— again—never turn your back on the ocean.

Objects on the beach also merit caution. Large drift logs can easily roll, even those that seem firmly imbedded in the upper beach. Logs that have recently washed up or are awash in the surf are especially hazardous because incoming waves, even in shallow water, can propel them or spin them forcefully. Even small chunks of driftwood, no larger than a piece of firewood, become battering rams when propelled by breakers. Also be wary around large rocks embedded in the beach because wave action gouges out a ring of deep water around them. Finally, if you find an object or creature washed up on the beach and you're unsure as to whether you should touch it, err on the side of safety. Potentially dangerous objects should be reported to the nearest authority.

It probably goes without saying to avoid cliff edges, but on the Oregon coast, cliffs can be especially hazardous. Those made from sandstone or other soils frequently reshape themselves, caving in and sloughing off

Warning

Structure is Not Designed for Public Access

Deadly Waves at Any Time

Massive winter storm waves hammer the Oregon coast. Photo by Erica Harris/OSU/CreativeCommons

sections of all sizes. Many such cliffs are undercut, hollowed out just beneath the top, and the weight of a person on the edge can collapse them. Entire housing developments have fallen prey to collapsing sea cliffs in Oregon, bearing witness to the dynamic erosive power of the surf.

Seasonality, weather, and tides also play significant roles in beach safety considerations. Winter storms tend to generate huge waves and rugged, highly unpredictable surf, but even during summer, high winds, and both offshore and inshore storms can generate powerful shore breaks. Combined with high tides, some beaches can disappear under water entirely for a few hours each day. Incoming tides can (and do) trap people on surf-zone rocks and headlands, in worst-case scenarios requiring immediate rescue before their precarious perch is completely underwater, or in best-case scenarios requiring waiting several hours for the water to recede. That's why beach explorers should know the tide times and levels for the day.

One last warning applies to the southern Oregon coast: poison oak abounds. It thrives on southerly exposures, including slopes leading right down to beach edges. All parts of the plant are toxic, and cause most people to break out in rash and severe itching within a few days of exposure. Learn to identify and avoid it. If you must hike through areas with heavy poison oak growth, wear long pants and long sleeves and then remove your clothes and seal them in a plastic garbage bag until you can wash them. The best policy is avoidance—keep a sharp eye peeled for poison oak and avoid brushing against it.

In any beach emergency, especially in uncrowded, out-of-the-way areas, the best way to assure a timely response is to call 911 and give the official beach number, which is posted on big yellow signs on many beaches, as well as on the official Oregon State Parks information signs that welcome visitors to most state park recreation areas, day-use sites, and waysides that have access to the beach.

Despite such voluminous warnings, Oregon's beaches truly are quite safe for all but the most foolhardy or naïve visitors, and accidents are quite rare. A little common sense coupled with a basic understanding of potential threats assures a safe and uneventful visit. Know the tide cycles for the days you visit the beach, so you know when water levels will rise. And of course, never turn your back on the ocean.

Rules and Regulations

Oregon Beaches are public property, a legacy all beachgoers share, but that public ownership also carries responsibility. Common-sense rules, such as don't litter and don't use the beach as a personal bathroom, are obvious, but often disregarded by selfish individuals; but in addition, Oregon State Parks, often in cooperation with other agencies, provides beach rules and regulations that can vary depending on the location. Other than informal sites, virtually all beach access sites have rules posted on large signs erected by Oregon State Parks.

Many beach activities and some beach access is restricted by rules to prevent disturbing threatened western snowy plovers during their nesting and chick-rearing season in spring and summer. These tiny shorebirds nest in the upper beach area, scraping out a slight depression in the sand for the nest, and sitting on the eggs in the open, relying on camouflage to avoid predators. In most areas, snowy plover beach restrictions are in effect from March 15 to September 15, and signage is usually obvious at beach access points and in many places on the beaches themselves in the form of bright yellow signs with a plover profile. In all areas covered by the March 15 to September 15 restrictions, the designated area is off limits to dogs (even on leash), motorized and nonmotorized vehicles (including bicycles), kites, and drones. In addition,

pedestrian and equestrians are limited to the wet-sand portion of the beach only. In a few places, restrictions are in effect from March 15 to July 15 and on these beaches, dogs are allowed on leash at that time. For complete up-to-date information, visit www.oregon.gov/oprd/NATRES/Pages/plover.aspx.

Obviously western snowy plover restrictions affect a variety of beach activities in regulated areas, but there remains plenty of beach open to all forms of recreation. All the beaches are governed by these basics:

Beach camping: In most locations—but not all—camping on the beach is not allowed, particularly on state-parks beaches and within the city limits of most beach communities. Beaches where camping is allowed tend to be remote. Naturally if you camp on one of the remote beaches where overnighting is allowed, be sure to make camp well above the high-tide line, far up against the upper beach. Intrepid backpackers who hike portions of Oregon's coast can find wonderful places to camp along some beaches, and have such places all to themselves, but when in doubt, simply check Oregon State Parks signs at beach access sites.

Beach restrictions to protect western snowy plovers are in place at many locations along the coast.
Photo by Jason Crotty/CreativeCommons

Dog rules vary considerably on Oregon Beaches. Some beaches require leashes and on others dogs can run free provided they are well behaved and the owner has firm voice control. Photo by John Shewey

Fires: Beach fires are allowed unless posted rules indicate otherwise, but fires must be west (seaward) of the vegetation line on the upper beach and only small driftwood pieces may be burned (no large logs). During summer, when dry conditions persist, increasing the risk for wildfire, managing agencies sometimes enact complete fire bans on Oregon's beaches. Notifications of such bans are posted at beach access sites and on the Oregon State Parks web pages for individual beaches.

Beach driving: Some beaches and parts thereof are open to vehicle traffic, with specific rules depending on location. In many areas, vehicles on the beach are banned or restricted at certain times of year, largely because of western snowy plover restrictions. Signage and well-used beach-access roads meant for vehicles indicate those beaches where vehicles are legal.

Dogs on the beach: Western snowy plover restrictions dictate that many beaches are off limits to dogs between March 15 and September 15, but otherwise, Oregon's beaches are actually quite dog friendly. State parks signs at beach-access locations tell whether dogs must remain on leash, and if not so designated, they are free to run provided the owner has firm voice control. In addition to having a great time romping on the beach, beware that dogs can also get into trouble. The waves wash up lots of temptations, both dead and alive—jellyfish, birds, crabs, fish, and more. Dead animals frequently stink, just the kind of stuff many dogs love to eat, mouth, roll in, or frolic with. So be mindful and keep an eye out.

Moreover, during spring and summer, mother harbor seals often leave their pups on the beach while out feeding; dog owners need to be especially vigilant that their pets do not harass or approach these fully protected marine mammals. In addition, beaches attract lots of birds, and some dogs love to chase them. Gulls, crows, and ravens are ubiquitous on the beaches, but from July through April, Oregon beaches are stopover grounds and wintering areas for migratory shorebirds, which often occur in large flocks; dog owners need to prevent their pets from chasing these birds, which many dogs love to do.

Naturally only well-behaved, well-socialized, and well-controlled dogs should be allowed off leash on the beaches. Of course Oregon's incredible sand beaches are great places for dogs, but owners should never endanger a dog by allowing it to roam the rocky shores and headlands—a dog can be swept away as easily as a person. Many Oregon State Parks beach access sites have dispensers with doggy bags and it's imperative that owners clean up after their dogs.

Local laws: Most beachside towns have their own city ordinances regarding beach properties, most of which mirror state parks rules, although in some cases they address additional topics. Seaside, for example, dictates that "No person shall play or practice playing golf or driving golf balls along or upon the ocean beach within the corporate limits of the city," and in Cannon Beach, the local police issue short-term beach access permits for vehicles being used to gather firewood for personal use. Most beach communities ban fireworks on the beach. In fact, municipal rules governing beaches are fairly uniform all along the coast

CHAPTER

2

Opposite: Flying kites at Lincoln City. Photo by Nathalie Owen/Creative Commons

OREGON BEACH ACTIVITIES

Many people visit Oregon's scenic beaches to do little more than bask in the natural splendor of this rugged, beautiful coastline. Simply taking time to walk down to the beach, breathing in the cool, salty air, and listening the mesmerizing crashing of the breakers on sand or stone is incredibly revitalizing. But Oregon's beaches also present a tantalizing array of outdoor pursuits, all of which attract many adherents.

From hiking and biking to surfing and windsailing, many people visit Oregon's beaches for active outdoors sports; Seaside, in fact, is home to one of the world's largest beach volleyball tournaments, and the Oregon coast also hosts several board-sports competitions throughout the year, including events for long boards, windsurfing, and tow-in big-wave surfing. For hikers, the Oregon Coast Trail, as its various remaining unfinished segments are completed, is rapidly becoming a major draw for outdoors enthusiasts who enjoy lacing up the boots to visit myriad coastal wonders along the route. Runners and joggers, both visitors and coastal residents alike, love striding along Oregon's lengthy sand beaches, especially during early morning and evening, when they enjoy respite from crowds on popular beaches, along with abundant wildlife, and surreal scenery.

Oregon's rocky beaches are remarkable treasure troves of intertidal organisms. Consequently exploring tide pools at low tide—"tide-pooling" —is an extremely popular and educational activity. So too is beachcombing, the act of scouring the beach for all manner of items, natural and manmade, washed up by the waves and the tides.

Beachcombing

Beachcombing means different things to different people. For some, beachcombing is an intense hobby; for others, a casual affair. Some beachcombers hunt for specific items—sand dollars, unique pieces of driftwood, even very rare Japanese glass fishing-net floats, a few of which are still found even though they have not been used in decades. Other beachcombers revel in the variety of things that wash up on Oregon's beaches, from unusual shells and bizarre dead fish, to old foreign bottles and even stones bearing fossilized plants and animals.

Beachcombing is a year-round activity, though many people prefer to roam the beaches after winter storms, when heavy seas might deliver treasures from far offshore. But even during summer, each new receding tide leaves promise of new items of intrigue washed up on the beach. In beachcombing, however—despite the changing tides and shifting sands—often the early bird does in fact get the worm, for the first person to hike along a beach each morning enjoys the best chance of collecting unique items. Dedicated beachcombers get out early, especially on popular beaches.

Shells, of course, are a favorite among beachcombers of all ages and interests, and no shell is more popular on the Oregon coast than that of the sand dollar. The eccentric sand dollar (Dendraster excentricus) is a species of flattened sea urchin that inhabits sandy seafloors, where it burrows just under the surface, and tends to group densely together. Sand dollars vary in color, from gray or brown to purple to nearly black. The animal's skeleton, called a test, often washes up on sand beaches, sometimes in tremendous numbers. These tests range from pale gray to white. Recently deceased sand dollars, still bearing color and some of the animal's fuzzy outer coat (composed of fine, tubelike feet with cilia) also wash up on the beaches, and are undesirable because their remaining flesh will soon begin to smell rancid if you take the dead creature home. Many of the tests are damaged by tumbling in the surf, making intact, undamaged sand dollars the prize for beachcombers. Nearly any of Oregon's extensive sand beaches will produce sand dollars, but the best—those with the most sand dollars—include Seaside Beach, especially close to the mouth of the Necanicum River, and the remaining sand beaches stretching all the way north to Clatsop Spit; the sand beaches on both sides of the Nestucca River (Bob Straub State Park on the north and Wakonda Beach on the south); the long stretch of sand from Yaquina Bay south to Seal Rock State Park; Waldport area beaches; and the extensive sand between Florence and North Bend.

Left: Sand dollar. Photo by John Shewey
Right: Clam fossils. Photo by John Shewey

Sand dollars are obvious—they wash up on open sand beaches, where they stand out. Fossils, however, are easy to miss. They are found on open sand beaches as well as rocky shores, and they come in myriad forms, including clams and scallops, snails, petrified wood, and even bones of marine mammals; one Oregon beachcomber found a fossilized ancient marlin skull, and another found a fossilized mammoth tooth. The key is to look closely, examining any rocks with unusual patterns and colors. Fossils can be found anywhere along the coast.

Likewise, agate hunting is a popular hobby on the Oregon coast, and the agatized treasures come in all shapes and sizes and many colors. Gravel beaches are best for finding wave-polished agates, and most dedicated agate hunters search the gravels at low tides. Any beach with gravel beds is likely to have agates, but the most extensive gravel beaches are found from Yachats southward, all the way to Brookings-Harbor. Many of the southern Oregon gravel beaches are seldom visited by agate enthusiasts simply because there are so many options for agate hunting on the south coast.

Because Oregon's beaches are state-owned public property, beachcombers are allowed to keep nearly anything they find. The exception is live organisms, except those harvested legally, as well as dead (or live) birds or marine mammals, all of which are protected. Live birds and mammals are fairly common on the Oregon beaches. Baby seals are often left on the beach while their mothers feed, and well-meaning beachgoers often try to "rescue" the pups, fearing they are lost or injured. The best policy is to leave the pup alone and keep

A beautiful agate-bearing pebble. Photo by Richard O'Neill

your distance; do not touch the animal or venture too close, and if you have a dog, leash it, and warn others to do so as well. The mother, no doubt feeding offshore nearby, is only likely to return to her pup if people are not around. Prime time for seal pups on Oregon beaches is April through August.

On the other hand, every once in a while, a whale, porpoise, or dolphin becomes stranded in the surf, and with immediate aid from trained personnel, the animal—at least the smaller species, such as harbor porpoise and Dall's porpoise—might possibly survive. Bystanders lacking proper training and equipment should keep their distance because a large thrashing mammal can be very dangerous, as can the cold, unforgiving Oregon surf. Most beaching events in Oregon involve gray whales and porpoises, though some rare and memorable whale beachings have occurred, including several in recent memory, such as the incredibly rare blue whale that washed up, already dead, north of Gold Beach in 2015, and a Baird's beaked whale that washed up live at Seaside in 2003.

But the most famous—or rather infamous—was the dead sperm whale that washed up near Florence in 1970. Unsure how to dispose of the massive, rotting carcass, state highway division personnel opted to use explosives, thinking that they could blast the remains somewhat seaward into small enough bits that gulls and other scavengers would soon finish the cleanup. Unfortunately the explosive charge—a half ton of dynamite—seemed far too much for the job at hand, at least as judged by Walter Umenhofer, a military veteran with explosives training who happened to be in Florence that day.

Harbor seal pup sleeping on the beach. Photo by Pam Rivers/BLM

Umenhofer's warnings went unheeded and upon the massive explosion, whale blubber and parts were launched as far as 800 feet inland, showering bystanders and even crushing one automobile—Umenhofer's brand-new Oldsmobile, which coincidentally, he had purchased during a "Get a Whale of a Deal" promotion in Eugene. Television news reporter Paul Linnman, who went on to enjoy a long career in Portland broadcast journalism, reported epically and hilariously from the scene, and during his voiceover to cameraman Doug Brazil's footage, Linnman quipped that the "...blast blasted blubber beyond all believable bounds." Today, the footage is easy to find on the internet and well worth enjoying; simply do a web search for the Oregon exploding whale.

Alongside marine creatures, manmade items, in addition to the aforementioned oriental glass floats, frequently wash ashore as well, and while much of it— unfortunately—is common garbage, often having been dumped at sea, the occasional oddity or even treasure is found. With both manmade and natural items, if you're not sure whether you should touch it, caution is always wise, and in cases of rare truly dangerous items, call authorities.

Beachcombing gear is straightforward: if you're walking the sand in search of sand dollars or other easily retrieved goodies, a pair of flip-flops or sandals in summer or shoes in winter, along with season-appropriate clothing suffices. If you're walking the surf line, wading through inches-deep water at times, rubber boots are handy. A walking stick to use for probing and flipping objects over can save a lot of bending down to pick things up, and a bucket or mesh bag will carry whatever you want to take home. Once at home, clean your items carefully; a mild bleach solution works wonders on sand dollars, not only helping to clean them, but also turning them white.

Hunting for agates. Photo by John Shewey

Exploring tide pools. Photo by Bob Wick/BLM

Tide-pooling

Landlubbers and first-time visitor to the Oregon coast might find the term "tide-pooling" rather foreign; but they also tend to eagerly embrace the activity once exposed to it on Oregon's fertile rocky beaches. Tide pools form in the rocks when the tide ebbs: the high tide covers the rocks and the low tide exposes them, leaving pools and pockets of all sizes filled with seawater and the life it sustains. Many Oregon beaches provide ready low-tide access to tide pools, allowing curious beachgoers to explore by sight, sound, and feel. Children tend to love tide-pooling, discovering mysterious creatures, making this a wonderful family activity.

Understanding the tides themselves is key to tide-pooling. The simple version is this: tide pools are exposed at low tide, and Oregon's coast experiences two low tides and two high tides each day, with the peak tides (high and low) spaced by about six hours. So to explore tide pools, you must consult a tide chart and plan to be on the beach at low tide, ideally an hour or so before the tide recedes to its lowest point.

More accurately, however, there are two high and two low tides every lunar day. A lunar day is the time needed for a specific location on Earth to rotate from a precise point under the moon back to the same point under the moon—a period of 24 hours and 50 minutes, unlike the 24-hour solar day. The tide cycles completely from high to low or low to high every six hours and 12.5 minutes, the moon's gravitational pull being the primary influence on tides. The size of each tide—essentially the level to which the ocean rises and falls along the shore—is largely determined by the moon's positon relative to the sun and Earth. During full and new moon phases each month, the Earth, moon, and sun are aligned (a state known as syzygy), creating maximum tide range because the sun's gravitational pull is coupled with the moon's gravitational pull. These tides are called "spring tides," the name deriving from the word spring in the context of jumping forth. Conversely, when the moon is in its first and third quarters each month, the sun and moon are at 90 degrees to each other as viewed from Earth and their respective gravitational pulls work against one another, in effect creating minimum tides. These are called "neap tides," from an archaic word meaning "without the power."

During spring tides, water exchange, measured in feet, between low and high tides is maximal. During neap tides, water exchange between the tides is minimal. Oregon's highest tides, sometimes called "king tides," measure in at 10 feet or more, but they are rare; 9-foot high tides are typically among the highest of the year in most locations. The highest tides always correspond with

the lowest tides, and it's those lowest tides that create the best tide-pooling opportunities. The lowest tides are called "minus tides" or "negative tides" because they are measured in feet below the mean sea level. They occur, of course, during spring tides (full moon and new moon phases).

Minus tides reveal incredible treasures along the Oregon coast, with the sea water dropping low enough to expose areas normally inaccessible to beachgoers. These seldom-exposed areas are home to organisms rarely encountered in the upper surf zone. Tide-poolers exploring during the lowest tides of the year, when low tides reach minus-2 feet or lower, may find species of sea stars, anemones, urchins, crabs, shellfish, and other creatures rarely seen without aid of diving gear; you may even luck upon an octopus or a surprisingly large fish, such as a kelp greenling, rock greenling, cabezon, or rockfish. Even at modestly low tides, Oregon's tide pools are treasure troves of unique and exotic organisms that keep beachgoers riveted.

Tide-poolers, of course, need to keep an eye on the ocean at all times and understand when and how the tide is changing. The best time to begin tide-pooling is one to two hours prior to the low tide, during the ebb current, when the tide is falling. Upon reaching low tide, the changeover to the flood current—the beginning of the rising tide—can happen quickly and above all, you don't want to be stranded offshore by the rising water. Always know what time the tide will turn at your location (tide tables are available online and in the form of booklets widely available from coastal merchants and tourism centers), and always abide by the old adage, never turn your back on the ocean.

Ochre stars come in shades of purple, orange, and red. Photo by Jerry Kirkhart/Creative Commons

Kelp crab. Photo by Jerry Kirkhart/Creative Commons

A colorful tide pool at Yaquina Head. Photo by Bob Wick/BLM

Any time storms occur offshore in the Pacific or along the coast, wave surges, unpredictable surf conditions, sneaker waves, and storm-enhanced tidal currents become imminent threats to beachgoers, making tide-pooling a risky endeavor. Summer offers the best conditions, but periods of calm weather during the balance of the year can also be excellent.

In addition, exposed rocks in the intertidal zone can be incredibly slippery, especially those covered with eel grass, kelp, and other seaweeds. Stick to sand and bare rocks. Wear shoes or boots, and pants, that can get wet; avoid sandals or flip-flops as they don't provide enough stability and traction, the exception being closed-toe, hard-sole sandals designed for aquatic use. Boots, shoes, or aquatic sandals with felt soles (or other soles meant to grip slippery rocks) are ideal. Many rocks are encrusted with barnacles or mussels and walking on them can destroy these organisms, so use good judgement and encourage others to do likewise.

A hiking stick is useful in maintaining balance on the rocks, but otherwise keep your hands free by stowing cameras, phones, and other items in a jacket pocket (inside a plastic bag if they are not water resistant). Young children should always wear a life vest, and don't let them wander too far. For groups of children, use the buddy system, and charge at least one adult with keeping a constant watch on the ocean and the group.

Marine organisms tend to be delicate and fragile and die quickly when removed or even moved. Some creatures can pinch or sting, so watch those fingers. Touching tide-pool creatures can be great fun, and educational, but be gentle. Otherwise encourage children to look and study, but not to remove organisms from the water. Often, simply lifting strands of seaweed out of the way can reveal extraordinary things in the tide pools, and likewise, sometimes if you simply hold very still and motionlessly watch a tide pool, all manner of swimming and crawling creatures come out of hiding.

The Oregon coast offers dozens of great tide pool locations, the best-known of which almost always draw crowds during minus tides, especially during summer. But many others remain under the radar. On the north coast, top tide pool locations include Ecola State Park, Haystack Rock (Cannon Beach), Oswald West State Park, and Cape Lookout. On the central coast, prime spots include Yaquina Head State Natural Area, Seal Rock State Park, Yachats, Cape Perpetua, Neptune, and Strawberry Hill. The rocky south coast is rich in tide pools, with top spots including Sunset Bay State Park, Cape Arago State Park, Coquille Point, Port Orford, Lone Ranch Beach, and Harris Beach State Recreation Area.

Beach Hiking and Biking

Some of Oregon's sand beaches seem to go on forever, stretching for miles. They are terrific venues for people who enjoy hiking along the ocean. Whether you hike (or jog or run) for pleasure or fitness or both, these sandy shores provide year-round opportunity and along the way you're likely to see wildlife close up and enjoy beautiful views. Moreover, Oregon State Parks, the Bureau of Land Management, and the U.S. Forest Service have established many coastal trails that lead to amazing places near the beaches, including headlands that provide incredible panoramas, old-growth forests and other unique habitats, and myriad historic sites.

Among the many coastal trails is a relative newcomer, the 425-mile-long Oregon Coast Trail (OCT). Depending on location, the trail—which spans the state from the Columbia River to the California border—runs along the beach, along Highway 101 and other roads, and along designated and maintained trail segments. Nearly 40 percent of the trail is on beaches, and another 40 percent is on paved roads. In places, the trail route requires hikers to ford streams, especially where they cross beaches, making tide tables crucial (many stream deltas are only crossable at low tide). Parts of the trail are open to horse riders and bicycles, and parts are use-restricted during the summer western snowy plover nesting season (generally meaning no dogs, camping, bicycles, motorized vehicles, and hiking on wet-sand beach only).

Though few people trek the entire Oregon Coast Trail, many hikers tackle segments of it, using campgrounds (many of which have inexpensive hiker/biker camping areas) or, in some places, legally camping on the upper beach. The completion date for the entire route is 2021, so until then, hikers need to plan connecting routes for OCT segments not yet constructed. Also, ferry service is required to cross Nehalem Bay, Tillamook Bay, and Winchester Bay. For complete details, including maps and help in planning OCT hiking expeditions, visit www.coasttrails.org.

In recent years, cyclists have increasingly embraced Oregon's beaches, riding along the wet-sand portions (or even the dry sand for a substantial workout). A bicycle is a great way to quickly explore lengthy beaches, and specially equipped "fat-tire" bicycles are now commonplace, even available for rent in some beachside communities. Critically, be sure to thoroughly wash all parts of the bicycle soon after you finish riding—saltwater is highly corrosive.

Special beach bicycles have extra-wide tires. Photo by John Shewey

Windsurfing the Oregon surf. Photo by Kevin Pritchard

Board Sports and Boating

Oregon has long attracted surfers, both locals and visitors who revel in the state's dramatically scenic beaches. Despite furtive starts at the sport dating back to before World War I, surfing got its big start in Oregon in the early 1960s when Scott Blackman bought his first board and tested it on the waves at Agate Beach just north of Newport. Blackman founded the Agate Beach Surf Club and famously documented the burgeoning sport with his photographs. Years later he and his wife, Sandy, authored the photo-rich Oregon Surfing, Central Coast (2014), a look back at the genesis of the sport in Oregon.

These days, surfers are ubiquitous along the entire coastline, from popular surfing beaches to little-known breaks in out-of-the-way places. In addition to surfboarders, Oregon beaches attract many stand-up paddle-boarders, boogie boarders, skim boarders, kite boarders, sand surfers, and windsurfers. The state hosts a variety of competitive boarding events, such as the Cape Kiwanda Longboard Classic, Agate Beach Surf Classic, and the Nelscott Reef Big Wave Classic, a tow-in event held offshore when the massive break at Nelscott Reef hits 30 or more feet. Oregon's popular surfing beaches, north to south, include The Cove at Seaside, Indian Beach, Short Sands Beach, Cape Kiwanda, Roads End, Otter Rock, Agate Beach, South Beach, Florence South Jetty, Bastendorff Beach, Battle Rock and Hubbard Creek Beaches at Port Orford, Pistol River, Sport Haven Beach (Brooking–Harbor south jetty), to name a few. Some of these spots are also popular with stand-up paddle-boarders (e.g. Cape Kiwanda) and windsurfers (e.g. Pistol River/Myers Beach).

Surf shops serve a number of Oregon coast communities, selling and renting the best gear, offering lessons, and doling out expert advice; various web sites, easy to find with a search engine, provide up-to-date surf conditions and forecasts, and some beaches even have web cams. One of the best sources of general information is the website www.oregonsurf.com.

Likewise, kayak rentals, guided kayak trips, and kayaking lessons are readily available along the Oregon coast, where kayaking has become increasingly popular, so much so that many aficionados now routinely use their boats for fishing and crabbing, customizing them to fit the task. In some places, kayakers can easily launch from the beach. Sunset Bay near Charleston is a good example—the cove here is frequently so calm that launching a kayak is easy even for beginners. Not only do sea kayakers enjoy exploring Oregon's varied and incredibly scenic coastline, but some enjoy kayak surfing—paddling kayaks along the face of the same kinds of breaks sought by surfers. Veteran sea kayakers even explore the arches and caves along the rugged coastline.

Oregon is not Hawaii or Southern California: the water here is cold. Very cold. Hypothermia-inducing cold. Oregon surfers routinely wear full wet suits and booties. Oregon sea kayakers usually wear cold-weather layered clothing beneath full dry suits and PFDs, and paddlers exploring anywhere near rocks wear helmets. Coastal paddlers should always carry a compass and/or GPS, and emergency equipment stowed in a watertight compartment, including cell phone and headlamp. An emergency safety kit or bailout kit is a wise inclusion. One excellent resource for paddlers is the Oregon Ocean Paddling Society, www.oopskayak.org. In all ocean paddle sports and board sports, participants should never exceed their ability level without expert guidance—Oregon's coastal waters present many hazards. Lessons and guided trips are available for virtually all board sports and paddling sports on the coast and are great ways to learn more and gain valuable experience.

Stand-up paddle-boarding on the calm waters of Sunset Bay. Photo by Mason Marsh/www.masonmarsh.com

Kayaking a coastal estuary. Photo courtesy of Visit Tillamook Coast

Photo by Parker Knight

Driving the Beach

Some stretches of sand beach in Oregon are open to vehicle use, though many Oregon coast enthusiasts question the wisdom of driving on the beach, citing both ecological consequences and safety concerns. In some places—at Cape Kiwanda, for example—vehicles on the beach hardly seem to create any negative impact. Indeed, at the beach at Cape Kiwanda, where trucks launch fishing boats through the surf, and where surfers frequently gather, vehicles on the beach are part of the scene, so to speak; part of the local flavor and mystique. Farther north, where some 10 miles of uninterrupted sand stretches from Fort Stevens State Park south to Gearhart, beachgoers drive out onto the beach from several access sites (Peter Iredale Beach, Sunset Beach, Del Ray Beach, 10th Street in Gearhart, and sometimes DeLaura Beach), but seldom wander far from those locations, with only a small percentage of beach drivers making lengthy drives on the sand north to south or vice versa.

A few other locations along the coast are also open to vehicles, with seasonal vehicle closures in effect to protect nesting western snowy plovers in several places. In most cases, signage and well-used vehicle-entrance roads indicate those beaches open to vehicle use. Seasonal restrictions and closures are clearly marked. Some beaches allow street-legal vehicles but not ATVs, and some allow only ATVs.

Driving on the beach carries inherent hazards and dangers. Four-wheel-drive is essentially mandatory and even then, many vehicles get bogged down in soft sand, both dry and wet. Unless you drive a specially beach-equipped vehicle with all the tools and tricks needed to extricate yourself from being stuck in the sand, always stick to the heavily-driven areas as indicated by numerous tire tracks. If you get stuck in the sand, find people to help push you out; if necessary, let some air out of the tires to create a wider tire-to-surface base, which helps the vehicle stay more atop the sand. Full tires tend to dig deeper into the sand. If you get mired in dry sand, beyond letting air out of the tires, try dumping buckets of water on the sand around each tire to make the surface firmer. Be especially wary of driving the wet sand at or below the tide line. Vehicles that get mired down below the high-tide line may very well be inundated by rising sea water before they can be extricated—and the extrication will be expensive.

Saltwater and street vehicles don't mix very well. Salt is corrosive, or course, and that salty sand and seawater tends to infiltrate just about every nonsealed part of vehicles that spend any amount time on the beach. A thorough freshwater washing should follow any beach-driving adventure. Complete descriptions of beach vehicle access areas and restrictions are available at http://arcweb.sos. state.or.us/pages/rules/oars_700/oar_736/736_024.html.

Birdwatching at the Beach

Oregon's beaches host a diverse array of nesting birds during spring and summer, many more species pass through during spring and fall migration, and a variety of species overwinter along the Oregon coast.

Gulls—aka "seagulls"—are ubiquitous of course, but many people don't realize that the Oregon beaches attract a number of different gull species, including the robust and handsome western gull, the most abundant year-round member of the tribe. Similar species, such as the glaucus-winged gull, herring gull, and Thayer's gull, along with smaller (but still similar) California gull, mew gull, and ring-billed gull, spend considerable time along the Oregon coast outside of their late-spring/summer breeding seasons. One species, the Heerman's gull, differs substantially from these other species, being dressed in handsome shades of slate-gray, silvery-gray, and warm brown, and with a bright-red bill; Heerman's gulls disperse northward from their Mexican breeding grounds, wandering north to Oregon during summer.

Gulls, depending on species, require two to four years to acquire full adult plumage, and some species readily hybridize—hence it's little wonder why properly identifying gull species proves tedious and frustrating even for experienced birdwatchers. For beachgoers not particularly keen to identify the individual species, gulls can nonetheless provide intrigue and wonder, whether mobbing a sea lion or pelican for its catch, dropping shellfish onto rocks to break them open, or flying off with a captured starfish seemingly way too big to be eaten. Similar to gulls, terns also prowl the skies above coastal waters. Caspian terns are most common. These striking and acrobatic birds plunge-dive for small fish and have established massive breeding colonies near the mouth of the Columbia River, where they are implicated in preying heavily on juvenile imperiled salmon and steelhead.

The aforementioned pelicans—brown pelicans—disperse northward from their California and Mexican breeding range and arrive in Oregon during mid- to late summer. They often fly low over the surf in single file lines, but when they find prey, these massive birds put on a spectacular display, plunge-diving into the water.

Oregon's rocky beaches, headlands, and seastacks provide nesting sites (rookeries) for tufted puffins, common murres, three species of cormorant, cavity-nesting pigeon guillemots, black oystercatchers, and a few other species. During spring and summer, many "colony rocks" fill to capacity with nesting seabirds—particularly puffins, murres, and cormorants—creating must-

Left: Glaucus-winged gull. Photo by John Shewey
Right: Heerman's gull. Photo by Alan Schmierer

Caspian tern. Photo by Tim Blount

see spectacles all up and down the Oregon coast. Great places to see these colonies include Goat Island (Harris Beach State Park), Heceta Head, Yaquina Head (Newport), Haystack Rock (Cannon Beach), and Three Arch Rocks. Such concentrations of seabirds attract predatory birds: bald eagles and peregrine falcons, both of which hunt the sea cliffs, headlands, and seastacks. Visitors to such places during spring and summer might get to watch bald eagles target seabirds on and near the rookeries.

Eagles and peregrines also target ducks, and the Oregon coast is home to several varieties of sea ducks, the most common of which are the three species of scoter—surf scoter, white-winged scoter, and black scoter. These robust, mostly black ducks breed in the far north of Canada and Alaska, but they are common throughout coastal Oregon during fall, winter, and spring. They often fly in lines low over the surf, and feed within or just outside the breakers. Likewise, the striking harlequin duck, named for a colorfully-dressed character in commedia dell'arte, feeds within the surf, perfectly at home in the crashing breakers.

In addition to the seabirds and ducks, Oregon beaches attract numerous so-called shorebirds—sandpipers, plovers, and their relatives. Only two species—the dainty western snowy plover and sometimes its larger cousin, the familiar killdeer—breed on Oregon's sandy beaches, but many more species pass through in migration and overwinter. From fall through early spring, one denizen of the sand beaches is especially fun to watch: the sanderling is a small sandpiper that travels in flocks, and when feeding,

Brown pelican. Photo by John Shewey

Left: Pelagic cormorant. Photo by John Shewey
Top Right: Pigeon guillemots. Photo by Roy Lowe/USFWS Bottom Right: Tufted puffin. Photo by John Shewey

A bald eagle attacks a colony of common murres at Yaquina Head. Photo by Roy Lowe/USFWS

Black turnstone. Photo by John Shewey

frequently follows the upper edge of incoming waves lapping up on the beach. Frenetically, the wave-chasing flocks of little birds—often measuring in the dozens and sometimes in the hundreds—alternately chase and retreat from the water line. The aforementioned black oystercatcher nests on rocks, and frequents rocky beaches, searching the intertidal zone for prey. Despite its name, the oystercatcher rarely if ever eats oysters on the Oregon coast, instead seeking limpets, mussels, chitons, and gastropods. Large, conspicuous, and often boisterous, black oystercatchers are generally easy to find at rocky locations such as Ecola State Park, Cape Meares, Depot Bay, Yaquina Head, Seal Rock State Park, Bob Creek Wayside, and many places on the south coast.

Birdwatching enthusiasts can attend two different birding festivals on the Oregon coast. In late April, Pacific City hosts its annual Birding and Blues Festival (www.birdingandblues.org), and in September, the Oregon Institute of Marine Biology serves as headquarters for the annual Oregon Shorebird Festival (www.fws.gov/refuge/Bandon_Marsh/visit/visitor_activities/ shorebird_festival.html). Both events include a variety of field trips to area birding hotspots. In addition, the Oregon Coast Birding Trails website, www.oregoncoastbirding.com, provides detailed information on birding hotspots all along the coast.

From the Columbia River to the California border, the Oregon coast provides outstanding birdwatching, with ample intrigue for diehard birdwatchers and casual observers alike; and the simplicity of this hobby is endearing: all you need are a good pair of binoculars and a regional field guide, such as *Birds of the Pacific Northwest* by John Shewey and Tim Blount (Timber Press).

Sanderling. Photo by John Shewey

Watching Marine Mammals

Oregon's coastal waters are home to a variety of marine mammals, ranging from massive whales to the diminutive harbor porpoise. The most common species are harbor seals and sea lions, which are ubiquitous and often found hauled out on beaches, jetties, intertidal rocks, docks, and buoys. California sea lions are well known for hauling out at docks at the historic bay front in Yaquina Bay and notorious for swimming far up the Columbia River to feed on salmon and steelhead congregated by Bonneville Dam. Northern fur seals and northern elephant seals are occasionally seen in Oregon.

Harbor seals are year-round residents and haul ashore at about three dozen sites along the coast, commonly on beaches, sand bars, and bay shores, but also on shoreline rocks. They congregate at these haul-out sites but are generally solitary or in small groups when in the water. They commonly feed within the surf zone, so beachgoers with keen eyes might spy a seal, just its head above water, studying them from the breakers. During spring and early summer, female harbor seals often leave their pups on the beach as they feed just offshore. Well-meaning visitors to the beach often assume these pups are stranded or injured, but the best course of action is always to leave them be and keep a discrete distance. The mother is no doubt nearby and will retrieve her pup when she's ready, provided no humans (or dogs) are nearby.

Several species of whales occur along the Oregon coast, but most are rarely seen from shore. The gray whale, however, frequently migrates along the coastline, easily seen from land at many locations. Gray whales migrate between the plankton-rich waters of the North Pacific and their breeding grounds in Baja Mexico, where they spend less than a month. Thousands of them migrate along the Oregon coast, with the peak of migration occurring in late December and early January. However, the migration season is drawn out and lasts from late summer through mid-spring. The whales are southbound in fall and winter and northbound in spring, when females frequently have their calves with them.

The easiest way to spot whales is to watch for their spouts—a tall puff of mist that appears like white spray—when the animals surface from a feeding dive. The spouts, or blows, are distinctive for each species of whale. A gray whale dives for three to six minutes and then surfaces to make three to five successive blows, each of them 30 to 50 seconds apart. At times, pods of whales stop to feed for considerable lengths of time at one location near shore, providing onlookers an excellent opportunity to watch them. Sometimes they show their tails (flukes) above water, and lucky observers may get to see a whale protrude its entire head vertically out of the water, a behavior called spy hopping. Several coastal ports offer whale-watching expeditions by boat.

Harbor seals hauled out on the beach. Photo by Ian McKellar/Creative Commons

Left: Photo by Oregon Department of Fish and Wildlife/CreativeCommons Top Right: Orca at the mouth of the Columbia River. Photo by Dan Lewer/OSU Marine Mammal Institute/CreativeCommons Bottom Right: Steller's sea lions. Photo courtesy of Oregon Department of Fish and Wildlife

Both killer whales (orcas) and harbor porpoises occur close to shore in Oregon. Orcas occasionally invade Yaquina Bay and other inshore waters to hunt sea lions. Harbor porpoises, just 4 or 5 feet long, tend to by shy, unlike their boat-following larger brethren, such as Pacific white-sided dolphin, bottlenose dolphin, and Dall porpoise, all of which occur well offshore.

Many people are surprised to discover that sea otters—iconic in the North Pacific—are missing from Oregon. They have never recovered in Oregon's coastal waters after populations nearly worldwide were decimated by the fur trade in the 1700s and 1800s. Protection came with the passing of the International Fur Seal Treaty (1911), the Marine Mammal Protection Act (1972), and the Endangered Species Act (1973). Nonetheless, while other states have made concerted efforts to recover sea otters, Oregon has yet to do so. Every once in a while, a sea otter shows up in Oregon, probably having wandered down from Washington or up from California. But these sightings are very rare. Far more common are river otters, which feed and frolic on some Oregon beaches, even swimming in the surf.

Harbor seal. Photo by John Shewey

Dungenous crab. Photo by Lincoln City Visitor and Convention Bureau

Crabbing and Clamming

Oregon's fertile coastal waters foster a rich assemblage of shellfish, from coveted razor clams of the sand beaches, to the incredibly flavorful Dungeness crab that has long supported a commercial crabbing industry. Coastal visitors can easily partake in this ocean bounty with a modicum of information. A shellfish license is required for anyone age 12 or older to harvest any types of shellfish. Licenses are available at any Oregon Department of Fish and Wildlife (ODFW) licensing agent, and online at www.dfw.state.or.us/online_license_sales/index.asp. The ODFW, which regulates harvest of shellfish, provides excellent and detailed how-to/where-to information on its web site, www.dfw.state.or.us/fish. Click on the "Fishing" tab, and then the "Crabbing and Clamming" tab.

Recreational crabbing is primarily done from various docks and piers in Oregon bays and estuaries, and most coastal communities provide ready access and ample information for crabbers. Moreover, you can rent crabbing gear at numerous locations (inquire locally through visitors bureaus, chambers of commerce, and hotels). The basic set-up is a crab ring or crab trap, baited with dead fish or other bait (available from places that rent crabbing gear), a bucket for keepers, and a crab measuring device (also available anywhere you rent equipment).

Crabbing is a year-round activity, though many people consider late summer through fall to be the best time. Slack water, the period when the tide is shifting from high to low or low to high is generally the best time, although this varies to some extent on location. The basics are simple: secure the rope that is attached to your crab ring or crab trap to the pier railing or stud, toss the ring or trap in the water, and wait. With rings, check every 20 or 30 minutes or so, and with pots, allow an hour or two.

Dungenous crabs are most prized of the myriad crab species found in Oregon; red rock crabs are also commonly caught by recreational crabbers. Only male Dungenous crabs may be harvested, and minimum size is 5.75 inches across the widest part of the carapace (for information on differentiating between male and female Dungenous crabs, and identifying species of crabs, see the aforementioned ODFW web site). Harvest limits for Dungenous and red rock crabs are posted in the ODFW shellfishing regualtions.

Of all the clam species found in Oregon, razor clams generate the most interest and excitement. Properly prepared, they are a delicacy. More than 95 percent of Oregon's razor clam harvest occurs on the Clatsop County beaches, which hold the state's densest, most stable populations. Other productive beaches

(north to south) include Indian Beach (Ecola State Park), Cannon Beach, Cove Beach, Short Sands Beach, Cape Meares Beach, Agate Beach, North Beach and South Beach (Newport), Waldport-area beaches, the north spit at Winchester Bay (Sparrow Park Beach), Coos Bay North Spit, Bastendorff Beach, Whiskey Run Beach (Bandon), and Meyers Creek Beach (Gold Beach). Seasons and harvest limits are tightly controlled, and in-season closures occur when biologists monitoring and testing razor clams (and other shellfish) detect the presence of naturally occurring domoic acid or paralytic shellfish poisoning, both of which are powerful, naturally occurring toxins. To check for closures, call the shellfish harvest hotline at (800) 448-2474.

In addition to razor clams, Oregon's coastal waters provide opportunity to harvest a variety of other clams, as well as mussels, and various other edible marine invertebrates. The ODFW classifies gaper, cockle, butter, littleneck, softshell, and purple varnish clams as "bay clams" because they tend to occur in various estuary habitats, from deep, gooey mud, to gravelly substrates. Digging for them requires precise knowledge of locations, techniques, and tides—and frequently high-top rubber boots. Mussels, on the other hand, adhere to surf-zone rocks, often forming large, dense colonies. Again, the ODFW "Crabbing and Clamming" web site offers excellent and detailed information.

Crabbing and clamming are fun, rewarding, educational family activities that allow all comers to get down and dirty, so to speak, on Oregon's beaches and bays. And a successful outing means delicious eats, fresh from the ocean.

Clam digging at Taft in Lincoln City. Photo by Lincoln City Visitor and Convention Bureau

Left: Cockle. Photo by Oregon Department of Fish and Wildlife/CreativeCommons
Right: Razor clam. Photo by Oregon Department of Fish and Wildlife/CreativeCommons

Surf Fishing

Oregon's sand-bottom beaches are home to a variety of fishes that, surprisingly perhaps, thrive in the tumultuous surf zone. Chief among them, from an angler's perspective, is the redtail surfperch (Amphistichus rhodoterus), aka "pinkfin." These schooling, saucer-shaped fish reach about 2 pounds, and often feed in the near-shore surf, darting into the shallows in pursuit of mole carbs and other prey, or prowling troughs and trenches—slightly deeper areas within the sandy surf. Anglers catch them on both live bait and lures (typically jig heads rigged with plastic baits), and while heavy surf rods are popular, some intrepid devotees prefer lightweight spinning rods to enhance the sport in catching these hard-fighting, handsomely marked fish. Fly fishers have even forged a minor presence on Oregon's surfperch angling scene, seeking gently-sloping beaches and periods of gentle surf to cast weighted jiglike flies for pinkfins. Still, the heavy rods traditionally used for surfperch, even if seeming like overkill for a fish measured in ounces, allow you to launch your offering well out into the breakers and keep it there amid the crashing waves.

Veteran surfperch anglers generally use 2- to 6-ounce pyramid sinkers, which anchor in place better than other types of sinkers. These are attached to the terminal end of the line, and above them are rigged one or more bait hooks on short dropper lines attached to the main line by three-way swivels or knots. The idea is to keep the bait anchored in place on the bottom so the fish can find it. Anglers who fish jig-heads with spinning gear use active retrieves, making a few casts in likely areas and moving on, systematically covering the water to locate fish.

Primetime for surfperch fishing is spring and early summer when the fish congregate for spawning in the near-shore shallows. Unlike most fish, which lay eggs, surfperch bear live young—an adaptation to their rough-and-tumble habitat that leaves little opportunity to lay eggs in a spawning bed on the bottom like fishes of less-dynamic environs. Opinions vary as to the best tides for surfperch fishing, but the last two hours of the incoming tide is often best; the first two hours of the incoming tide can also be excellent. Low light seems even more important than tide stage, with early morning being best. Fishing at dawn on an incoming tide is ideal, so surf fishers need to pay attention to local tide charts. Low tides are ideal for learning the beach—look for depressions, called troughs, running parallel to sand bars and remember their locations; also look for cuts in the sand bars where trenches slice through them perpendicular to or at angles to the shore; in places, wide holes, from a few inches to a few feet, can develop along the shore. When the higher tide returns to fill them

Fishing for redtail surfperch near Bandon. Photo by John Shewey

with water, all such "structures" can attract surfperch, so if you can scout out such locations, return at the incoming tide and target these areas.

Surfperch fishing carries an inherent risk: the surf can be rough and unpredictable. Always err on the side of safety and follow the old adage, never turn your back on the ocean. The safest surf occurs during a convergence of settled weather and minimal water exchange between high and low tides (neap tides, which occur at quarter-moon phases). Many surf anglers wear knee boots, hip boots, or waders—the water on the Oregon coast is cold. Most of the time you can remain high and dry, but your feet are certain to get wet regardless. Surf anglers often "chase waves" by running out after a receding breaker to add a little distance to their cast, and then retreating while allowing line to spin off the reel as the next breaker comes in. However, bear in mind that surfperch often feed very near shore, sometimes nearly at your feet, so don't neglect to fish in close.

A variety of smaller surfperch species thrive on the sand beaches, while a host of other fish are available in the rocky intertidal zone. Favorites among anglers include the colorful and hard-fighting striped seaperch (Embiotoca lateralis), which feeds on crustaceans, worms, and mussels, and which is often found near mussel beds. Also popular are the inshore bottomfish—rock greenling (Hexagrammos lagocephalus), kelp greenling (H. decagrammus), cabezon (Scorpaenichthys marmoratus), the occasional lingcod (Ophiodon elongates), and various species of rockfish (Sebastes). Rockfish, especially the black rockfish (S. melanops), are colloquially known as "black bass," "sea bass," and "rock bass."

Redtail surfperch. Photo by Steve Morey/www.theoutershores.com

Fishing off coastal rocks is potentially dangerous, but much less so for anglers who understand tidal movements and currents, study their favorite beaches thoroughly, and above all, stay well above the water level. In other words, never fish from low perches near the surf. Stay well up out of harm's way and use rods and line stout enough to haul fish up out of the water. Wear shoes or boots with excellent traction, and wear a life vest when prowling the rocks. The rocky intertidal zone tends to be most productive on incoming tides. Like surfperch, most denizens of the rocky shores will take bait and artificial lures, though striped seaperch are decidedly easier to take on bait.

The ODFW typically allows liberal harvest of surfperch and striped seaperch (15 per person per day as of this writing), despite acknowledging that surfperch population dynamics are not well understood. Surfperch make excellent table fare when served fresh, so keep enough for a dinner or two, but consider carefully releasing fish when you've captured enough for your uses (barbless hooks help immeasurably in releasing fish, and artificial lures are much easier to remove than bait hooks). For a great deal of information about surfperch, visit Steve Morey's web site, www.theoutershore.com. Catch limits on other species—rockfish, greenling—are far more restrictive, vary by species, and are subject to change, so check the current fishing regulations from the ODFW.

The Pacific mole crab, or sand crab, is a favorite food of redtail surfperch and beaches with lots of mole crabs usually offer good fishing. Photo by Pavel Kirillov/CreativeCommons

Fourth of July fireworks at Gold Beach. Photo courtesy of Oregon Coast Visitors Association

Oregon Beach Events

Coastal communities from Astoria to Brookings host a variety of fun, entertaining, and educational events throughout the year, and many visitors plan beach trips specifically for favorite festivals, competitions, and celebrations. Many Oregon beach towns host Fourth of July festivities complete with fireworks displays, and visitors who've never seen spectacular fireworks bursting over ocean or bay are in for a special treat.

Beach towns also host a variety of events focusing on cuisine, regional wines, and local ales. One of the oldest and biggest occurs each winter in Newport: the Newport Seafood and Wine Festival, and this megalithic party only hints at the many other such events that celebrate Oregon seafood, such as salmon, crab, and even albacore tuna, which provide an offshore fishery every summer. Other annual events focus on natural or cultural history—for example, the Oregon Shorebird Festival based in Charleston, Yachats Village Mushroom Fest, Depoe Bay Indian-style Salmon Bake, Pacific City Dory Days. Up and down the coast, music, art, and theatre festivals celebrate the arts.

In addition to these celebrations, Oregon's coast hosts a variety of competitive events, including several prominent board-sports contests, such as the Pistol River Wave Bash and the Cape Kiwanda Longboard Classic. The town of

Seaside annually hosts one of the world's largest beach volleyball tournaments, and serves as the festive finish line for the state's famous Hood to Coast Relay. Other running events are also held annually at a variety of locations, and they range from short fun runs to the Oregon Coast 50 kilometer race. Oregon beaches also host sandcastle competitions and kite festivals, artistic and colorful events that are fun for all ages.

Many prominent annual events are listed in the appendix herein, but check with chambers of commerce and visitors' bureaus, as well as the Oregon Coast Visitors Association, www.visittheoregoncoast.com, for information on the many other events and celebrations hosted by coastal communities. Oregon beach events tend to be well attended, some of them massively attended; lodgings can sell out months in advance of the biggest extravaganzas, such as the Seaside Beach Volleyball Tournament and the Newport Seafood and Wine Festival. Be sure to make arrangements well in advance, then dive into the fun and celebrate the things that make Oregon's coast unique and alluring.

CHAPTER

3

Twin Rocks at the south end of Rockaway Beach. Photo by Michael Mattingley/Oregon Coast Visitors Association

NORTH COAST BEACHES: CLATSOP AND TILLAMOOK COUNTIES

Oregon's north coast is, in some ways, a study in contrast: Clatsop County is home to the tourist-driven beachside towns of Seaside and Cannon Beach, two of the busiest beach playgrounds in the state. An easy drive from the Portland area via US Highway 26, the two communities bustle with busy streets, crowded sidewalks, and popular sand beaches during the summer season, and tend to remain busy enough during the so-called off season that would-be visitors are well advised to make lodging reservations well in advance no matter the month. Conversely, Tillamook County remains recognizably more agrarian, its county seat, Tillamook, a working town, set inland on the east side of Tillamook Bay. Tillamook County's best-known touristy enclaves still attract plenty of visitors—after all, Portland and the northern Willamette Valley are not so far away—but the county nonetheless offers a number of alluring off-the-radar beaches.

Seaside is a versatile community, catering to all ages; Cannon Beach is a bit more upscale, a great place to enjoy a fine meal, but also entirely family friendly. Tillamook, home to the famous Tillamook Cheese Factory and the Tillamook Air Museum, still retains its small-town charm and its working-class roots while providing ample services and attractions for visitors. Clatsop County's 30-odd-mile stretch of Highway 101 largely hugs the coastline, but on its 70-mile run through Tillamook County, the highway courses inland to skirt Tillamook Bay and remains distant from the coast for 40 miles, leaving beach access to secondary routes, often resulting in uncrowded beaches near a series of tiny, charming beachfront communities, such as Oceanside and Tierra Del Mar.

North coast beaches come in myriad forms, from broad sandy expanses to inaccessible cobble shorelines carved into precipitous headlands. Clatsop County features a continuous 20 miles of sand beach from Clatsop Spit at the mouth of the Columbia River south to "The Cove" at the south end of the beach at Seaside. Briefly interrupted by rugged Tillamook Head, the glimmering sand beaches continue just north of Cannon Beach and run another dozen miles down to the county line at Falcon Cove. Tillamook County's beaches are more diverse, as the coastline traces a convoluted path, forming towering headlands, sand beaches, inlets, rocky shores, and broad estuaries. State parks and recreation areas abound on the north coast, including popular and sprawling Fort Stevens State Park, Ecola State Park, Oswald West State Park, and Cape Lookout State Park. Happily, Clatsop and Tillamook County beaches range from hyper-popular with easy access, to hidden and secluded with less-obvious access.

Beach volleyball at Seaside. Photo by John Shewey

Astoria
Warrenton
Westport 30
CLATSOP
Mist
COLUMBIA
Seaside
Cannon Beach
Elsie
Vernonia
Saint Helens
47
Arch Cape
Scappoose
53
Manzanita
Timber 26
WASHINGTON
Glenwood
Burlington
Rockaway Beach
6
PORTLAND
TILLAMOOK
Forest Grove
Hillsboro
Fairview
Troutdale
MULTNOMAH
Hood River
Odell
Mosier
84
City of the Dalles
Parkdale
Tillamook
Beaverton
Gresham
HOOD RIVER
47
219
Tigard
Milwaukie
Sandy
35
Dufur
Tualatin
Lake Oswego
Rhododendron
WASCO
197
Beaver
YAMHILL
Newberg
Oregon City
Estacada
Wamic
Donald
99E
213
211
Pacific City
McMinnville
Canby
Maupin
219
Molalla
26
216
Wapinitia
18
Amity
Woodburn
CLACKAMAS
Willamina
99W
Gervais
211
Otis
22
219
Scotts Mills
18
Keizer
Silverton
Simnasho
Lincoln City
22
Dallas
SALEM
MARION
Valsetz
Monmouth
Elkhorn
Depoe Bay
Independence
223
Stayton
Gates
Warm Springs
99W
Jefferson
Mill City
Idanha
Willo
Siletz
226
JEFFERSON
101
Adair Village
Crabtree
22
Madras
Newport
Eddyville
20
Corvallis
Albany

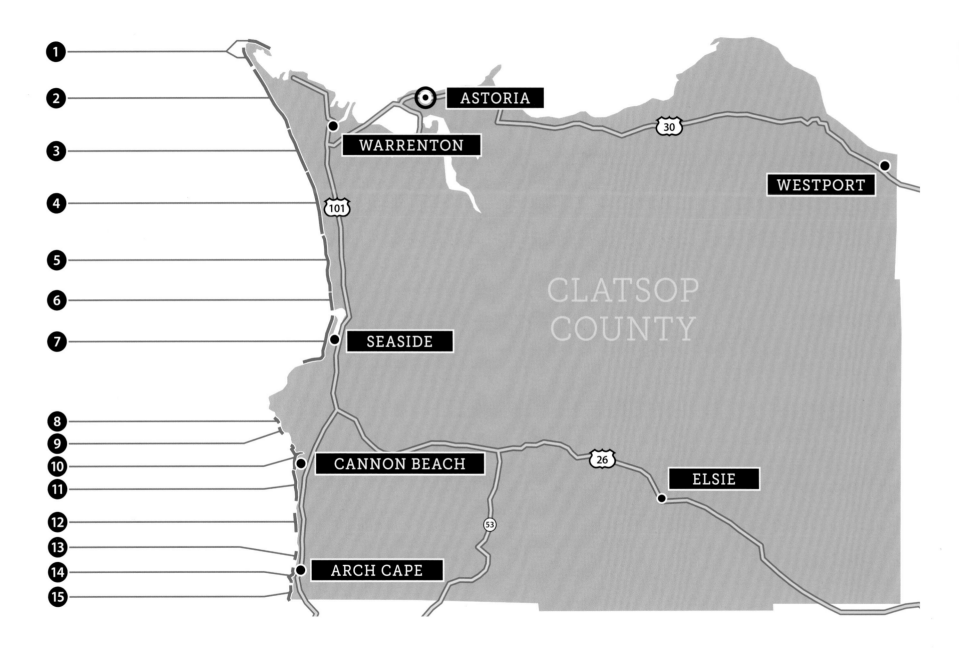

North Coast Beaches - Clatsop County

ASTORIA

WARRENTON

WESTPORT

101

30

SEASIDE

CANNON BEACH

26

ELSIE

53

ARCH CAPE

1
2
3
4
5
6
7
8
9
10
11
12
13
14
15

CLATSOP COUNTY

CLATSOP COUNTY BEACHES

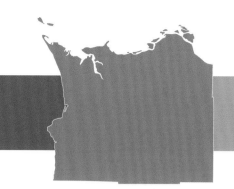

1. Clatsop Spit Beaches
2. Fort Stevens Beach
3. DeLaura Beach
4. Sunset Beach
5. Del Ray Beach
6. Gearhart Beach
7. Seaside Beach
8. Indian Beach
9. Crescent Beach
10. Chapman Beach
11. Tolovana Beach
12. Arcadia Beach
13. Hug Point Beach
14. Arch Cape Beach
15. Cove Beach

Clatsop Spit/Fort Stevens Beach

Location: Fort Stevens State Park, 14 miles northwest of Astoria, 18 miles north of Seaside, at the mouth of the Columbia River.

Access: Several parking areas within Fort Stevens State Park provide short trails to the beach; seasonal vehicle access to beach.

Facilities: Huge campground with 170 full-hookup RV sites, 300 electrical sites with water, 15 yurts (10 with universal access), 11 cabins (eight with universal access), hiker/biker camp, flush toilets and showers, RV dump station.

Fees: Camping fees apply.

Contact: Fort Stevens State Park, (503) 861-1671, www.oregonstateparks.org; Astoria Warrenton Chamber of Commerce, (503) 325-6311, www.oldoregon.com.

In addition to historic intrigue, abundant wildlife, and a sprawling campground, Clatsop Spit is widely known as perhaps the best razor clam beach on the Oregon coast, offering more than 4 miles of clean sand that, during prime times, attracts clam diggers by the hundreds. Clatsop Spit (aka Clatsop Beach and Fort Stevens Beach) continues southward and includes the contiguous beaches to the south, which go by their local names—DeLaura and Sunset Beaches, Del Ray Beach, Gearhart Beach, and Seaside, respectively—creating a virtually uninterrupted 18-mile-long strip of prime clamming beach. In addition to clamming, the beach at Clatsop Spit, from the base of the Columbia River south jetty south to Delaura and then Sunset Beaches, offers excellent prospects for surfperch, and the south jetty itself is popular for anglers seeking rockfish, greenling, sea perch, and surfperch. Moreover, the lengthy stretch of attractive sand beach here offers fun beachcombing, with sand dollars quite abundant, especially between late fall and early spring when few people roam the beach.

Fort Stevens State Park preserves a sprawling 4,247 acres, including its namesake, the site of a Civil War earthen fort completed in 1865, its intent to guard the mouth of the Columbia River against attack by Confederate and British gun boats. The fort was named for Union Army Major General Isaac I. Stevens, first territorial governor of Washington, who died in 1862 at the Battle of Chantilly in Fairfax County, Virginia. The fort continued to serve as Oregon's only coastal defense facility during the Spanish-American War, World War I, and World War II. On June 21, 1942, Fort Stevens was attacked by Japanese

submarine I-25, carrying a crew of 97 and armed with a 140 mm deck gun, becoming the only military fort in the United States to be fired upon by a foreign enemy since the War of 1812. The attack did little damage and claimed no casualties.

The state park has a huge campground, 6 miles of hiking trails, 11 miles of paved bicycle trails, a freshwater lake with swimming areas, two smaller lakes ideal for fishing and canoeing, a military museum, historic concrete coastal gun batteries, and the famous shipwreck of the *Peter Iredale*. Tours of the old military facilities are available during summer through Friends of Old Fort Stevens, (503) 861-2000, www.visitftstevens.com. As part of its Living History schedule, the friends group holds a variety of other events at Fort Stevens State Park between May and September.

Frequently the subject of dramatic photographs, the wreck of the *Peter Iredale* stands like a steel skeleton on the beach west from the campground via well-marked Peter Iredale Road. The 285-foot, four-mast sailing vessel was sailing from Salina Cruz,

Clatsop Spit and the wreck of the *Peter Iredale*. Photo courtesy Oregon Coast Visitors Association

○ Clatsop Spit/Fort Stevens Beach *(continued)*

Mexico, bound for Portland, when, on September 26, 1906, it was driven ashore by a powerful squall. All hands made it safely to shore, and plans were drawn to tow the ship back to sea, but before favorable weather arrived weeks later, the ship had listed badly, becoming deeply imbedded in the sand. Much of her remains were sold for scrap. The bow section, some ribs, and mast sections remain buried in the beach. The best time to visit the wreckage is during winter or early spring, when the beach has been scoured of much of the sand that accumulates during summer, revealing more of the ship's skeleton.

Fort Stevens State Park also includes the beaches on the Columbia River, from the north side of the south jetty around to the east (inland) side of Clatsop Spit. Heavily tidal influenced, the mouth of the Columbia here attracts lots of wildlife, especially birds, and is one of the best sites on the north coast to look for migrants, overwintering species, and pelagic birds driven shoreward by powerful Pacific storms. Access to these beaches is from the south jetty parking lot near the north end of Jetty Road, and from the last parking area at the terminal end of Jetty Road. From

the jetty parking lot, an observation tower provides a commanding view of the beach to the south, and a jetty trail leads west along the base of the jetty and out to the wide swath of sand beach stretching around the north tip of Clatsop Spit.

Between the jetty access parking lot on the north and the *Peter Iredale* beach access to the south, two additional parking areas provide immediate access to the beach along Clatsop Spit, both located along Jetty Road.

Street-legal vehicles (no motorcycles or off-highway vehicles) are allowed on the beach at Fort Stevens south of the *Peter Iredale* road access; the 4-mile stretch of beach from the *Peter Iredale* beach access north to the south jetty is closed to vehicles from noon to midnight between May 1 and September 15. In addition to the *Peter Iredale* access at Fort Stevens State Park, additional vehicle access points are located to the south at DeLaura Beach (difficult), Sunset Beach, Del Rey Beach, and off 10th Street in Gearhart.

A banded Caspian tern on the beach at the Columbia River south jetty in Fort Stevens State Park. Photo by John Shewey

The wreck of the *Peter Iredale* on Clatsop Spit. Photo courtesy Oregon Coast Visitors Association

○ DeLaura Beach

Location: Warrenton, 2 miles south of Fort Stevens State Park.

Access: Rugged, 0.25-mile pedestrian/vehicle access road.

Facilities: None.

Little-known DeLaura Beach is a gorgeous stretch of coastline, backed by tall vegetated dunes, and seldom visited other than by a handful of sand-driving enthusiasts who love the challenge of navigating the steep access road and then the soft, powdery, tire-grabbing sand. If that sounds like your brand of beach fun, don't underestimate this deep sand—it can mire down the best of four-wheel-drive vehicles. The access road itself, about a quarter mile long, can be problematic. During late summer and early autumn it is usually dry, rocky, and rutted, but during wet weather and from the onset of autumn rains until early summer, expect gooey mud at best and impassable flooded road at worst. The road tunnels through coastal scrub forest—alder, willow, and pines—and then reaches the vegetated dunes

DeLaura Beach. Photo by John Shewey

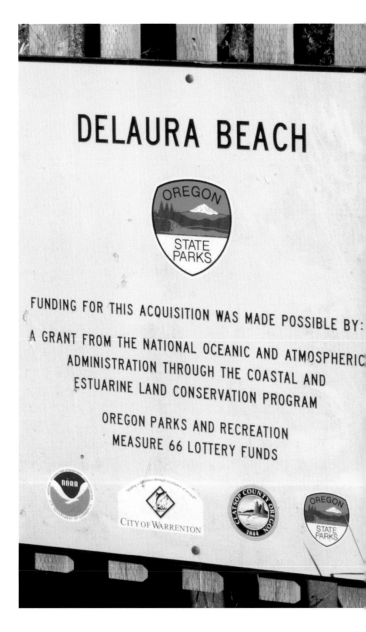

above the beach. If your vehicle is not well-equipped for sand driving, park here and walk to the beach; otherwise, scout the descent to the beach on foot, and then drive down. If you don't like the prospects for driving back out the way you came, you can drive north on the beach about 2 miles to the vehicle access road at the *Peter Iredale*.

Naturally, DeLaura Beach is a great place for pedestrians as well as vehicles. You can walk the access road, or drive it as far as the back side of the dunes, where a small turnaround area has room for parking. The total distance, from the west end of DeLaura Road to the beach itself, is about one-third of a mile. Because so few people walk this stretch of sand, it's a great place for beachcombing, with sand dollars fairly common, and a variety of other shells washing up often. Like the more accessible beaches nearby, DeLaura Beach is an excellent location for both razor clams and redtail surfperch.

The key to the quietude of DeLaura Beach is a complete lack of signage on Highway 101 and the fact that the beach sits about 3 miles off the highway.

The road to Fort Stevens State Park (State Route 104) departs Highway 101 at milepost 11.5 at the south end of Warrenton. From there, go north about 0.3 miles and veer left onto Columbia Beach Road/Ridge Road. Go north 1.5 miles and turn left onto DeLaura Beach Lane, and follow it west 0.7 miles to the wide gravel parking area and sign announcing DeLaura Beach. From there, the 0.25-mile access road continues west.

Entrance sign at the road leading to DeLaura Beach. Photo by John Shewey

○ Sunset Beach

Location: Sunset Beach State Recreation Site, Highway 101, milepost 13.5, 5.5 miles north of Gearhart.

Access: Trail and road access to beach, along with wheelchair-accessible boardwalk to beach viewing point.

Facilities: Outhouse.

Contact: Sunset Beach State Recreation Site, (503) 861-3170 ext. 21, www.oregonstateparks.org.

Especially popular for digging razor clams, with easy access by foot or vehicle, Sunset Beach is the middle portion of the uninterrupted sand beach stretching from the Columbia River south jetty at Fort Stevens State Park south to Seaside. The site has two parking areas near the west end of Sunset Beach Lane, which turns off Highway 101, 2 miles south of the Highway 101/State Route 104 junction and 5.5 miles north of Pacific Way in Gearhart. The first parking lot serves the Fort to Sea Trail, which retraces a route used by the Lewis and Clark Corp of Discovery, which wintered in the area at Fort Clatsop during the winter of 1805-06 (see www.nps.gov/lewi/planyourvisit/forttosea.htm).

Sunset Beach offers good prospects for surfperch anglers. Photo by John Shewey

The second parking area is along both sides of the road's west end where it ramps down to the beach. Generally Sunset Beach is easy to drive on, and the 3.5 miles down to the vehicle access at Del Ray Beach presents few problems. Going north can be a bit trickier, especially because of increasingly soft sand around DeLaura Beach. During winter, when few people wander this stretch of sand, Sunset Beach can be great for beachcombing, particularly following storm-driven high tides.

Sunset Beach is one of the state's top razor clam locations. Photo by Steve Cota

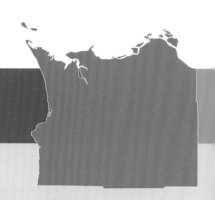

Del Ray Beach and Gearhart Beach

Location: Gearhart, just north of Seaside.

Access: Pedestrian access at the west ends of most east-west streets in Gearhart; primary access points at Pacific Way and 10th Street (vehicle access at 10th Street). Pedestrian and vehicle access at Del Ray Beach State Recreation Site, Highway 101 milepost 17.

Facilities: None.

Amenities: Gearhart offers a handful of appealing eateries and lodging options, as well as a popular golf course.

Contact: City of Seaside Visitors Bureau, (503) 738-3097, www.seasideor.com; Del Ray Beach State Recreation Site, (503) 861-3170, www.oregonstateparks.org.

The mouth of the Necanicum River separates Gearhart Beach from Seaside Beach just to the south; otherwise there is little to differentiate the two wide, long stretches of sand except that the Gearhart stretch tends to attract fewer people, though its lack of pedestrian traffic comes with the caveat that north from the 10th Street beach access, vehicles are allowed on the beach and they tend to show up in droves during the summer season. However, 10th Street is located about 1 mile north of the Necanicum River, leaving lots of wide, sandy beach open for those who prefer to escape the vehicle traffic.

The area around the mouth of the river is one of the best places on the entire coast to find sand dollars, but during summer, get there early in the morning to beat the crowds. During winter, the beaches are much quieter, especially Gearhart Beach. Access is easy, with limited parking and a wide beach-access trail at the end of Pacific Way, the primary entrance to Gearhart from Highway 101 (just north of milepost 19). Follow Pacific Way due west to the beach trail (if you arrive in the morning, stop first for coffee and excellent pastries at Pacific Way Bakery). Parking is limited at this location, but streetside spots are nearby.

At the Pacific Way beach access, Ocean Avenue heads south, and about a quarter mile down this road are beach trails tucked in between the houses at the west ends of E Street and G Street. Parking is minimal so be careful not to block driveways, impose on private property, or impede traffic.

To the north of Pacific Way, via North Marion Avenue, beach trails thread between houses at the west ends of most east-west streets, with the major access point being 10th Street. Here, a wide, easy-to-drive beach-entry road serves vehicles (four-wheel-drive is

best, though two-wheel-drive vehicles can cautiously wander the harder sand within easy reach of the entryway). For four-wheel-drive vehicles, the drive-on access at Del Ray Beach is just 1 mile to the north. Del Ray Beach stretches northward, uninterrupted, to meld into Sunset Beach, DeLaura Beach, and Clatsop Beach. The beach drive from Del Ray to Sunset Beach covers about 3.5 miles.

In addition to the aforementioned Pacific Way Bakery, Gearhart is the site of one of the dozens of eclectic Mcmenamin's brewpubs: Gearhart Hotel and Sand Trap Pub, (503) 717-8150, sits about a block off the beach and serves up the pub fare and fine ales that have made the Mcmenamin brothers famous in the Northwest brewery world. Adjacent to the Sand Trap is the popular Gearhart Golf Links, www. gearhartgolflinks.com.

Top: Del Ray Beach. Photo by Tony Webster/Creative Commons
Bottom: Gearhart Beach. Photo by John Shewey

○ Seaside

Location: Approximately 80 miles west of Portland via U.S. Highway 26 and 101.

Access: 1.5-mile long walkway (the Promenade) follows along the beach, providing numerous access points; all east–west-oriented streets in Seaside lead to the Promenade; additional access south of town.

Facilities: Restrooms, as well as showers to hose off seawater and sand, are located at the base of the Turnaround (end of Broadway Street) below the stairwells.

Amenities: Numerous restaurants, shops, hotels, rental houses, and attractions are located within easy walking distance from the beach.

Contact: City of Seaside Visitors Bureau, (503) 738-3097, www.seasideor.com.

Seaside rivals Cannon Beach, Lincoln City, and Newport as the busiest coastal town in Oregon, and may well draw more summertime tourists than any of the others—any summer weekend, the downtown beach district swarms with visitors, its sidewalks and shops crowded, its streets lined with slowly moving vehicles. More than 2 miles of wide sandy beach fronts the town proper, stretching from the mouth of the Necanicum River south to The Cove (the colloquial name for the south end of this stretch of beach). Increasingly rocky down toward The Cove, Seaside's beach is otherwise composed of fine, dense, soft sand; at low tide it stretches more than a quarter mile wide from the 1.5-mile-long Promenade—the city-maintained paved pedestrian pathway stretching along the upper beach—to the surf line.

On summer days, the crowded summer streets, naturally, spill out onto the sprawling beach, which attracts walkers, runners, beachcombers, surf anglers, surfers, wakeboarders, volleyball players, kite enthusiasts, dog walkers, bicyclers, and more. Surprisingly, however, the beach crowds are slow to assemble, and visitors who head for the sand at sunup can enjoy quiet and solitude, sharing the beach with just a handful of people even on the busiest summer weekends. The most popular access point in town is the Seaside Turnaround at the end of Broadway Street. Streetside parking in the area fills quickly, but the city maintains public parking options, the best and biggest being a large lot one block north of Broadway between Edgewood and Columbia Streets—an easy walk of a few hundred yards to the beach. Each east–west-oriented street in Seaside ends at the Promenade, so from wherever you park, simply walk west to access the beach.

While the core downtown tourist district of Seaside and its adjacent beach draw the biggest crowds, often you can find ready parking and fewer people at the south end of town, at the west end of U Street (the so-called "U Street District"), which turns west off Highway 101 on the south end of town (across from Les Schwab). From U Street, you can also turn south on Edgewood Street, Downing Street, or Ocean Vista Lane, which converge to form one road that runs alongside The Cove and provides immediate beach access with plenty of roadside parking. Once on the beach in The Cove, you can wander southward to enjoy the rocky tidepools, which are best on minus-tides. The Cove is also Seaside's most popular surfing area, as well as an excellent spot for birdwatching, particularly from late summer through early spring.

Like the south end of the beach at The Cove, the north end, at the mouth of the Necanicum River—diminutive on summer low tides—draws far fewer visitors than the beach within sight of the Turnaround. A morning walk north to the broad swath of sand at the Necanicum delta is decidedly pleasant at any time of year. Additionally, a pair of little-known informal

The annual Seaside Beach Volleyball Tournament is held each August. Photo courtesy of Oregon Coast Visitors Association

○ Seaside *(continued)*

parking areas allow immediate access to the delta. One is located at the north end of North Franklin Street, and the other at the north end of North Columbia Street. Both of these access sites are located in a residential neighborhood, so avoid blocking driveways or otherwise impeding local traffic. The Necanicum delta is another good birdwatching location, and one of the best places on the Oregon coast to find sand dollars.

End to end, Seaside's wide, flat, sand beach is one of the state's top beaches for digging razor clams (be sure to check the latest Oregon Department of Fish and Wildlife regulations). This beach is also a top destination for redtail surfperch, and early morning incoming tides often find wader-clad surf anglers plying their craft in the oft-gentle surf of late spring and summer.

Seaside hosts a number of big events during the summer, including one of the world's largest beach volleyball tournaments that runs for three days during the second full weekend in August. But come winter, even seemingly ever-busy Seaside calms

substantially and visitors who don't mind the cooler weather can often find the beach deserted and the city itself much quieter. In fact, any time from late autumn through early spring can be a decidedly pleasant time to find the town and its beaches in a state of calm, the frenetic energy and bustling crowds of summer but a memory.

Aerial view of Seaside Beach. Photo courtesy of Oregon Coast Visitors Association

The Cove at the south end of Seaside. Photo courtesy of Oregon Coast Visitors Association

Indian Beach and Crescent Beach (Ecola State Park)

Location: Ecola State Park, just north of Cannon Beach.

Access: Short, easy trail to Indian Beach; long, difficult trail to Crescent Beach.

Facilities: Restrooms, picnic tables.

Fees: State park day-use fee, payable at entrance booth, or recreation pass required.

Contact: Ecola State Park, (503) 436-2844, www.oregonstateparks.org; Cannon Beach Chamber of Commerce, (503) 436-2623, www.cannonbeach.org.

The two beaches at Ecola State Park present two different opportunities: Indian Beach is easy to reach, save for the limited parking, while Crescent Beach requires a more substantial hike. Consequently beautiful Indian Beach absorbs most of the beach-going traffic, while equally picturesque Crescent Beach is lightly visited. Crescent Beach stretches about three-quarters of a mile, bordered by Chapman Point to the south and Ecola Head to the north. Slightly shorter, postcard-pretty Indian Beach is enclosed by dramatic Indian Point to the north and Bald Point to the south.

The road through Ecola State Park terminates at the parking area for Indian Beach, with a scenic overlook and short trail down through the cobble and onto the sand. This mesmerizing beach attracts a few surfers, some early-morning beachcombers, and lots of tourists. Parking is limited and the narrow, winding road through the park gets busy quickly on summer days and on weekends much of the year. Go early in the morning or face lines at the entry booth and the possibility of no available parking. Once past the entry station, Ecola Point parking area is just off to the left, and well worth a stop for the views, while the park road continues northward to Indian Beach.

Indian Beach. Photo by Chris/CreativeCommons

The trail to Crescent Beach departs the Ecola Point parking lot and runs about 1.5 miles; it's steep, muddy in places, and relatively difficult. Few visitors make the hike. However, low tides present an easier alternative: relatively few people realize that at low tide you can walk around Chapman Point at Cannon Beach and directly onto Crescent Beach. Use any of the beach-access sites in Cannon Beach. The easiest is at the end of 7th Street, just a short walk from Chapman Point. The lower the tide the better (but it needn't be a minus-tide), and watch your clock and the water level to make sure you get back south of Chapman Point before the tide returns.

Moreover, on a summer (daylight) minus-tide, you can walk all the way from Indian Beach, to Cannon Beach, hiking around Bald Point, through Ecola Point, and then around Chapman Point. To make this one-way through-hike on a minus-tide, start at the Indian Beach parking area in Ecola State Park about 30 minutes prior to peak low tide so you are rounding Bald Point at the lowest water level. The total distance is about 2 miles. Naturally you'll need a way to get back to your vehicle at the end of the hike (it's a 3-mile hike back up into the park once you head off the beach south of Chapman Point at the west end of 7th Street in Cannon Beach).

The two beaches and associated headlands of Ecola State Park abound in wildlife, especially birds and tidepool creatures. Low tides—and especially minus-tides—are fantastic at both Indian and Crescent Beaches. The rocks at the feet of the headlands on both beaches are loaded with sea stars, anemones, and myriad other animals. The near-shore rocks and surf attract many species of seabirds, from harlequin ducks and surf scoters to brown pelicans and pelagic cormorants, as well as numerous shorebirds between late summer and late spring.

The well-signed entrance for Ecola State Park is at the north end of Cannon Beach. The twisting and turning road is unsuitable for RVs and trailers, and the only turnaround points for cars are at the two parking lots, 1.2 miles into the park, and then 1.5 miles beyond that point, and Indian Beach.

Crescent Beach. Photo courtesy of Oregon Coast Visitors Association

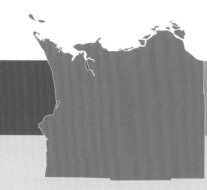

Cannon Beach Area (Chapman Beach and Tolovana Beach)

 Location: Cannon Beach; Highway 101, mileposts 28–30, 80 miles west-by-northwest from Portland.

 Access: Numerous beach access points within the town of Cannon Beach.

 Facilities: Restrooms, picnic tables.

 Amenities: Numerous restaurants, lodging options, and shops within walking distance of beach.

 Contact: Cannon Beach Chamber of Commerce, (503) 436-2623, www.cannonbeach.org.

One of Oregon's busiest coastal tourist communities, idyllic Cannon Beach fairly brims with activity nearly all year round, emanating a palpable resort-town vibe, especially on sunny summer days. Its narrow streets, keenly kempt sidewalks, eclectic shops, intriguing watering holes, and alluring restaurants are almost always abuzz with visitors, and of course the crowds spill out onto the town's beautiful sandy beaches, where massive Haystack Rock provides a frequently photographed backdrop. The sand stretches for 4 miles, from Chapman Point on the north end of town, south past Silver Point at the south end of town, and down to Humbug Point,

the dividing line between the beaches of Cannon Beach and Arcadia Beach.

The northern stretch of this beach is called Chapman Beach, its southern half, Tolovana Beach, though few people use those names, instead referring to the entire stretch as simply Cannon Beach. At the midpoint of the beach, Haystack Rock rises 235 feet above the surf, its tide-pools within reach at low tides. A public parking lot on Gower Avenue in Cannon Beach's midtown district is just a short walk from Haystack Rock, but most westbound streets in Cannon Beach and conjoined Tolovana Park lead

to beach trails. The trick is finding parking, and the solution is to plan your beach visit for early morning. The town has several public parking lots, plus plenty of streetside parking, but the spots tend to fill quickly beginning in mid-morning. Tolovana Beach Wayside (exit Highway 101 about a quarter mile south of milepost 30) provides access to the southern half of the beach, and from here, you can walk a mile south to Silver Point. At low tide, you can easily walk around Silver Point and continue down to Humbug Point.

Cannon Beach offers a wide array of lodging options, but make reservations well ahead of time—and that goes for any time of year. Likewise, call ahead for seating if you want to sample one of the town's highly-reputed restaurants, such as Stephanie Inn, Lazy Susan Café, The Irish Table, Wayfarer, Sweet Basil Café, or Newman's at 988. Even the friendly pubs and lunch stops tend to be plenty busy. But save time for the beach: the wide swath of clean golden sand at Cannon Beach is ideal for nearly every beach activity, from early morning beachcombing to flying kites in the afternoon breeze to enjoying a summer picnic with a spectacular view.

Cannon Beach and Haystack Rock. Photo by Tom Dixon/CreativeCommons

Arcadia Beach. Photo courtesy of Oregon State Parks.

Arcadia Beach

 Location: Highway 101, milepost 32, 3 miles south of Cannon Beach.

 Access: Short trail down to beach from forested parking lot.

 Facilities: Restrooms, picnic tables.

Contact: Arcadia Beach State Recreation Site, (503) 368-3575, www.oregonstateparks.org.

Framed by two minor headlands, Humbug Point to the north and Hug Point to the south, mile-long Arcadia Beach is a gorgeous stretch of clean sand ideal for beachcombing, picnicking, surf fishing, and even board sports. The 8-acre Arcadia Beach State Recreation Site includes a small parking area with picnic tables set beneath a canopy of Sitka spruce. Many visitors swing into the parking lot for a quick view of the beach below, but surprisingly few bother to walk down to the sand. That's not to say Arcadia Beach isn't busy at times—this is the north coast after all—but during the offseason, from October to April, don't be surprised to find this beach deserted. To the south, at low tides, you can cross over Hug Point on the old beach road (see next entry) to reach Hug Point Beach, and you can walk north around Humbug Point to visit the south extent of Tolovana Beach.

Surf fishing at Arcadia Beach. Photo by John Shewey

Hug Point Beach

Location: Hug Point State Recreation Site, Highway 101 milepost 33.5, 4.5 miles south of Cannon Beach.

Access: Short stairwell trail to beach.

Facilities: Restrooms, picnic tables.

Contact: Hug Point State Recreation Site, (503) 368-3575, www.oregonstateparks.org.

Family-friendly Hug Point Beach, with its colorful sandstone and basalt bluffs, firm sand, and wave-battered intertidal rocks attracts substantial crowds during the summer tourism season, but not nearly the number of people who crowd into Cannon Beach to the north or Oswald West State Park to the south, mainly because the Hug Point parking lot is large enough for only a few dozen vehicles. This intriguing beach takes its name from the fact that in the days before the coast highway was constructed, the beach served as the road, and coach and vehicle traffic had to run right along the rock headland here—hug the rocks, in other words—at low tide to get around the point. At low tide, the rocks farthest north of the trail access—Hug Point itself—still bear the carved-out road bed used long ago.

Low tide, in fact, opens access to the entire north end of the beach, including a secluded pocket beach with a big cave in the sandstone and a veil-like waterfall on aptly named Fall Creek that spills over a small bluff above and onto the beach during the rainy season. During summer, this sheltered cove begs for an old-fashioned beach party, and sure enough, many weekends find a group of beachgoers with chairs set up, Frisbees, footballs, surf boards, and all the other typical accoutrements. High tide brings the water up against Adair Point

Beach hikers walk the old road carved into the headland at Hug Point. Photo by Eli Duke/CreativeCommons

(the headland just north of the parking lot), sealing off the pocket beach, so visitors need to watch the tide and the time or wait until the water again recedes with the next ebb.

The northernmost end of the beach, along the base of Hug Point, has nice tide pools at low tide, and of course hikers can walk around the point, using the old stone roadway, to reach the gleaming sand beach to the north. The beach hike between Hug Point and the beach access at Arcadia Beach State Park covers about 1 mile. The sand is firm enough along the water that during summer, some visitors use bicycles to make the journey between the two state parks. At higher tides, surf anglers sometimes fish from the old carved-out roadway.

North end of Hug Point Beach. Photo by Traveling Otter/CreativeCommons

Arch Cape Beach

 Location: In and near the small community of Arch Cape, along Highway 101, 5.5 miles south of Cannon Beach.

 Access: Short trails lead to the beach within town.

Facilities: None.

 Amenities: Variety of lodging options.

 Contact: Arch Cape and Falcon Cove Community Club, www.archcape.com.

The decidedly pleasant community of Arch Cape tends to offer a respite from the bustling crowds of Cannon Beach just 5 miles north. This small town has a core of year-round residents intermingled with numerous vacation rentals, as well as several luxurious B&B-type establishments, the highly regarded Arch Cape Inn and Retreat (www.archcapeinn.com), Inn at Arch Cape (www.innatarchcape.com), and Ocean Point Inn (www.oceanpoint-inn.com). Otherwise, Arch Cape offers few services, although eclectic Jack's Thrift Shop is always worth a visit.

The idyllic sand beach at Arch Cape, largely out of view of the highway, stretches for more than a mile, from Point Meriwether at Hug Point State Park south to scenic Arch Cape itself, a precipitous headland (that the highway tunnels through) with a triangular sea stack sitting in the surf just off its foot. During low tides, a strip of sand between the headland and the sea stack allows egress to Cove Beach to the south (see next entry), but get back before the water rises or you face a long walk or long wait. Arch Cape Beach is seldom crowded and frequently deserted; it's a fine place for beachcombing, particularly on receding tides after winter storms.

Several access points provide short trails to the sand. The west end of West Ocean Lane (turn west off the highway at Jack's Thrift Shop) has room for four or five vehicles on the south side of the street against the trees and a secluded picnic table along the short trail to the beach. Another public trail is located 0.2 miles north along Pacific Road, just south of Donlon Street, but parking is minimal. At the south end of town, only a short walk from the cape, Leech Lane has ample parking, and is the closest access site to Cove Beach just to the south.

Left: Cooking a shellfish shore lunch. Photo by John Shewey
Right: Arch Cape Beach. Photo by John Shewey

Cove Beach. Photo by John Shewey

Cove Beach (aka Falcon Cove Beach, Magic Rocks Beach)

 Location: Highway 101 milepost 37, 2.5 miles south of the town of Arch Cape and 3.3 miles north of Neahkahnie Viewpoint.

 Access: Short, steep trails down to cobblestone upper beach at the end of Columbia Street along Tide Avenue.

Facilities: None.

Hidden well off Highway 101 behind a forested, beachfront residential area just north of Cape Falcon, Cove Beach goes by any of several names, including Falcon Cove Beach and occasionally Magic Rocks Beach. This latter moniker derives from the vast fields of volcanic cobble that make up much of this pristine, seldom-visited beach that stretches from the little cove at the northernmost foot of Cape Falcon north to the rocks that form Arch Cape. These dense cobbles click and clack together as the breakers drain off them, producing a truly magical, unique sound.

The north end of the beach is accessible through the rocks at Arch Cape at low tide levels—use the Leech Lane access, then walk south across Arch Cape Creek and through the rocks. But the better part of this beach—the magic rocks stretch—is farther south, accessed via

secondary roads: at milepost 37, turn west off Highway 101 onto Falcon Cove Road. Go about half a mile to a Y-intersection and take the right-hand fork (Columbia Street) and follow it downhill for 0.4 miles to its end at Tide Avenue. The trail is directly ahead across from Columbia Street. A second beach-access trail, with a stairwell, is located a tenth of a mile north on Tide Avenue. Neither location can accommodate more than two cars, so be careful not to impede local traffic (which is very light). These two access points lead directly down to the narrowest part of the beach, where high tides swallow the sand that borders the cobblestone upper beach.

The dilemma is when to visit: low tide exposes a gorgeous stretch of narrow sand beach, often littered with enough shells to make for fun beachcombing. Moreover, the first two hours of an incoming tide on a

calm, late-spring morning presents solid prospects for surfperch fishing, as this beach typically hosts a solid population of mole crabs (favorite food of redtail surfperch). High tide, on the other hand, eliminates much of the sand beach, but brings the breakers up onto the cobble so you can hear the magical jangling of click-clacking stones. In fact, while you cannot access the beach during a big winter storm, you can certainly hear the cobble and watch massive breakers from the two access trails.

South a short distance from the two access points, the beach ends at the foot of Cape Falcon amid a jumble of boulders. Low tides reveal tide pools and intrepid, sure-footed, mountain-goat-type visitors can explore quite a ways southward along the cliffs, but be careful not to get cut off by the incoming tide.

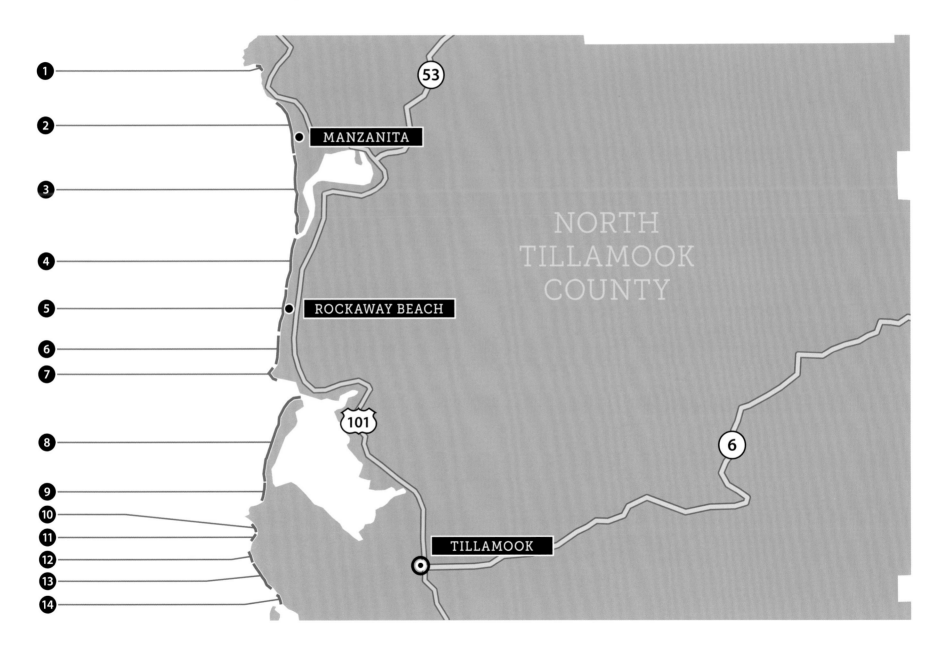

1

2 **MANZANITA**

3

4

5 **ROCKAWAY BEACH**

6

7

NORTH TILLAMOOK COUNTY

101

8

6

9

10

11

12 **TILLAMOOK**

13

14

NORTH TILLAMOOK COUNTY BEACHES

1. Short Sand Beach
2. Neahkahnie Beach
3. Nehalem Spit
4. Nedonna Beach
5. Rockaway Beach
6. Twin Rocks Beach
7. Barview Jetty County Park
8. Bayocean Peninsula

9. Cape Meares Beach
10. Short Beach
11. Lost Boy Beach
12. Tunnel Beach
13. Oceanside Beach
14. Netarts

1

2

3

4

5 BEAVER

6

7

8 PACIFIC CITY

9

10

SOUTH TILLAMOOK COUNTY

101

22

SOUTH TILLAMOOK COUNTY BEACHES

1. Netarts Spit
2. Cape Lookout State Park Beach
3. Cape Lookout South Beach
4. Sand Lake Recreation Area
5. Tierra Del Mar
6. McPhillips Beach
7. Kiwanda Beach
8. Bob Straub State Park
9. Winema Beach
10. Neskowin Beach

103

○ Short Sand Beach

 Location: Oswald West State Park, along Highway 101, 10 miles south of Cannon Beach, 5 miles north of Manzanita.

 Access: Fairly easy 0.5-mile trail to the beach.

Facilities: Restrooms, picnic tables.

Contact: Oswald West State Park, (503) 368-3575, www.oregonstateparks.org.

Short Sand Beach, or "Shorty's" to use the parlance of those who frequent this beautiful pocket beach, is one of the most popular walk-in beaches on the north coast, always drawing a substantial crowd on summer weekends. The only accessible beach in spectacularly scenic 2,484-acre Oswald West State Park, Short Sand Beach is popular with surfers. Despite being hemmed in and protected from the wind by headlands that jut well out into the sea on both ends to form Smuggler's Cove, Short Sand Beach is angled just right to absorb a consistent and often beginner-friendly break, with more challenging breaks often peeling off both headlands. Among the surfers, boogie boarders and stand-up paddle-boarders also frequent Shorty's

and the cove often transforms into a classic, almost California-style "beach scene," complete with plenty of dogs.

The short, pleasant hike to Short Sand Beach courses through mature Sitka spruce forest, and is an easy walk ideal for families even with young children. The trail begins at the southern parking lot for Oswald West State Park, on the west side of Highway 101 just south of the large parking area on the east side of the highway. On any day between May and the end of September, get there early or risk finding no room to park (in which case, park at the big lot and use the Short Sands North Trail). A short distance farther south

Short Sand Beach. Photo by Eli Duke/CreativeCommons

from the Short Sands South Trail, another trailhead, for the Necarney Creek Trail, leads down to the beach trail, and all the trails in Oswald West State Park interconnect, so in reality, any of the four trailheads will get you to the beach. The main trail includes a narrow suspension bridge over Short Sand Creek.

Short Sand Beach is typically uncrowded during winter and while its gravel beds, if they remain uncovered during summer, are routinely picked over for agates during the busy season, an early morning low tide during winter—especially midweek—sometimes delivers solitude, and agate hunting all to yourself. Usually, with the spring and summer wave patterns depositing sand onto the beach, Shorty's is virtually all sand (except for the upper fringe of cobble), the beach shaped by angular sandbars and shallow troughs at low tides. In winter, however, the gravel beds are usually revealed. The walk in and out of Shorty's is easy enough that photographers can linger for vibrant sunset photos and then make it quickly back up to the parking lot. Because Oswald West State Park attracts so many visitors, it also attracts a few thieves, so don't leave anything of value in sight in your vehicle.

Short Sand Beach. Photo by Eli Duke/CreativeCommons

Neahkahnie Beach (aka Manzanita Beach) and Nehalem Spit

Location: Neahkahnie, Manzanita, and Nehalem Bay State Park; Highway 101, 14 miles south of Cannon Beach, 17 miles north of Garibaldi.

Access: Numerous access points in Neahkahnie/Manzanita; beach trails from Nehalem Bay State Park campground and day-use area.

Facilities: Nehalem Bay State Park campground has 265 electrical sites with water (three with universal access), 18 yurts (two pet-friendly), hiker/biker camp, horse camp with 17 primitive sites, air strip and airport camp with primitive sites, hot showers/flush toilets, RV dump station; day-use sites has restrooms.

Amenities: Manzanita offers a variety of good restaurants, interesting shops, and lodging options.

Fees: Day-use fee or recreation pass required for Nehalem Bay State Park; camping fees apply.

Contact: City of Manzanita, www.exploremanzanita.com; Nehalem Bay State Park, (503) 368-5154, www.oregonstateparks.org.

Verdantly forested Cape Falcon juts splendidly out into the sea a few miles south of Cannon Beach, but viewed from a distance on a clear day, this scenic headland appears to be nearly enveloped by massive 1,680-foot Neahkahnie Mountain looming above. Highway 101 wraps around Neahkahnie's west slope, providing a spectacular view to the south of mile after mile of gleaming white sand and the beachside communities of Neahkahnie and Manzanita. Here, 6 miles of popular and poetically

pretty beach extend from the foot of Neahkahnie Mountain south to the mouth of the Nehalem River. Despite the summer crowds that enjoy these welcoming towns, Neahkahnie Beach (also called Manzanita Beach) hardly ever seems crowded, and its southern extension—Nehalem Spit—frequently offers genuine solitude for those who hike a mile or two south down the beach from sprawling Nehalem Bay State Park.

Situated on the narrow spit, the state park encompasses shoreline on both Nehalem Bay and the ocean, with a network of trails—including a 1.8-mile-long biking/hiking path—that allow visitors to branch out and explore a variety of habitats, including the wildlife-rich estuary. The state park offers a large campground and a day-use area (which requires a daily fee), and is popular with equestrians who enjoy riding along the beach. Oregon Beach Rides, www.oregonbeachrides.com, operates a concession

at the day-use site during summer, offering guided beach and trail rides. Moreover, Nehalem Bay is a popular fishery for clams, crabs, and salmon (boat rentals are available at the marinas on the inland side of the bay).

To reach Nehalem Bay State Park from the north, turn off Highway 101 at Laneda Avenue in Manzanita, go one block west and turn left on Classic Street, which becomes Gary Street leading into the state park. From the south, turn west off Highway 101 at Necarney City Road, following its windy path to a left turn on Gary Street leading into the park. To reach the day-use area (and the boat ramp on Nehalem Bay) follow the main road past the campground entrance and continue for about 1 mile heading south.

Back to the north, in the community of Manzanita and its northern outskirt, Neahkahnie, beach access abounds, and a variety of restaurants and lodging options, as well as an eclectic shopping district along Laneda Avenue, sit within walking distance of the sand. The two primary exits off Highway 101 are at Nehalem Road near milepost 43, and a third of a

Neahkahnie Beach and Nehalem Spit from the viewpoint on Highway 101 north from Manzanita. Photo by John Shewey

○ Neahkahnie Beach (aka Manzanita Beach) and Nehalem Spit *(continued)*

mile farther south at Laneda Avenue (the local visitors center is near the west end of Laneda). Both streets head west to meet Ocean Road, which runs along the beach for more than half a mile and provides numerous parking pullouts. At its juncture with Ocean Road, Nehalem Road swings north and becomes Pacific Boulevard, which offers further pullouts for beach parking.

South from Ocean Road, beach access is available at nearly every west-running street off of north–south-oriented Beach Street: from the west end of Laneda Avenue, go east 200 yards and turn south on Carmel Avenue, go three short blocks, and turn right (west) on Edmund Lane to find the first and northernmost of these short access trails that squeeze between houses. The next three are each a block apart, at Treasure Cove Lane, Beeswax Lane, and Pacific Lane. South of Pacific Lane, two more access trails branch off Beach Lane in the next quarter mile. Then Sunset Lane/Necarney Boulevard branches left off Beach Lane, heads inland a short

North end of Neahkahnie Beach. Photo by John Shewey

distance, and turns south; each of the 10 roads running west from this road offers beach access. These residential-neighborhood access locations, though plentiful, offer only scant parking, primarily curbside, so be respectful and avoid blocking driveways or impeding traffic.

The broad sand beach from Neahkahnie south to Nehalem Spit attracts all kinds of beach enthusiasts—beachcombers, surfers, hikers, beach cyclists, equestrians, kite fliers, picnickers, sunbathers, and visitors who just want to breathe in the marine air and enjoy the gorgeous coastal views. One local business, Bahama Mama's (www.manzanitabike.com) rents surfboards, boogie boards, paddle boards, and fat-tire beach bicycles.

The gleaming white sand at Neahkahnie Beach. Photo by John Shewey

○ Nedonna Beach (aka Manhattan Beach)

Location: North end of Rockaway Beach, Highway 101 milepost 48.8.

Access: Short trails through coastal dunes from state wayside and from signed access points along Beach Drive.

Facilities: Restrooms and picnic tables at Manhattan Beach State Wayside; outhouse at Nedonna Beach/South Jetty parking area.

Contact Manhattan Beach State Recreation Site, (503) 368-5943, www.oregonstateparks.org; Rockaway Beach Chamber of Commerce, (503) 355-8108, www.rockawaybeach.net.

Along many stretches of beach in Oregon, names are somewhat confusing: in some places, one sand beach melds seamlessly into the next with little to demarcate their borders, and other beaches go by more than one name. In the case of scenic, driftwood-littered Nedonna Beach, which stretches south from the south jetty at Nehalem Bay, the name Manhattan Beach is really not accurate, but is nonetheless the name of the state park wayside (Manhattan Beach Wayside), located just off Highway 101, at the southern end of the beach. Manhattan Beach is an unincorporated community at the north end of the town of Rockaway Beach; its post office was decommissioned in the 1970s.

Manhattan Beach Wayside. Photo by John Shewey

The name remains, however, and is often applied to the entire stretch of beach on the north half of Rockaway Beach. In reality, though, the beachfront at Manhattan Beach is Nedonna Beach, and it stretches from the mouth of Nehalem Bay south about 1 mile to the outlet of Crescent Lake. Thereafter comes Rockaway Beach (see next entry).

Surprisingly, Nedonna Beach is only lightly visited, especially its scenic north end near the jetty. Access is available from Manhattan Beach Wayside at the south end of the beach (Highway 101 milepost 48.8), from the south jetty parking area near the north end of the beach at the north end Beach Drive, and from several trails that squeeze between beach houses in between those two bookends (look for small, white "Beach Access" signs along Beach Drive). The northernmost access area has a large gravel parking lot from which several trails head through vegetated dunes to reach the beach and the jetty. This short jetty is a good bet for fishing for perch, rockfish, and salmon, but be very careful—rogue waves often sweep up the narrow bay mouth and surge onto the north face of the jetty. The south face can also absorb some dangerous breakers. During periods of relative calm, however, the jetty (especially the south face) is a pleasant place for fishing.

This area is quite popular with dog owners, providing a broad swath of clean, white sand with plenty of driftwood perfectly sized for a game of fetch. However, be very careful that water-loving dogs do not get anywhere near the bay mouth on the north side of the jetty—the currents are nasty and could easily sweep a dog out to sea. Play it safe and stay well down to the south away from the jetty. The state wayside at the south end of the beach near the highway offers tree-sheltered picnic sites and several trails leading a short distance to the beach.

Nedonna Beach. Photo by John Shewey

Rockaway Beach (aka Manhattan Beach) and Twin Rocks Beach

Location: Highway 101, mileposts 49–52, 12 miles south of Manzanita, 5 miles north of Garibaldi.

Access: Numerous access points from west ends of streets and from prominent wayside.

Facilities: Restrooms, picnic tables, information center at Rockaway Beach Wayside.

Amenities: Rockaway Beach offers several dining and lodging options, along with a variety of eclectic shops strung along Highway 101.

Contact: Rockaway Beach Chamber of Commerce, (503) 355-8108, www.rockawaybeach.net.

Highway 101 courses inland to wrap around both Nehalem Bay and Tillamook Bay, but between those two points, the highway runs beachside through the eclectic, scenic, and welcoming community of Rockaway Beach. The community stretches for 3 miles north to south, and provides numerous access points to its gorgeous and lengthy sand beach, which is anchored on its south end by Twin Rocks—a pair of sea stacks, one with a prominent arch.

Almost everyone swarms to the centrally located and spacious Rockaway Beach Wayside—and why not?

The parking area opens out onto this scenic beach, with benches, picnic tables, and a Veterans of Foreign Wars memorial. Moreover, the Rockaway Beach Chamber of Commerce visitors center—a bright-red caboose in the parking lot—is staffed during peak tourism times, so local intel is immediately available. And if you need a break from all that sand and surf, the Sand Dollar Restaurant & Lounge, adjacent to the parking lot, offers back-patio seating overlooking the beach.

On the other hand, if you prefer seclusion and solitude, Rockaway Beach offers numerous beach-access

locations that are hardly used at all, even with ever-busy Highway 101 running nearby. Basically, just about every west-running street in town, whether branching off Highway 101, or off the frontage roads on the west side of the railroad tracks that parallel the southbound lane of 101, leads to a public beach access trail. Some locations have plenty of parking, others can accommodate two or three vehicles, and some have no parking, but nearby streetside parking. The farther you venture north or south from Rockaway Beach Wayside, the fewer people you'll find on the beach.

On the south end of town, Twin Rocks Beach is a true gem, a beautiful stretch of sand with a commanding view of the Twin Rocks and a popular beach for people who enjoy Zen-like calm and meditating on the beach with a wonderful view. The access closest to the rocks sits at the end of Minnehaha Street, with a gravel lot that can accommodate perhaps eight vehicles (and rarely gets that many). However, because of its orientation to the shoreline, the arch at Twin Rocks is somewhat obscured from this head-on view; it's more obvious and photogenic (with a telephoto lens) from a bit farther north, such as the access point at the west end of Washington Street or 8th Avenue, or from the little-known Twin Rocks Turnaround on Breaker Avenue: turn west off Highway 101 at Washington Street, drive a short distance west and turn right on Breaker Avenue, and drive north about 100 yards to the small park, which has two designated handicap parking slots and a paved wheelchair-accessible path to the top of the beach.

Fourth of July fireworks at Rockaway Beach. Photo courtesy of Visit Tillamook Coast

Rockaway Beach. Photo by John Shewey

The beach at Barview Jetty, Photo by GrannyFanny2009/CreativeCommons

Barview Jetty County Park

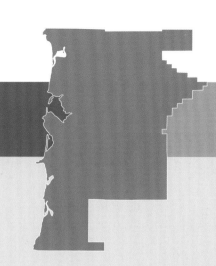

 Location: 2 miles northwest of Garibaldi, near Highway 101 milepost 54.

 Access: Short trail to the beach from gravel parking lot atop the Tillamook Bay south jetty (Barview jetty); additional beach trails from adjacent campground.

 Facilities: Adjacent Barview Jetty County Campground has 84 campsites (71 full-hookup and three universal-access), hiker/biker camp, restrooms, showers, RV dump site.

 Fees: Camping fees apply.

 Contact: Barview Jetty County Park, (503) 322-3522, www.co.tillamook.or.us/gov/parks/campgrounds.htm

Barview Jetty—the Tillamook Bay north jetty—is well known as a productive fishery for black rockfish and other species. As with all jetties in Oregon, anglers must use caution and common sense fishing the Barview Jetty. Its outer end is especially hazardous, but even along the inner section near the little community of Barview, waves can sometimes wash well up onto the rocks, endangering anglers perched on the jetty. Barview Jetty also forms the southern boundary of the 6-mile stretch of sand beach between the Nehalem River and Tillamook Bay.

A day-use area, with parking atop the jetty, provides access to the wide sandy beach abutting the north side of Barview Jetty. Moreover, Barview Jetty County Park features an expansive campground, which is especially popular during late winter and early spring when steelhead ascend the local rivers, and in early autumn, when fall chinook salmon arrive in Tillamook Bay. The north edge of the bay, from Barview east through Garibaldi, is also excellent for clam digging at very low tides, and much of the bay offers fine prospects for crabbing (mostly by boat). The fishing,

clamming, and crabbing in Tillamook Bay accounts for many of the campers at Barview Jetty County Park, so often the beach west of the park is fairly quiet. To get to the beach, turn into Barview from Highway 101 at Barview Store; follow the signs for the campground, then follow Jetty Road to the large parking area above the beach. This beach is especially quiet during winter, when it's a fun beachcombing area, and any time of year it is a fine place to exercise dogs, being well-removed from any busy roads.

The beach at Bayocean Peninsula. Photo by Traveling Otter/Creative Commons

Bayocean Peninsula and Cape Meares

Location: 8 miles northwest of Tillamook.

Access: Hike-in access only.

Facilities: None.

Contact: Tillamook County Tourism, (503) 842-2672, www.tillamookcoast.com.

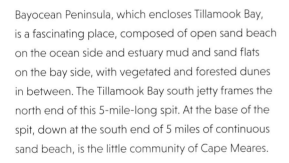

Bayocean Peninsula, which encloses Tillamook Bay, is a fascinating place, composed of open sand beach on the ocean side and estuary mud and sand flats on the bay side, with vegetated and forested dunes in between. The Tillamook Bay south jetty frames the north end of this 5-mile-long spit. At the base of the spit, down at the south end of 5 miles of continuous sand beach, is the little community of Cape Meares.

This broad spit was once the site of grandiose plans: real estate developer T.B. Potter, and his son, Thomas Irving Potter, designed and built a vacation community, called Bay Ocean Park, on the spit, beginning in 1906. Potter envisioned the resort

Cape Meares Beach. Photo by Cindi Brooks/CreativeCommons

○ Bayocean Peninsula and Cape Meares (continued)

as the Atlantic City of the West, and by 1914, 600 lots had been sold along platted streets; houses sprung up alongside commercial properties, including a natatorium housing a large, heated swimming pool. A hotel "annex" was erected amid plans for a much larger, palatial hotel to serve as the centerpiece of Bay Ocean. But soon the Pacific Ocean began exerting its dynamic power on the low-laying peninsula, washing away the sand under the footings of the natatorium; the walls began to sag, the facility was closed; the roof collapsed in 1936, and the building was demolished by 1939. Homes were swallowed by the ocean and the town soon evaporated, its remaining buildings torn down and/or burned. By the late 1950s the resort community was a memory. Little remains today, most signs of the town washed away, buried by sand, or swallowed by the densely vegetated dunes.

The gorgeous sand beach that made Bayocean so attractive remains, sometimes serene and inviting, other times battered by raging Pacific storms. Drive-in access to the spit was closed off long ago in favor of creating a more remote experience for visitors.

Trail along the west edge of Tillamook Bay on the Bayocean Peninsula. Photo courtesy of Visit Tillamook Coast

You can hike the beach or the old Bayocean Dyke Road on the bay side of the spit, which leads 3 miles to the Tillamook Bay south jetty: in Tillamook, turn west on 3rd Street to Netarts (State Route 131) and go 1.8 miles to a right turn onto Bayocean Road and follow it along the southwest shore of Tillamook Bay for 5 miles to a right (north) turn onto Bayocean Dyke Road, which leads 1 mile to the parking lot. From there, hike the road north along the bay to Kincheloe Point, the north end of the spit. This hike is great for birdwatchers, especially at a moderately low tide in fall or spring when exposed mud flats attract shorebirds.

The beach hike to Kincheloe Point covers about the same distance, beginning at a designated trailhead in northwest corner of the parking lot and coursing west through the vegetated dunes about 0.25 miles to the beach. Two more main trails cut west across the spit to the beach within the first mile of the dyke road. Or you can start on the beach in the little community of Cape Meares, at the west end of Meares Avenue, adding about 1.5 miles to the hike north up the beach.

The Tillamook Bay south jetty and the rock dyke extending inland from it offers good fishing for perch, rockfish and other bottomfish, and the occasional salmon, but be very careful of big waves and slippery rocks. Intrepid clam diggers who understand the dangers of gooey bay mud can enjoy fine harvests along the bay side of the spit, but whether fishing or clamming on Bayocean Peninsula, bear in mind the relative isolation of the area—if you encounter trouble at the hands of waves, rocks, tides, or mud, help is a long ways off. The long beach between Cape Meares and the south jetty is great for beachcombing, especially after winter storms. Other than in the little residential community itself, this beach never seems to draw crowds.

Trails connect the beach and the bay on the Bayocean Peninsula. Photo courtesy of Visit Tillamook Coast

Short Beach and Lost Boy Beach

Location: 1 mile north of Oceanside.

Access: Steep stairwell trail down to Short Beach; Lost Boy Beach accessible only at extreme low tides once or twice per year.

Facilities: None.

Contact: Tillamook Area Chamber of Commerce, (503) 842-7525, www.tillamookchamber.org.

One of the north coast's relatively hidden beaches, Short Beach escapes the notice of most visitors because it is only marginally visible from the road and there are no signs announcing it. This gorgeous sand beach is studded with rocks of all sizes, including a massive onshore sea stack that looks something like a miniature version of Cannon Beach's Haystack Rock, but with a wind-gnarled spruce tree actually growing on top of it. At high tide, the sea reaches up over the sand part of the beach, leaving a cobblestone fringe, but at the lowest tides, you can walk all the way around the large central rock. The monolith itself is part of the Oregon Islands National Wildlife Refuge and is therefore off limits to would-be climbers.

Above the beach, Short Creek pours down onto the beach from a manmade viaduct, creating a scenic threadlike waterfall. But the real treat for waterfall enthusiasts is at the north end of the beach, where Larson Creek forms a photogenic two-tiered wispy waterfall to reach its delta on the beach. Short Beach stretches nearly one-half mile to the north from the access trail, finally ending at a precipitous headland at the base of Cape Meares. The gravel expanses on Short Beach, most prominent during winter, provide excellent rock-hounding and agate hunting.

The headland that encloses the south end of Short Beach blocks access to a small pocket beach called

Sunset at Short Beach. Photo by John Shewey

Lost Boy Beach because reputedly a boy was once lost for an entire day on the beach when he was trapped by the incoming tide. Lost Boy Beach is impossible to reach at all but the lowest tides of the year. The easiest way to get there is to walk around the headland at the south end of Short Beach, but this is only possible on the lowest minus-tides—below minus-2 feet and often only at lower tides even than that because the dynamic nature of beach composition and wave patterns changes the beach often. If that sounds like a lot of trouble—waiting for the one or two daylight minus-2-foot or lower tides of the year—consider that this little beach is punctuated by cavernous, three-entryway Lost Boy Cave. It's a gorgeous, seldom-seen spot, replete with great tide pools, but once you get there, explore quickly and then retrace your steps before the tide begins to flood.

The single access location for Short Beach is just minutes north from Oceanside. Measuring from the intersection of Pacific Avenue (SR 131) and Cape Meares Loop Road at the south end of Oceanside, go 1.3 miles north and watch for a chain-link fence on the right (east) side of the road and a guardrail on the left (west side) just before you reach Radar Road. Park on either side of the road, in the pullouts, near the north end of the guardrail. The trail leads steeply down to the beach, but is reinforced with stair-step railroad ties throughout—entirely the work of local residents.

The stairwell down to Short Beach. Photo by John Shewey

◯ Oceanside Beach, Tunnel Beach, and Netarts

Location: Oceanside and Netarts.

Access: State park access site at Oceanside Beach with easy hike north to Tunnel Beach; access to the beach from Netarts is at the end of Happy Camp Road and at the west end of Crab Avenue.

Facilities: Restrooms.

Contact: Oceanside Beach State Recreation Site, (503) 842-3182, www.oregonstateparks.org; Tillamook Area Chamber of Commerce, (503) 842-7525, www.tillamookchamber.org.

The idyllic little town of Oceanside, with about 400 residents, is an unincorporated community composed of numerous vacation rental properties that swells to five times that population during prime summer weekends. Its waterfront is anchored by Oceanside Beach State Recreation Site and a small headland called Maxwell Point.

In 1921, entrepreneurs J.H. and H.H. Rosenberg bought 160 acres from the estate of John W. Maxwell, founding the town of Oceanside. Within months they began platting the settlement and selling lots.

Oceanside Beach. Photo by John Shewey

Remarkably, they built a 3-mile-long wooden plank road between the new vacation settlement and Netarts just to the south, completing the project in 1925, and opening the road on July 3. "By evening of that day, 500 tents had been set up, and Oceanside was ready to play," wrote historian Ulrich H. Hardt for The Oregon Encyclopedia. The inventive and ingenious Rosenbergs also decided to blast out a tunnel through the base of Maxwell Point to create pedestrian access from the easy-to-reach beach on its south side to the cliff-guarded beach to the north.

Opened in 1926, the tunnel remains in use today: simply walk north from Oceanside Beach State Rec Site, walk through the cement-reinforced bunkerlike tunnel entrance, then scramble through the rocks in the heart of the tunnel, and emerge on what is now frequently called Tunnel Beach—a mesmerizing conglomeration of cobble, sand, boulders, and scenic surf-zone sea stacks. At low tides, explore along the edges of the big rocks, which host dense colonies of anemones and sea stars (at minus tides, you can often walk around Maxwell Point). Tunnel Beach is locally well known for its propensity to produce good agate hunting at all seasons, but especially during winter, when wave patterns remove sand from the beach and reveal extensive cobble and gravel beds. It's also a nice place for early morning beachcombing and birdwatching just about any time of year. Don't linger at the tunnel entrances as loose rocks often fall from the cliffs above, especially in wet weather.

The Rosenbergs—whose descendants are somewhat ubiquitous in Tillamook County—also decided to create egress to the next beach to the north, Lost Boy Beach (see previous entry) and built an elevated plank walkway around the headland that blocks access to this small pocket beach at all but the lowest tides. Apparently the walkway was short-lived, no surprise considering the batter-ram surf that hammers these small headlands.

Just south of Oceanside, the quaint little community of Netarts provides additional beach access as this beach stretches uninterrupted from the mouth of Netarts Bay north to Maxwell Point. A stairwell trail at the west end of Crab Avenue leads down to the

Tunnel Beach from the mouth of the tunnel. Photo by John Shewey

○ Oceanside Beach, Tunnel Beach, and Netarts *(continued)*

The beach at Netarts. Photo courtesy of Visit Tillamook Coast

edge of the bay mouth, and from there you can walk out to the beach proper. The Crab Avenue access has parking room for only two or three vehicles, but a more spacious beach access site sits a short distance north at the downhill end of Happy Camp Road (at the north end of town). Happy Camp is a great place for kayaking, flying kites, setting up a picnic, or exploring the beach.

Netarts Bay is well known for crabbing and clamming, with ample shoreline access for clamming; Netarts Bay Drive wraps around the inland side of the bay, hugging the shoreline and providing plenty of places to park and walk out onto the clamming flats at low tide. Crabbing is mostly done by boat, with a county launch in town (Netarts Boat Landing) and a private launch, with rental boats and crabbing gear, just east of town at Netarts Bay Garden RV Resort (www. netartsbay.com).

Stairwell in Netarts leading to the beach along the mouth of Netarts Bay. Photo by John Shewey

Cape Lookout and Netarts Spit

Location: Cape Lookout Road, 5 miles south of Netarts, 13 miles north of Pacific City.

Access: Two beaches, one on each side of the cape; easy trail access to the north-side beach; lengthy trail access to the south-side beach.

Facilities: Day-use site with restrooms and picnic tables; campground with 38 full-hookup sites, 170 tent sites, 13 yurts (one pet friendly), six cabins (one pet friendly), hiker/biker camp; two sites, one cabin, and nine yurts with wheelchair-ramp access; restrooms, hot showers; RV dump station.

Fees: Day-use fee or recreation pass required; camping fees apply.

Contact: Cape Lookout State Park, (503) 842-4981, www.oregonstateparks.org.

Cape Lookout, a narrow, forested, cliff-bound lava headland that protrudes 1.5 miles into the Pacific, provides a spectacular panorama for visitors who hike the trail out to its western end. The 2.8-mile trail begins at a designated trailhead and parking area along Cape Lookout Road, 2.7 miles south from the entrance to Cape Lookout State Park campground. From the end of the cape trail, visitors often see migrating gray whales as well as sea lions and a variety of seabirds.

Netarts Spit. Photo by John Shewey

The sprawling year-round campground at Cape Lookout State Park is located on the north side of the cape and includes campsites just a few steps from the beach and others set back in the trees. The day-use site, which requires a daily fee or recreation pass, is located just past the entrance to the campground.

The beach here stretches north more than 4 miles, from the north foot of Cape Lookout to the end of Netarts Spit, which is directly across Netarts Bay from the town of Netarts. The only access to the spit (other than by boat) is from the beach, but at high tides, the southern end near the day-use site usually disappears underwater; under such conditions, hike north along a trail on the upper dunes into the campground, then north through the camping areas and continue on an old service road running up the middle of the spit. When the road ends, cut over to the beach and continue northward. The narrow spit itself has a number of informal trails, but the area is brushy so beach walking is easier (although a few other sections can get swallowed up at high tides). South from the day-use area, you can walk a short distance down to the cove at the foot of Cape Lookout at low tide.

Seldom busy other than during summer weekends, the beach stretching from Cape Lookout to the north end of Netarts Spit offers ample solitude for visitors willing to hike north from the campground or day-use area, especially at the distant end of the spit at the mouth of Netarts Bay. This scenic spot is often occupied by hauled-out harbor seals, and it's a good birdwatching location. Allow plenty of time to make the hike up and back; an early-morning start about halfway through an ebb tide allows you to remain on the beach rather than coursing through the dunes on the way north and on the return walk south around low tide or shortly into the incoming tide.

The beach on the north side of Cape Lookout. Photo Courtesy of Visit Tillamook Coast

Cape Lookout South (aka Boy Scout Beach, Scout Camp Beach)

Location: South side of Cape Lookout.

Access: 1.8-mile-long trail switch-backing down 800 feet of elevation to the beach.

Facilities: Restrooms.

Contact: Cape Lookout State Park, (503) 842-4981, www.oregonstateparks.org.

The Cape Lookout trailhead (see previous entry) also serves the trail for the seldom-visited beach on the south side of the cape. This beach is among the most secluded on the north coast because much of the shorefront is part of the Boy Scouts of America's Camp Meriwether, leaving visitors only two access options: hike the 1.8-mile switch-backing trail 800 feet down from Cape Lookout or hike up the beach from the Sand Lake Recreation Area (see next entry) parking lot on the south end of this 4-mile-long stretch of sand. The trail from the cape provides some nice scenic views along the way and deposits you near the north end of the beach, and is a slightly shorter round-trip walk, but it's steep enough in places, despite numerous switchbacks, to be a little

hard on knees, while the walk up the beach from Sand Lake is flat.

Both routes have their strong suits—an early morning low-tide walk north along the beach from the south often means 2 miles of untouched beachcombing, especially once you get beyond the boundary for driving on the beach at the south border of the Boy Scouts property. On the other hand, the long drop down the mountainside on the trail from Cape Lookout, coursing through beautiful coastal Sitka spruce forest, deposits you at the north end of the beach, in the rocky cove at the foot of the cape. Along the way, stop to look up into the largest spruce trees, whose branches host clusters of ferns.

The rocky north end of the beach presents boulder-field tide pools—you must use care exploring them because incoming breakers wash up into the rocks, but at minus- or near-minus low tides, the area is fascinating. Moreover, low tide allows egress quite a ways out along the base of Cape Lookout. Be sure to wear shoes or boots that can get wet rather than open-toed sandals as you'll be walking on rock most of the time. Other than the rocky north end, however, the remainder of the beach is clean sand, with a smattering of small gravel fields. The surf here is good habitat for redtail surfperch, but few people venture down to fish the area.

Additionally, this lonely and scenic beach, with Cape Lookout as a spectacular backdrop, is popular with the few surfers who don't mind the long walk to get in and out. As early as the 1970s, surfers from the Newport area had discovered the big, clean breaks just south of Cape Lookout, and would sneak through the Boy Scout property to avoid the long hike, and often camp on the upper beach. As part of Arcadia Publishing's *Images of Modern America series*, Scott and Sandy Blackman, with *Oregon Surfing, Central Coast*, provide a photo-rich insider's look at those halcyon days of Oregon surfing, telling the story of surfing at the "Boy Scout Camp."

North end of Boy Scout Beach at the foot of Cape Lookout. Photo by John Shewey

Sand Lake Recreation Area

 Location: 15 miles southwest of Tillamook, between Cape Lookout and Cape Kiwanda.

 Access: Beach access via foot/ATV trails adjacent to camping and day-use areas.

 Facilities: Three campgrounds totaling 139 campsites, restrooms, dispersed sand camping, day-use site.

Fees Camping and day-use fees apply.

 Contact: Sand Lake Recreation Area, (503) 392-5100, www.fs.usda.gov/recarea/siuslaw/recreation/recarea/?recid=42689.

Sand Lake Recreation Area is best known as an expansive sandy playground for dune buggies, to use the antiquated term for all-terrain vehicles designed to drive on sand dunes. Recreational sand drivers of all ages and experience levels enjoy the 1,076 acres of dunes, coastal lodgepole pine forest, and adjacent sand beach, all of which is anchored by three campgrounds, a dispersed-camping area, and a day-use site. The area is popular and the three campgrounds fill up almost every weekend from May through September. All-terrain vehicle rentals are available nearby from Sand Lake Tsunami ATV Rentals, (503) 965-6572, www.sandlaketsunamiatvrental.com.

The beach adjacent to the Sand Lake dunes is composed of clean, bright sand, with occasional gravel beds exposed during winter. Happily for visitors who prefer beaches without vehicles, off-road vehicles cannot drive the beach north of the southern boundary of the Boy Scouts of America's Camp Meriwether, which leaves almost 2 miles of pristine sand past the scout camp and up to Cape Lookout (see previous entry). It's a nice early-morning walk, especially midweek or offseason, during a low tide. During winter, you'll usually have the north end of the beach to yourself. To the south, vehicles are prohibited on the beach at the tip of Sand Lake's

north spit, an area that tends to attract lots of bird life. The mouth of Sand Lake is crossable on foot at peak low tide during summer but be careful and use common sense.

ATV Riders just above the beach adjacent to Sand Lake. Photo courtesy of Rick Cunningham/ Sand Lake Tsunami ATV Rentals

Tierra Del Mar

 Location: 3.5 miles north of Pacific City on Sand Lake Road.

 Access: Roadside parking north of town; short trails to the beach in town.

 Facilities: Outhouse at Tierra Del Mar main beach access on south end of town.

Contact: Pacific City Nestucca Valley Chamber of Commerce, (503) 965-3633, www.pcnvchamber.org.

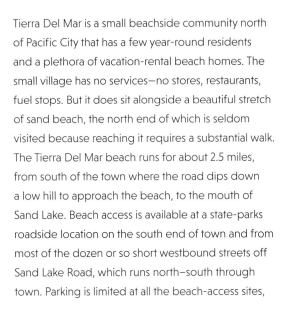

Tierra Del Mar is a small beachside community north of Pacific City that has a few year-round residents and a plethora of vacation-rental beach homes. The small village has no services—no stores, restaurants, fuel stops. But it does sit alongside a beautiful stretch of sand beach, the north end of which is seldom visited because reaching it requires a substantial walk. The Tierra Del Mar beach runs for about 2.5 miles, from south of the town where the road dips down a low hill to approach the beach, to the mouth of Sand Lake. Beach access is available at a state-parks roadside location on the south end of town and from most of the dozen or so short westbound streets off Sand Lake Road, which runs north–south through town. Parking is limited at all the beach-access sites,

especially at the roads within town, and visitors must use care to obey "no parking" signs and to avoid blocking driveways. Even with minimal parking, however, these street-end access sites are great because few tourists use them. Walking the short trail to the beach from the west end of Pollock Avenue, for example, cuts well over half a mile off the hike to the mouth of Sand Lake, though this access site has room for only two or three vehicles.

The beach at Tierra Del Mar is open to vehicles, but with restrictions in place that provide plenty of opportunity for beach hikers who prefer solitude. From the mouth of Sand Lake south to the approximate north boundary of Cape Kiwanda State

Park property near the state-parks Tierra Del Mar beach access along Sand Lake Road, motor vehicle travel is prohibited May 1 through September 30, and from sunrise to sunset on legal holidays, and on Saturdays and Sundays between October 1 and April 30. From the state-park beach access site, there are no restrictions on driving on the beach south to Cape Kiwanda. High tide, however, can block vehicles from passing around Miles Creek Point just north from the drive-on access at McPhillips Beach (see next entry).

Sand Lake's south spit and the beach leading up to it offers intrigue for wildlife enthusiasts, especially birdwatchers. The area attracts flocks of gulls, terns, and pelicans, along with cormorants and scoters;

shorebirds, such as sanderlings, dunlin, and western sandpipers frequent both the beach and the Sand Lake shoreline and mudflats, and the lake's shallows are also favorite hunting grounds for herons. The north end of the spit forms an expansive sand beach, especially at low tide, and visitors can hike over the vegetated dune above to view Sand Lake. This entire area, including the spit and its beach, are part of one of Oregon's newest state parks, the Sitka Sedge State Natural Area.

The beach at Tierra Del Mar. Photo by Erin/CreativeCommons

McPhillips Beach

Location: Cape Kiwanda State Natural Area, north side of Cape Kiwanda, north of Pacific City.

Access: Unmarked access road 1.3 miles north of Cape Kiwanda parking lot in Pacific City; vehicles allowed on beach.

Facilities: None

Contact: Pacific City–Nestucca Valley Chamber of Commerce, (503) 965-3633, www.pcnvchamber.org; Kiwanda Beach State Natural Area, (503) 842-3182, www.oregonstateparks.org.

Lesser known than the ever-busy beach at Pacific City just over the hill to the south, the 2-mile-long stretch of sandy shore from the north side of Cape Kiwanda up to the outskirts of Tierra Del Mar frequently offers a quiet respite for visitors looking for a picnic spot on the sand or a great place for an early-morning or evening stroll. This stretch of sand is called McPhillips Beach, and intriguing natural wonders await intrepid explorers who venture among the rocks on the north side of Cape Kiwanda, which forms the beach's southern terminus. The semisecret access to McPhillips Beach is unmarked: from the main parking area for Cape Kiwanda Beach (the site of Pelican Pub), continue 1.3 miles north on Kiwanda Drive,

which becomes McPhillips Drive, and turn left on an unmarked access road just past a white crosswalk painted on the road (if you reach the intersection with Sand Lake Road, you have driven about 800 feet too far north). Follow this road steeply downhill and either park in the gravel cul-de-sac on your right or, if you prefer and have four-wheel drive, continue downhill as the pavement turns to wet sand, gravel, rock, and mud, and drive out onto the beach.

Driving south along the upper beach is easy (stay in the existing vehicle tracks to avoid soft sand) and leads to some interesting rock formations down near the north face of Cape Kiwanda. Driving north

requires a creek crossing just up from the access road—it's best to stay up high on the beach and cross the creek on firm sand and cobble rather than the soft sand farther down the creek. Just beyond the creek delta, a bluff of multihued rocks called Miles Creek Point interrupts the expansive sand—the escarpment is easy to climb and provides a nice perch to enjoy a morning coffee when the wind is down. McPhillips Beach is also fairly popular with dog owners, and because the beach is backed by steep bluffs and cliffs, even the most adventurous dogs can't get into much trouble other than maybe scarfing down crabs and crab parts that often wash up on shore.

Left: McPhillips Beach, with Cape Lookout in the distance. Photo by John Shewey
Right: The access road to McPhillips Beach. Photo by John Shewey

Kiwanda Beach

Location: Pacific City.

Access: In Pacific City, go west across the Nestucca River on Pacific Avenue and turn right (north) on Cape Kiwanda Drive; continue 1.3 miles to the large parking lot on the left (which can become crowded on prime summer and holiday weekends).

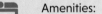

Facilities: Restrooms, beach-access route for vehicles.

Amenities: On-sight brewery/pub, lodging, and other dining options; beach-launch charter fishing.

Contact: Pacific City–Nestucca Valley Chamber of Commerce, (503) 965-3633, www.pcnvchamber.org; Kiwanda Beach State Natural Area, (503) 842-3182, www.oregonstateparks.org.

Cape Kiwanda, with its colorful layers of sandstone, shares the limelight with a massive near-shore sea stack called Haystack Rock to create a postcard-pretty scene at Kiwanda Beach, on the ocean side of Pacific City (as opposed to the inland side of town on the east side of the Nestucca River). Long-beloved Pelican Pub & Brewery occupies the upper beachhead at the parking lot that serves this popular beach, honoring the location with one of its most popular beers, Kiwanda Cream Ale.

Kiwanda Beach draws throngs of tourists on summer weekends and holidays for just about every Oregon beach activity, plus at least one that is unique: the surf here on the south side of Cape Kiwanda is frequently calm enough that expert boat operators launch dories directly from the beach, navigating over the breakers on the way out and riding them in to slide up on the beach on the return trip. The Pacific City dory fleet has fished these waters since the early twentieth century and reached its zenith in the 1960s and 70s, when this small coastal town ranked among the state's major

salmon fishing ports. Originally the dory boats were powered by oars, but motorized craft eventually took over. Recreational fishermen have likewise taken over the dory fleet, as many once-prolific fish populations can no longer withstand widespread commercial fishing. Tighter restrictions on harvest and shorter seasons on a variety of fish have made commercial fishing far less tenable than during the heyday of the dory fleet, so many dory boat operators fish for sport, catching bottomfish, salmon, dungenous crab, and other species. Charter fishing trips are readily

available, allowing visitors to experience dory fishing out around monolithic Haystack Rock and beyond. Book well ahead of time with Eagle Charters Fishing (www.eaglechartersfishing.com), Haystack Fishing (www.haystackfishing.com), or Pacific City Fishing (www.pacificcityfishing.com).

A few dory boat owners still fish and crab commercially, their catch often going to local restaurants. The Pelican Pub offers dory-caught fish whenever the boats can launch, and also commemorates the local fleet with its Doryman's Dark Ale. Seating at the pub is difficult on busy weekends, so reserve a table ahead of time; or walk across the street to excellent-but-lesser-known Dory Pizza (the inland side of town offers myriad additional dining and lodging options). The city itself celebrates the dory fleet with two annual events: the Blessing of the Dory Fleet in early June, and the Dory Days Festival in mid-July. The latter features a surprisingly robust and popular parade and a variety of activities centered around the dory boats and their heritage. In addition to ocean fishing, Pacific City offers excellent prospects for catching salmon and steelhead

The beach at Pacific City. Photo courtesy of Visit Tillamook Coast

○ Kiwanda Beach *(continued)*

Left: Surfing the Kiwanda break at sunset. Photo by Ian Sane
Right: Waiting for a wave at Kiwanda Beach. Photo by John Shewey

(and also searun cutthroat trout) migrating into the Nestucca River. Numerous fishing guides work the river, from tidewater well upstream. Public boat-launch sites are conveniently scattered along the river, the lowermost on the downstream end of Pacific City, well below the head of tide. Fishing for fall chinook salmon begins in late summer, while winter steelhead fishing runs from December through early spring.

Cape Kiwanda Beach is also a popular surfing location, with a big near-shore break, and also popular with stand-up paddleboarders and kayakers; stand-up paddleboards and kayaks can be rented in town at Nestucca Adventures, (503) 965-0060. The beach here is the site of the annual Cape Kiwanda Longboard Classic surf contest, www.capekiwandalongboardclassic.com, which draws substantial and jovial crowds and includes a beer-garden-style brewfest featuring a number of regional microbreweries. Pacific City itself offers everything a beach town needs and more, from an array of lodging options, a variety of restaurants, a surf shop, bait and tackle store, eclectic shops, and even a wine bar.

Cape Kiwanda Beach is open to vehicles for a length of about a quarter mile south from the parking lot. That leaves about a mile of beach, down to Pacific Avenue, free of vehicle traffic for hikers, beachcombers, and others who prefer a quieter experience. During winter, scenic Cape Kiwanda Beach is much less crowded and following winter storms can offer good beachcombing all along its entire length, but especially the southern half extending down to the mouth of the Nestucca River within Bob Straub State Park.

Playing on the big dune at Cape Kiwanda. Photo by John Shewey

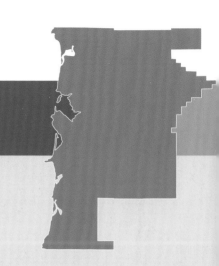

Bob Straub State Park

Location: Pacific City, stretching from the mouth of the Nestucca River north to Sunset Drive (a south turn off Pacific Avenue).

Access: Trails branch off from central parking area to explore the beach, dunes, and river.

Facilities: Restrooms, pinic tables, established trails.

Contact: Bob Straub State Park, (503) 842-3182, www.oregonstateparks.org; Pacific City–Nestucca Valley Chamber of Commerce, (503) 965-3633, www.pcnvchamber.org.

A short distance south and much quieter than the ever-busy beach at Cape Kiwanda in Pacific City, Bob Straub State Park encompasses the Nestucca River spit, which stretches more than 2 miles south from the river's final bridge crossing, at Pacific Avenue (the primary east–west road in Pacific City). The spit is largely vegetated with a mix of low shore pine and grassy dunes, and narrow to a sandy point at the mouth of the river. Harbor seals frequently haul out on the sand at the southernmost end of the spit. The inland side of the spit forms expansive mud flats at low tide levels along the river, with a few areas where salmon anglers can fish from shore between Pacific

Avenue and the county boat ramp area about 0.4 miles south on Sunset Drive (the road leads to the state park day-use area). Sunset turns south off Pacific Avenue just west of the bridge.

The day-use parking lot at the north end of the park feeds a network of trails, both through the dunes and to the beach. The trails, which are used by both pedestrians and equestrians, thread through both sides of the spit, providing views of bay and ocean. Local stables Green Acres Beach & Trail Rides, (541) 921-6289, offers guided horseback tours. From fall through spring, the area is excellent for birdwatching and during winter, the spit beach

is a fun place for beachcombing. The mouth of the Nestucca River is hazardous—don't venture into the water—but often very scenic.

Hiking Nestucca Spit. Photo courtesy of Visit Tillamook Coast

Winema Beach

Location: Highway 101, milepost 93.5 between Neskowin and Pacific City.

Access: Short trail to the beach from small parking lot at the end of Winema Road; adjacent parking areas are private property.

Facilities: Outhouse.

Many of Oregon's off-the-radar beaches remain secret and enigmatic because they are isolated by difficult, physically demanding access. But a few easy-to-reach beaches, such as beautiful Winema Beach between Neskowin and Pacific City, simply seem to defy discovery by the masses by serendipitous locations and lack of signage. From Lincoln City north to Bay City on the north shore of Tillamook Bay—a distance of 50 miles—Highway 101 courses inland, away from the coastline, leaving beach access to the secondary roads, and with no state park facilities to announce, the state has never erected signs directing visitors to Winema Beach. But hidden at the end of a short, winding access road, a tiny parking area adjacent to the Wi-Ne-Ma Christian Camp provides access to a gorgeous expanse of clean sandy beach with a domelike monolith, visible to the north as soon

as the short, sandy trail from the parking area spills onto the beach itself.

A short hike up the beach to the big rock reveals why Winema Beach is best at lower tide levels: at high tides, the water often penetrates beyond the monolith, filling a narrow sandy channel that separates it from the beach barrier cliff, blocking further northward hiking (or blocking the return trip if you've walked to the north end of the beach unaware of the tide stage). At low tides, the huge rock is accessible from all sides. Nearly a half mile farther north, the beach ends at the mouth of the Nestucca River (beneath a minor headland called Porter Point), a great location to look for harbor seals and birds, but stay out of the water, as the delta here creates dangerous currents. At the foot of Porter Point, a

cable "hand rail" installed in the cliff allows intrepid hikers to sneak around the point—at low tide—to a tiny, secluded beach at the edge of the river. Don't linger, or you'll be trapped for several hours until the next falling tide.

Winema Beach is a good bet for finding intact sand dollars as the tide ebbs; few people use this beach, but one or two shell collectors can sweep the beach clean of unbroken sand dollars, so get there early in the morning. Spring through mid-autumn is best; winter wave patterns reshape the beach, transferring substantial amounts of sand offshore and leaving deep troughs, helping create rugged surf that tends to shatter sand dollars. Even in summer, Winema Beach is cut by fairly deep troughs and channels, revealed at low tide, and

they help make this a productive location for surf fishing for redtail surfperch. Low tide stages are best because they reveal the rip currents and pockets in the surf that hold fish, but keep your distance from these features—cast into them, but don't wade near them. And keep a sharp eye on the tide stage and incoming water to avoid being trapped on a rapidly disappearing sand bar. Even on days with calm summer surf, the breakers tend to hammer Winema Beach because of its steep profile, especially on the incoming tide, so be careful.

To find Winema Beach, turn west onto Winema Road from Highway 101, 3.1 miles south from the Highway 101 turnoff to Pacific City, and 3.5 miles north of Neskowin (and 0.5 miles north of the signed viewpoint in the southbound lane). Just after turning off the highway, Winema Road forks; stay to the left and wind down the hill to the tiny parking area for the beach. Parking is at a small sand/gravel-surface lot with room for about six vehicles; adjacent parking areas are private property (church camp and private residences).

Winema Beach. Photo by John Shewey

○ Neskowin Beach

Location: Neskowin Beach State Recreation Site, Highway 101, milepost 97.

Access: Short trail leads from inland state parks parking lot to beach; additional access points along west edge of town.

Facilities: Restrooms, picnic tables.

Contact: Neskowin Beach State Recreation Site, (541) 994-7241, www.oregonstateparks.org; Neskowin Community Association, www.neskowincommunity.org.

With its signature sea stack, called Proposal Rock, the beach at Neskowin is one of the scenic treasures of this part of the coast, and the village itself, with a popular golf course, has long been a favorite vacation retreat; many of its houses are rentals, but the town has a year-round population of about 300 people. Other than the golfing facilities, Neskowin visitors are served by Neskowin Trading Company & Beach Club Bistro, and The Café on Hawk Street, both near Highway 101, across Oregon Street from the state park. Vacation rentals are easy to find on the internet.

The beach at Neskowin is a broad expanse of sand and usually very busy during summer, when the village's population can swell to 2,000 people or so. Naturally the easy-to-reach beach around Proposal Rock draws the most visitors. Neskowin Creek runs out onto the sand here, reaching the ocean in front of the massive near-shore sea stack. The creek is easy to cross, so beachgoers can explore southward to the foot of Cascade Head. Some years, if enough sand is hauled offshore during winter, a ghost forest emerges from the beach—the remnant trunks of a long-ago ocean-inundated forest.

While the beach around Proposal Rock is eminently popular, far fewer visitors realize that along Neskowin's beachfront residential strip that stretches

Neskowin Sunset. Photo by Pamela Carl/CreativeCommons

north along the coast for more than a mile, beach-access trails are located at the west ends of many streets. They offer very limited parking, but allow egress to the narrower, steeper—and substantially less crowded—section of beach well north of Proposal Rock. To locate these beach trails (only one, the Mount Angel Street access, has an Oregon State Parks access sign), go west from the state park parking lot on Salem Avenue and then turn right (north) on Breakers Avenue. Explore your way northward; after about half a mile, Breakers Avenue bends east as Corvallis Avenue and feeds into Hawk Street, which continues north.

Along these interior Neskowin streets, you'll begin to notice the eclectic collection of hand-painted signs asking drivers to slow down. Painted by local citizens at an annual sign-painting event, these oft-creative signs hint—loudly—at the fact that in Neskowin, the village street are also the sidewalks, used by children and pets. So heed their request and drive slowly.

Neskowin Beach. Photo by AbhinabaBasu/CreativeCommons

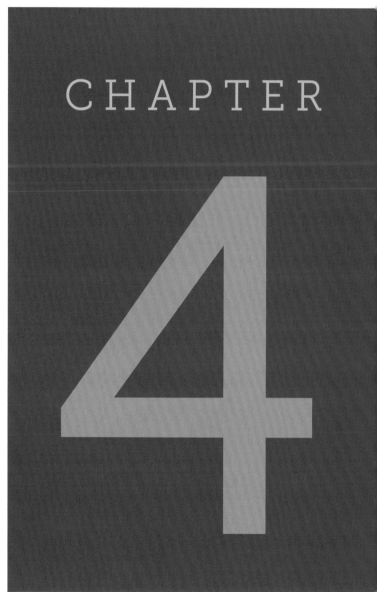

CHAPTER

4

Cobble Beach and Yaquina Head. Photo by Jim Bauer

CENTRAL COAST BEACHES: LINCOLN, LANE, AND DOUGLAS COUNTIES

Stretching for some 120 miles, Oregon's central coast, comprising the westernmost edges of Lincoln, Lane, and Douglas Counties, offers everything beach enthusiasts could ask for along the North Pacific Coast. This diverse section of the coastline boasts extensive sand beaches as well as rocky seashores, massive headlands, and significant estuaries. Along this entire stretch of the coast, only at Florence and Reedsport does Highway 101 route more than a mile from the beach, and for many miles, the road runs directly alongside the beach, providing excellent access.

Several tourist-friendly towns anchor the central coast. Lincoln City, Newport, and Florence are the largest, but equally appealing are smaller communities such as Depoe Bay, Waldport, and Yachats. All offer a wide variety of amenities, from luxurious hotels and inns to simple and modestly-priced accommodations, and from high-end restaurants to eclectic eateries to lesser-known chowder houses, breakfast joints, and pubs. Each of these towns has its own personality and identity. Lincoln City stretches along Highway 101 for 6 miles, its beautiful beaches largely hidden behind expansive residential and commercial districts, but easy to reach from numerous access points. Originally this 7 miles of coastline held several tiny communities; they are all interconnected now, and called districts, but their history remains alive and well. Southernmost of them is the historic Taft District, beautifully set along the north shore of oft-placid Siletz Bay.

Depoe Bay, 10 miles south of Lincoln City, ranks among Oregon's most scenic towns, set on a bluff above the rugged bay sharing its name. Its harbor connects to the bay through a narrow passage, and watching boats navigate the channel has long been a sightseeing attraction. Likewise, Depoe Bay is one of the best places on the Oregon coast for watching storm-driven waves collide violently with rocky shores. When heavy seas coincide with high tides, breakers hammer the rock bluff just below Highway 101, sending sheets of seawater up over the roadway and onto cars and onlookers.

Newport, the second-largest city on the Oregon coast with about 10,000 residents, is an old working harbor town, the longtime home to a sizable fishing fleet based in Yaquina Bay. Spanned by the iconic Yaquina Bay Bridge, designed by Conde McCullough and opened in 1936, the bay continues to serve both commercial and recreational fishing craft targeting everything from crabs and scallops to albacore and salmon. Newport is also home to two outstanding interactive marine science institutions, the Oregon Coast Aquarium (www.aquarium.org) and the Hatfield Marine Science Center (www.hmsc.oregonstate.edu). Located adjacent to one another on the south side of the bay, the two facilities are must-see attractions for all ages.

About 15 miles south of Newport, the quaint little community of Waldport sits astride the mouth of the Alsea River and annually attracts thousands of salmon anglers, along with crabbers and clam diggers. Ten miles farther south, eclectic Yachats is perched along one the most ruggedly dramatic stretches of the central coast and offers visitors an intriguing array of shops, eateries, and lodging options. South from Yachats, Highway 101 winds through a stunning stretch of seashore that includes Cape Perpetua, Heceta Head, and the long-popular Sea Lion Caves (www.sealioncaves.com), a private wildlife preserve famous for the largest sea cave in the Americas and the sea lions that haul out there. Visitors descend into the cave by elevator.

Florence, 25 miles south of Yachats, is the northern gateway to the Oregon Dunes National Recreation Area, a 40-mile-long expanse of coastal sand dunes with areas open to dune buggies and other sand-driving vehicles and other places reserved for foot traffic only. Florence's old-town district offers wonderful restaurants; its bayfront, on the Siuslaw River, is popular with anglers, crabbers, birders, and even surfers. South from Florence, Highway 101 skirts the dunes for about 20 miles down to the Umpqua River and Reedsport, a tourist-friendly community with a rich and storied history as a logging and mill town.

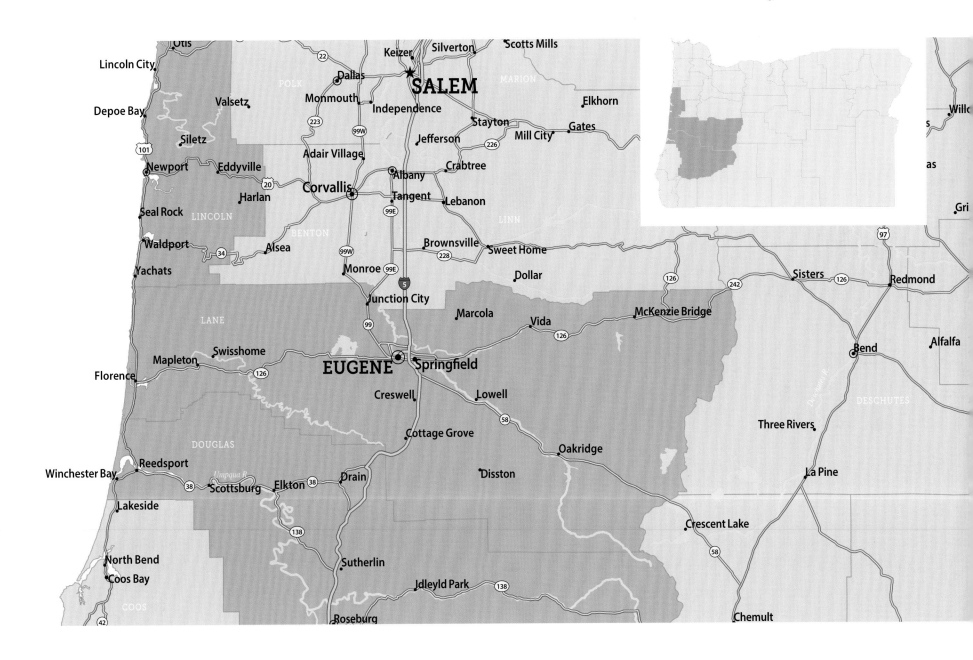

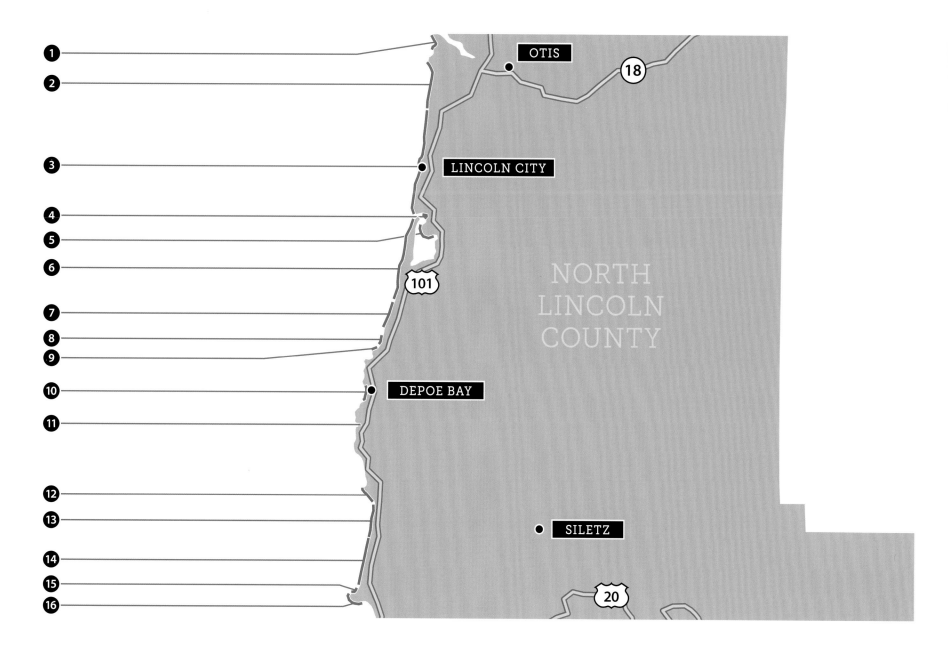

①

②

③ LINCOLN CITY

④

⑤

⑥

⑦

⑧

⑨

⑩ DEPOE BAY

⑪

⑫

⑬

⑭

⑮

⑯

OTIS

18

101

NORTH
LINCOLN
COUNTY

SILETZ

20

NORTH LINCOLN COUNTY BEACHES

1. Three Rocks Beach
2. Roads End Beach
3. Lincoln City Beaches
4. Schooner Creek Point
5. Cutler City
6. Gleneden Beach & Salishan Spit
7. Lincoln Beach
8. Fogarty Beach

9. Boiler Bay
10. Depoe Bay
11. Whale Cove
12. Otter Rock Beach
13. Beverly Beach
14. Moolack Beach
15. Starfish Cove
16. Yaquina Head & Cobble Beach

SOUTH
LINCOLN
COUNTY

NEWPORT

EDDYVILLE

20

SEAL ROCK

WALDPORT

34

YACHATS

SOUTH LINCOLN COUNTY BEACHES

1. Agate Beach
2. Nye Beach
3. Yaquina Bay State Park
4. South Beach
5. Holiday Beach
6. Ona Beach
7. Curtis Street Beach
8. Seal Rock

9. Holly Beach
10. Bayshore Beach
11. Keady Wayside
12. Waconda/Tillicum Beach
13. Yachats Beaches
14. Cape Cove Beach

○ Three Rocks Beach

Location: Mouth of the Salmon River, at the south base of Cascade Head.

Access: Only accessible by small boat from Knight County Park.

Facilities: Boat ramp for launching small craft.

Contact: Lincoln City Visitor and Convention Bureau, (541) 996-1274, www.oregoncoast.org.

One of Lincoln County's most picturesque beaches, Three Rocks Beach is accessible only by boat, with most visitors arriving by kayak. The beach sits at the mouth of the Salmon River, stretching southward from the sheer cliffs of magnificent Cascade Head to form a gorgeous cove tucked beneath a steep headland north of Lincoln City. The only access, however, is from the river's north bank at Knight County Park at the end of Three Rocks Road: from Highway 101, 1 mile north from the Highway 18/22 interchange, turn west on Three Rocks Road toward Cascade Head and continue 2.3 miles to a left turn into the park.

Knight Park has a boat ramp (and a small crabbing/fishing dock) from which you can launch kayaks and small boats for the short run across the river. The ocean is 1 mile downriver, and you can paddle down the river a ways to save walking time down the bank to the beach; however, do not approach the river mouth, as it tends to form dangerous currents and unpredictable breakers. Also mind the tides—incoming water is best for the return trip, especially if you paddle down the river a ways. Be sure to leave your boat well above the high-tide line. On the hill above the river's south bank, Camp Westwind, www.westwind.org, operates a variety of camp programs, primarily for youth. The

Three Rocks Beach/ Photo by Nate Angell/CreativeCommons

organization's cabins are available for rent when not in use for camp programs.

The beach at the mouth of the Salmon is typically sparsely populated and frequently deserted. It's well worth visiting, and during summer, the surrounding headlands usually block the wind, creating a beautiful haven for a beach picnic. Kayakers can further explore upriver (east) on the Salmon River through its broad tidal estuary, which is laced with tidal creeks, several of them large enough to paddle at high tide. Bird life abounds on the estuary, and elk often graze its grasslands and shallow tidal marshes. Kayakers will be happiest avoiding both the duck-hunting season (generally October through December), which brings a few hunters to the estuary, and the salmon fishing season (August through October), which draws substantial crowds when the runs peak.

The mouth of the Salmon River is a productive crabbing location, and both kayakers and small-boat operators get in on the action, but beware the extremely powerful current on falling tides, and avoid the river's mouth. Crabbers have drowned here in the past.

Three Rocks Beach looking north to Cascade Head. Photo by Nate Angell/CreativeCommons

Roads End Beach. Photo by EyeMindSoul/CreativeCommons

Roads End Beach

Location: North end of Lincoln City along Logan Road, 1 mile north of Highway 101.

Access: Short trail to the beach from large central parking area at Roads End State Recreation Area.

Facilities: Restrooms, picnic tables.

Contact: Roads Ends State Recreation Area, (541) 994-7341, www.oregonstateparks.org.

As its name implies, Roads End State Recreation Site sits near the end of the road in the north extent of Lincoln City—not really at the end of the road, but at the northernmost access site for the long stretch of sand extending more than a mile up to Roads End Point. This beach is popular for a variety of activities, from board sports to beach combing to running and dog walking. At low tides, the north end, at the base of the point, presents nice tide pools, and if the tide is low enough, you can scamper around the rocks to a tiny hidden pocket beach (but don't linger or you'll be stranded until the next tide low enough to allow return passage).

Roads End is no longer the quiet stretch of gleaming sand it used to be, attracting lots of visitors to a parking lot that can fill completely on summer weekends, but during the off-season, you can expect to share the beach with only a few others. Winter beachcombing can be fun here, but arrive very early in the day—this district of Lincoln City has lots of permanent residents and dozens of vacation rentals, so a few people always seem to be on the beach at dawn, whether looking for interesting things washed ashore, walking their dog, running for morning exercise, or enjoying a quiet stroll.

The day-use state parks parking area is 1 mile north of Highway 101 via Logan Road at the north end of Lincoln City: Logan Road heads north from the stoplight intersection adjacent to McDonalds, Safeway, and the Mcmenamins Lighthouse Brewpub (a nice lunch stop after a morning at the beach).

159

Lincoln City: Wecoma, D River, Nelscott, and Taft Beaches

Location: Lincoln City, west of Highway 101.

Access: Various access points as described below.

Facilities: Restrooms.

Amenities: Lincoln City offers numerous options for dining and lodging, along with a variety of shops and all services.

Contact: City of Lincoln City, (541) 996-2151, www.lincolncity.org; Lincoln City Visitor and Convention Bureau, (541) 996-1274, www.oregoncoast.org.

Admirably, Lincoln City has preserved excellent access to its beautiful beaches despite periods of rapid urban development. The beaches here are mostly clean, bright sand, ideal for just about everything that draws people to the Oregon beaches: picnicking, flying kites, jogging, hiking, running with the dog, playing with the kids, beachcombing, photography, wildlife watching, and more. Moreover, Lincoln City boasts an impressive array of restaurants, shops, and other forms of entertainment. Every Lincoln City regular could name a favorite lunch stop, chowder house, or dinner restaurant. In the latter realm,

Blackfish Café, www.blackfishcafe.com, at Highway 101 and 28th Street, is one of the best, and down south, the Bay House, www.thebayhouse.org, is reliably excellent. On the far north end of town, Mcmenamin's Lighthouse Brewery opened in 1986 and is more popular than ever for its regionally renowned ales. But those recommendations only hint at the options available to diners in this popular destination town of about 8,000 residents.

Stretching for some 6 miles north to south, mostly along Highway 101, Lincoln City is essentially divided

Sunset at Spanish Head in Lincoln City. Photo by Chris Brooks/CreativeCommons

into north and south halves, with the demarcation point being the D River (the world's second-shortest river at a mere 440 feet). At the mouth of the D River, D River State Recreation Site provides the most obvious beach access in the city, which is somewhat fortuitous for visitors who prefer a bit less beach congestion. The myriad other access points are scattered along the developed shoreline out of site of the highway and in places more than a quarter mile west from it.

North from D River, east-west streets are designated NW and south of D River, they are designated SW. Street numbers increase going north from D River and also increase going south from D River. In the north end of town, short beach-access trails are located at the west ends of NW 5th, 15th, 21st, 26th, 35th Court, and 37th, 40th, 44th, and 50th Streets. Limited parking is available at 5th Street; the 15th Street access includes maintained vehicle access and visitors frequently drive out onto the sand here, and this section of beach also has an extensive patch of exposed bedrock in the surf zone. The 21st and 26th Street access points both have just a few parking stalls

D River State Wayside. Photo by Oregon Coast Visitors Association

○ Lincoln City: Wecoma, D River, Nelscott, and Taft Beaches *(continued)*

and stairwell trails to the beach. The 35th Court access (On Jetty Avenue between 34th and 35th Streets) has five parking stalls and a broad sand trail down to the beach—the trail has supported vehicle entry to the beach in the past, but is usually too washed out to drive down. The 37th Street access (on Jetty Avenue just north of 37th) is a narrow trail squeezed between two houses, with no parking slots. The 40th and 44th Street access sites, with plenty of parking, are on the south and north sides, respectively, of the Chinook Winds Casino complex, and the 50th Street access has only street-side parking. Restrooms are located at the 15th and 26th Street locations.

South of the D River, beach access is available from 11th, 35th, 44th, and 51st Streets. The 11th Street access is at diminutive Canyon Drive Park, which has restrooms and parking for about a dozen vehicles; it's hidden and hard to find: from the highway, turn west on SW 12th Street, go three blocks, and swing north on SW Fleet Drive, which leads a short distance to a left turn on SW 11th Street and then 200 yards to the park. From the beach access here, it's an easy and pleasant half mile walk north to D River, and about the

Rare snow on the beach at Lincoln City. Photo by Oregon Coast Visitors Association same distance down to the rocky section of beach below low bluffs studded by homes at the Nelscott district (this area is called Nelscott Beach). Heading south, the next access, at the west end of SW 35th, has room for a few cars and is seldom used.

The remaining beach-access sites are all south of the Inn at Spanish Head (a prominent hotel and landmark along Highway 101). Southwest Beach Street, a west turn off Highway 101 just south of the Inn at Spanish Head, leads 200 yards down to the signed beach access at SW 44th Street (parking is curbside). The SW 51st Street access serves the north shore of Siletz Bay at the Taft district of Lincoln City, a wonderful little neighborhood with myriad restaurants and shops, including the Lincoln City Surf Shop, www.lcsurfshop. com, which sells and rents all manner of surfing gear, as well as Mo's Seafood, the chowder house made famous on the Newport bay front many decades ago.

The beach at Taft is typically serene, being inside the mouth of Siletz Bay and thus protected from the full force of the ocean. It's also very busy on most summer days, but a great place to hang out with friends, enjoy a picnic, or even crab from the public pier. Kayakers can launch from the beach to explore the bay and even cross over to the beautiful sand beach at Salishan Spit. Kayakers and boaters in Siletz Bay must beware of currents, stay away from the bay mouth, and watch the tide levels—much of the bay is shallow and at low tide reveals vast gooey mudflats that can hopelessly mire careless boaters.

Lincoln City, just north from the mouth of the Siletz River. Photo by Cody Cha/Lincoln City Visitors and Convention Bureau

Schooner Point at the south end of Lincoln City. Photo by Cody Cha/ Lincoln City Visitors and Convention Bureau

Schooner Creek Point and Cutler City

Location: South end of Lincoln City.

Access: Short trails to beaches from small public access sites.

Facilities: None.

Contact: City of Lincoln City, (541) 996-2151, www.lincolncity.org; Lincoln City Visitor and Convention Bureau, (541) 996-1274, www.oregoncoast.org.

Schooner Creek enters Siletz Bay at Taft, its mouth marked by a seemingly misplaced sea-stack-like rock escarpments protruding from the bay's northeast corner along Highway 101. Schooner Creek Wayside along the west edge of the highway (south of the Schooner Creek bridge) has trails leading down to the mudflats and rocks, which are only accessible at low tide. This spot is popular for clam digging, and also for birdwatching. Between late summer and mid-spring, the flats here, and throughout the bay, often attract shorebirds, ducks, grebes, herons and egrets, and various birds of prey, including bald eagles, merlins, and even red-shouldered hawks.

Just to the south, the highway departs the edge of Siletz Bay at the site of what was once called Cutler City, now part of Lincoln City. The Cutler City district occupies a broad peninsula protruding westward into the bay; it is fringed by a narrow sand beach that is easy to reach from Josephine Young Memorial Park at the end of 65th Street, and also from the ends of SW 66th, SW 68th, and SW 69th Streets, and from the south ends of SW Fleet and SW Galley Streets. The city park has only a few parking slots and elsewhere parking is limited to street-side in this residential neighborhood, so be mindful not to block driveways, and be respectful of property owners. These access points primarily serve clam diggers seeking softshell and purple varnish clams, but the beach here is

never crowded and a fun alternative to the bustling beaches in nearby Taft. On the inland side of Cutler City, just west of Highway 101, the Cutler Wetlands preserve has a network of trails that are excellent for birdwatching; access is from SW 63rd and SW 69th Streets, and SW Inlet Avenue.

Gleneden Beach and Lincoln Beach

Location: West of Highway 101, 1.1 miles south of Salishan Lodge, 2.7 miles north of Fogarty Creek State Recreation Area; near milepost 122, but many mileposts are missing on this stretch of the highway.

Access: Gleneden Beach State Recreation Site includes a short trail to the beach, with additional access at the west end of adjacent Wesler Street, and at the west ends of Laurel Street, Willow Street, and Tide Street (see below).

Facilities: Restrooms, picnic tables.

Even on busy summer weekends, lack of obvious highway signage generally assures only small crowds at Gleneden Beach State Recreation Site, which occupies a low bluff above the beautiful sandy beach on this stretch of the coastline. For several miles, through the communities of Gleneden Beach and Lincoln Beach, the beach remains out of view from the highway about 0.5 miles to the east, so this long strip of lovely sand remains quiet and pristine—even more so for beach hikers who stroll north 2 to 3 miles out onto Salishan Spit. A gated housing community occupies the spit, so the only access is via the beach (or by paddling over from Taft), and not many people walk that far north from Gleneden Beach. The beach

Gleneden Beach. Photo by Doug Kerr/CreativeCommons

near the state park area attracts a few surfers, and beachcombers roam the sand here in the early mornings, but you'll rarely, if ever, find a crowd, and to escape the few people on the beach near the day-use state park, you need only hike north or south.

To the south, the beach stretches more than 2 miles from Gleneden Beach State Wayside down to Fishing Rock, a scenic point that extends out into the surf to form the southern boundary of this lengthy strip of sand. Fishing Rock is just a short walk from the beach access trails at the west ends of Willow Street and Tide Street in Lincoln Beach, 2 miles south of Wesler Street. The Oregon Coast Trail climbs up from the beach to head south over Fishing Rock; atop Fishing Rock, the trail then meets Fogarty Street.

Access to Gleneden Beach State Wayside is straightforward: 1.1 mile south of the Salishan intersection or 2.7 miles north of Fogarty Creek, turn west off Highway 101 at Wesler Street (at the fire station in Gleneden Beach) and follow it a short distance west to the park. A second access point to Gleneden Beach—mostly known only to locals—is

located at the west end of Laurel Street: from the north, turn right onto Gleneden Beach Loop just south of the Salishan intersection and go south 0.4 miles to a right turn on Laurel Street; follow Laurel west to a small gravel parking lot on the left and an obvious path to the beach on the right. From the south, turn left onto Wesler Street, then right onto Gleneden Beach Loop and go north 0.5 miles to a left turn onto Laurel Street. If you intend to hike north up Salishan Spit, this secondary access carves more than half a mile off your walk.

Gleneden Beach Wayside. Photo by Doug Kerr/CreativeCommons

○ Fogarty Beach

◎ **Location:** Fogarty Creek State Recreation Area, Highway 101, milepost 125.

🚗 **Access:** Short walk under the highway from state park day-use area with ample parking (except on the busiest summer weekends).

🚻 **Facilities:** Restrooms, picnic tables, water.

📞 **Contact:** Fogarty Creek State Recreation Area, (541) 265-4560, www.oregonstateparks.org.

Scenic and popular little Fogarty Creek Beach occupies a small rocky cove sandwiched between two minor headlands. Because it's sheltered from the wind, this pleasant crescent of sand is popular with picnickers, and California-esque crowds of beach loungers often assemble on warm summer days, the throngs never really detracting from the charm of this spot. At low tide, the climbable, well-worn sea stack on the center of the beach provides a great perch for viewing the ocean beyond, and tide pools nearby beg exploration. During periods of calm surf, surfperch fishing can be good at this beach, specifically north of the Fogarty Creek delta, on the narrow strip of sand beneath the hotels perched on the bluff above; but stay out of the water when fishing because the sand drops off quickly, creating dangerous rips and a powerful shore break. The day-use state park on the east side of the highway is surprisingly expansive, with a network of trails winding through coastal woodlands and wooden footbridges spanning Fogarty Creek. It has two entrances, Fogarty Creek South and Fogarty Creek North, with the largest parking lot at the north section; footbridges over the creek connect the north and south parcels.

A Pacific loon in the surf at Foggarty Creek Beach. Photo by John Shewey

Fogarty Beach at Fogarty Creek State Recreation Area. Photo by Stephen J. Henrickson

Exploring tide pools at Boiler Bay. Photo by John Shewey

Boiler Bay

Location: 1.5 miles south of Fogarty Creek crossing on Highway 101.

Access: Small informal highway-side parking area (see below) with very steep, potentially dangerous informal trail down to the cove; low-tide access only.

Boiler Bay is named for an old steamship boiler, still visible at low tide, embedded in the mud in this small, rocky cove: in 1910, the 175-foot, 600-ton, oil-powered steam schooner J. Marhoffer caught fire and ran aground here at what was then called Brigg's Landing. The fire, accidentally started in the engine room, quickly became a shipwide conflagration and captain Gutsave Peterson ordered the ship abandoned after he steered it in toward the rocky coast from 3 miles out. All hands made it into the lifeboat, including Peterson's wife and the ship dog, but the cook died of his injuries when the crew attemped landfall at rugged Whale Cove. The ship itself soon became a floating inferno, drawing a local crowd to the bluffs above Boiler Bay and when it collided violently with the rocks and exploded, parts and pieces went flying in all directions. Atop the bluff at a small informal pullout, a section of the ship's hawsepipe (anchor pipe) remains imbedded in the soil.

The same rocks that ultimately wrecked the steamship create wonderful tide pools in Boiler Bay, but they are accessible only at low tide and worthwhile only at very low tides. Moreover, the trail down into the cove is perilously steep and rocky and slippery even when dry because of sand scattered over the rocks. It's no place for children or anyone not in excellent physical shape. The trail dives off the bluff at a small, unmarked, informal gravel parking area with room for about three vehicles. The pullout sits on the west side of Highway 101, where it makes a fairly sharp bend, about 0.3 miles north of Boiler Bay State Scenic Viewpoint and 0.7 miles south of where the highway crosses Fogarty Creek (signed). Be very careful pulling in and out of the parking spot—the highway curves away to the south, so oncoming traffic is difficult to see (prudence dictates always turning south from this pullout—if you are northbound, you can easily turn around down at the state scenic viewpoint).

The Boiler Bay tide pools are exceptional on minus tides, but only safe during periods of calm ocean conditions. Don't venture too far seaward (there's no reason to with the plethora of tide pools within the back of the cove) and keep a sharp eye peeled for rogue large waves. Boiler Bay is a designated intertidal research reserve and as such is closed to the harvest or taking of most intertidal organisms.

Depoe Bay

Location: Highway 101, milepost 128.

Access: No beach access, but excellent overlook along sidewalk and seawall; parking in designated stalls along the shoulder of Highway 101.

Facilities: Restrooms, picnic tables, whale-watching interpretive center.

Amenities: The town of Depoe Bay stretches alongside Highway 101, providing immediate access to dining and shopping, along with ocean-fishing and whale-watching charters; public launch site for ocean-worthy boats and kayaks.

Contact: Depoe Bay Chamber of Commerce, (877) 485-8348, www.depoebaychamber.org.

Ruggedly wild and scenic, Depoe Bay is a mile-long, quarter-mile-deep cleft carved out of the rocky headlands that characterize this part of the central coast, and while there is no accessible beach within this natural bay, the scenery alone mandates further exploration than is possible by just driving by on Highway 101. The roadway through the town of Depoe Bay sits atop a seawall, itself built upon a massive abutment of wave-hammered basalt, with a sidewalk on the ocean side of the highway providing superb views of the surging ocean below. During storms, especially those coinciding with high tides, breakers collide violently with the rock face below the road, sending massive spouts of seawater up and over the highway: fissures and caverns in the rock, called "spouting horns," forcibly redirect the incoming waves and propel water high into the air, often soaking onlookers and nearby vehicles. A running tradition of local humor in Depoe Bay suggests the spouting horns are to be permanently plugged with cement—but if these rumors raise your ire, note the typical release date of such news: April 1.

In addition to the spouting horns, Depoe Bay is also renowned for its spouting whales. Both gray and humpback whales occur here and can appear at any time of year; humpbacks rarely come near shore, but gray whales frequently enter the bay. Migration periods—late March, late August/early September, and late December—bring the most sightings, and sitting atop the seawall at Depoe Bay, the Whale Watching Spoken Here Interpretive Center provides copious educational material, as well as viewing windows and binoculars, on-site staff, and a gift store (proceeds from which help fund the center). A chalkboard at the center keeps tabs on daily, weekly, and monthly whale sightings, and annually about 1,000 humpbacks and more than 1,500 gray whales cruise past Depoe Bay; occasionally lucky onlookers are surprised to see a whale well inside the cove. Local boat captains offer inexpensive group whale-watching excursions, departing from the small harbor at Depoe Bay (a list of local whale-watching charters is available at the center). Boats departing and entering Depoe Bay harbor must navigate a narrow chasm in the rocks, passing beneath the highway bridge. Above the chasm and adjacent to the whale-watching center, a walkway and viewing platform allows visitors to watch the boats expertly navigate this perilous passage.

Depoe Bay also offers other scenic vistas, away from the hustle and bustle of downtown Depoe Bay. Although still within the busy zone, Depoe Bay Scenic Park and Depoe Bay Whale Park sit along the west side of the highway north of the downtown hub, the latter, across the highway from Bradford Street, easily located by the prominent whale sculpture and memorial wall, and the former occupying a partially wooded area across from Bechill Street; both parks have picnic tables, with those at Scenic Park sitting amid trees that

can provide a modicum of shelter from the wind. Far from the beaten path, at the west end of Vista Street (turn west from the highway in north Depoe Bay), a public trail leads to superb views of Pirate's Cove (and the seabird colony that nests on the rocks guarding its north side) and you can walk atop the rock bluffs above the pounding surf between Pirate's Cove and Depoe Bay to the south. Use extreme caution and stay well back from the edges (this is no place for children). The very limited parking is curbside, as this is a residential neighborhood; the trail is marked by a stone sign announcing, "Depoe Bay Scenic View Area." An additional public viewpoint sits just to the south (at the end of Alsea Street, well within walking distance if you park in the vicinity), overlooking Depoe Bay.

Of note, the city of Depoe Bay holds an annual Native American-style salmon bake each mid-September, with slabs of fresh salmon slow-roasted on cedar stakes in the traditional manor of the regional tribes. The salmon bake is so popular that each year, some 2,000 pounds of salmon is cooked and served. Native Americans from local tribes perform traditional ceremonial dances.

Pirate's Cove in Depoe Bay. Photo by John Shewey

Harbor seals hauled out in Whale Cove. Photo by Nicki Dugan Pogue/CreativeCommons

Whale Cove

Location: 1.5 miles south of Depoe Bay.

Access: None; inaccessible due to sea cliffs and private land; partial views from Highway 101.

Whale Cove is a diminutive but scenic marine reserve carved into the coastline between two minor headlands. At low tide, the north shore of scenic Whale Cove reveals an intimate little beach, but the only access is via sea kayak by expert ocean paddlers launching at Depoe Bay and coursing south around a broad headland. In 2015, 14 acres of land along the perimeter of the cove was converted to part of the Oregon Islands National Wildlife Refuge, protecting it from development (Bryce and Beebe Buchanan had purchased the land more than a decade prior with the idea of protecting it and then worked out a deal with government agencies to sell the land to the government for less than half its market value at time). The cove comes into view briefly as the highway wraps around its south side adjacent to Whale Cove Inn (www.whalecoveinn.

com), but otherwise only partial views are available from Rocky Creek State Scenic Viewpoint just south of the inn. The luxurious, expensive inn itself offers superb, expansive views of the cove.

Surf scoters in Whale Cove. Photo by John Shewey

Otter Rock Beach and Devils Punchbowl State Natural Area

Location: 8 miles north of downtown Newport, 5 miles south of Depoe Bay; Highway 101 milepost 132 (north entrance) and 133 (south entrance).

Access: Devils Punchbowl State Natural Area, a state park, covers about 5 acres at the headland, providing ample parking, and trails down to the beaches.

Facilities: Restrooms, picnic tables, viewing area for the punchbowl.

Amenities: Mo's Restaurant and Flying Dutchman Winery sit alongside the westernmost parking lot.

Contact: Otter Rock Marine Reserve, www.oregonmarinereserves.org/otter-rock.

At its north terminus, Beverly Beach runs up against a modest headland called Otter Rock, and atop this headland is the centerpiece of Devils Punchbowl State Natural Area, a natural gaping round hole that fills from beneath with swirling seawater. The hole is thought to be the remnant of a collapsed, wave-carved cave in the headland, and a fenced overlook allows visitors to peer down into the cavern, and also watch for passing whales offshore.

At very low tides, beachgoers can explore the cavern from below (but don't get caught down here by the incoming tide). The trail to the beach is poorly marked: the site has three designated parking areas; park at the first of these as you drive west on 1st Street, or if that lot is full, turn right (north) on C Avenue and look for the smaller lot on your left just past 2nd Street; after parking, walk north up C Avenue, past 3rd Street to where the trail to the beach forks off to the left (a tide pool interpretive sign and a metal post in the middle of the trail marks the spot). At the bottom of the trail, turn left and walk down the beach to reach excellent tidepools along the north foot of the headland, and if the

Devils Punchbowl from above. Photo courtesy of City of Newport

water is low enough, hike out around the front of the headland to reach the archway entrance to the bottom of the punchbowl.

The beach abutting the south side of Otter Rock, often protected by the wind and frequently carrying a consistent break, has long ranked among Oregon's most beloved surfing locations, especially popular with beginning surfers, boogie boarders, and skim boarders. In fact, each June, the Surfrider Foundation hosts the Otter Rock & Roll youth surf contest. The trail down to this beach is across 1st Street from the easternmost parking lot for Devils Punchbowl (just east of C Avenue, at the crosswalk).

Alongside the parking lot for the Devils Punchbowl overlook, perfectly positioned to intercept the lunch crowd, Mo's West Restaurant, (541) 765-2442, has been serving up its famous clam chowder and other seafood delights since 1972. Mo's West—the bright blue building at the parking lot—is open seasonally, from March through September, for lunch during weekdays and through early evening on weekends

Inside Devils Punchbowl at low tide. Photo courtesy of City of Newport

Moolack Beach & Beverly Beach

Location: 5 miles north of downtown Newport, alongside Highway 101 between mile markers 134 and 137 (but several mile marker signs may be missing from this stretch).

Access: Short walk to Beverly Beach from Beverly Beach State Park and to Moolack Beach from the Moolack Beach parking area (near milepost 135, west side of highway).

Facilities: Beverly Beach State Park Campground has 53 full-hookup sites, 75 electric/water-only sites, 125 tent sites, 21 yurts (two pet friendly), three seasonal group camping areas, flush toilets and hot showers, RV dump station, firewood for sale, yurt meeting hall, three campsites/six yurts with universal access; day-use picnic area; information center.

Fees: Camping fees apply.

Contact: Beverly Beach State Park, (541) 265-9278, www.oregonstateparks.org.

Perhaps the prettiest stretch of sand in the Newport area, conjoined Moolack and Beverly Beaches stretch for more than 4 miles between Yaquina Head to the south and Otter Rock to the north. Highway 101 runs alongside the beach, providing mesmerizing views that distract motorists all too easily. Adjacent sprawling Beverly Beach State Park includes a huge woodland campground and large day-use area and provides easy access to the beach via trail under the highway. The campground, which offers dozens of campsites, ranging from full-hookup RV sites to hiker/biker tent sites, tends to fill routinely during the summer, but its popularity hardly diminishes the excellent location adjacent to these beautiful beaches, and it's also a great central home base for exploring the central coast. And despite the summer crowds, easy-access

Beverly Beach. Photo by Tomas Quinones/CreativeCommons

Moolack and Beverly Beaches remain largely pristine, and during the winter, can be devoid of visitors. Hikers and runners can stretch their legs in both directions, picnickers can find a cozy spot on the beach head when the wind is down, kite enthusiasts can rely on that wind more often than not, anglers can ply the surf in the early morning and evening for surfperch, and surfers can ride the waves up at the north end of the beach near Otter Rock. The entire beach is good for early-morning or ebb-tide beachcombing, especially after storms, with the south end (Moolack Beach) generally best for finding agates during winter, and the middle mile or so better for shells, including sand dollars. The entire beach offers excellent views to the south of Yaquina Head and its lighthouse.

Wade Creek, easily forded, divides Beverly Beach to the north from Moolack Beach. The southern end of Moolack has a variety of intertidal rock formations, especially so during winter when sand is transported offshore. An intriguing layer of wave-carved bedrock leads like a rugged old European cobble road around Schooner Point and into Starfish Cove at low tides (see next entry). The rocks at Moolack Beach, and even more so in Starfish Cove, are laden with shellfish fossils.

The established parking area for Moolack Beach (1.5 miles south of Beverly Beach State Park) is a rutted gravel lot with two entrances about 100 yards apart, and from there, informal trails are incised through soft sandstone leading down to the beach. Nearby along the highway are two other informal parking areas—wide gravel shoulders—that usually provide beach access, but the bluff upon which the highway is built here is subject to continual deterioration at the hands of high surf, primarily in winter, so the narrow, steep pathways down to Moolack Beach can disappear readily.

Surfing at Moolack Beach. Photo by Oregon Coast Visitors Association

Starfish Cove. Photo by John Sparks

Starfish Cove

Location: North side of Yaquina Head.

Access: Two hidden, unmarked access sites; or low-tide-only hike for about 2.5 miles heading south from Moolack Beach parking area.

Facilities: Beverly Beach State Park Campground has 53 full-hookup sites, 75 electric/water-only sites, 125 tent sites, 21 yurts (two pet friendly), three seasonal group camping areas, flush toilets and hot showers, RV dump station, firewood for sale, yurt meeting hall, three campsites/six yurts with universal access; day-use picnic area; information center.

Lightly visited because the two easiest access points are hidden and unmarked, exotic little Starfish Cove is separated from the sprawling Moolack and Beverly Beaches to the north by Schooner Point, a minor headland only passable at low tide. The 5-mile-roundtrip hike down from the Moolack Beach access is a great low-tide trek for people who enjoy walking and exploring the surf line, but the shorter hidden access routes are much more expedient. Starfish Cove is carved into the north base of Yaquina Head, and composed largely of wave-etched mudstone and rock platforms, most of which bear fossilized mollusks. True to its name, Starfish Cove abounds in starfish, primarily ochre stars, specimens of which can be purple or orange in shade. The cove, at low

tide, provides good tide-pooling, and a variety of shorebirds frequent the rocks and beach, especially during the spring and fall migrations.

The quickest route to Starfish Cove is also somewhat perilous and only appropriate for the agile and fit: just north of the turnoff to Yaquina Head, turn west on NW 55th Street and drive to its end, turning right into a small gravel parking lot. From the parking lot, an informal trail leads steeply down the bluff: walk down it very tentatively and check to see if the route to the beach is safe—this sand bluff is subject to constant erosion. If this trail proves untenable, walk to the north end of the parking area and walk north on the trail that passes by the little brick utilities shed. Just past

the shed, before the trail rises up to NW 56th Street, watch for a bushwhacker trail diving off the slope through the trees toward the beach. Navigate the steep trail down to a small (but steep) stone-filled ravine that usually has water flowing down it. From there you can decide if the route is tenable (again, erosion alters the route fairly often). Note that you will need to carefully pick your way down the this steep creek bed to reach the beach.

The more northerly and much more user-friendly access to Starfish Cove is at the west end of NW 68th Street, a narrow, inconspicuous gravel road turning west off Highway 101 almost a mile north of the turnoff to Yaquina Head. A small parking area and

○ Starfish Cove *(continued)*

short trail to the beach here are seldom used except by locals. From there, the hike to southern extent of the cove is only about a mile and fascinating all along the way.

Ideally, begin your exploration of Starfish Cove about two hours before the ebb tide—even earlier if you decide to hike down around Schooner Point as soon from Moolack Beach. You'll have plenty of time to explore the diminutive cove and its natural wonders. However, beware this area during stormy weather or periods of high seas, as unpredictable surf can send heavy breakers into the cove. Naturally, the lower the tide, the better for exploring the tidepools. Clam and other fossils abound, and loose specimens are easy to collect, but do not remove them from the rocks— take photos and leave them intact for other visitors to wonder over.

Yaquina Head seen from the end of 55th Street at Starfish Cove. Photo by John Shewey

Looking north from the exposed bedrock at Starfish Cove. Photo by John Sparks

Yaquina Head & Cobble Beach

Location: North end of Newport, 4 miles north of Yaquina Bay, 4 miles south of Beverly Beach State Park.

Access: Turn west on Northwest Lighthouse Drive at the signs for Yaquina Head Outstanding Natural Area; long stairwell trail descends to Cobble Beach.

Facilities: Large interpretive center, restrooms, picnic tables, historic lighthouse, stairway trails to beach.

Fees: Daily fee required, payable at entry (self-pay kiosk available); federal recreational land passes and Oregon Pacific Coast Passport accepted.

Contact: Yaquina Head Outstanding Natural Area (BLM), (541) 574-3100, www.blm.gov/or/resources/recreation/yaquina/index.php.

Hulking Yaquina Head and its picturesque lighthouse sit entirely within the Bureau of Land Management's Yaquina Head Outstanding Natural Area—an appropriate name for this stunning and dramatic coastal headland. Of keen interest to beach enthusiast, the south side of the outer section of the headland, facing southwest, features one of the Oregon coast's natural wonders: a beach composed of basalt cobblestones. Black and glossy when wet, and dark gray when dry, the cobbles click and clack and ring enthusiastically when powerful waves wash up and then drain from the beach.

Cobble Beach is justifiably a major attraction among the many points of interest on Yaquina Head, and just to the west, in a sheltered rocky cove, low tide reveals wonderful tide pools full of intriguing sea life. Harbor seals bask on the low rocks here, and sea birds, such as pelagic cormorants and common murres nest in dense rookeries atop the sea stacks that rise up from the intertidal zone. The abundant seabirds attract both bald eagles and peregrine falcons and lucky visitors sometimes get to watch these predatory birds haze the seabird colonies, often snatching up a meal.

A lengthy set of stairs leads down to Cobble Beach and the adjacent tide pool area, but it's a substantial climb back up, so make sure you're up for the exertion. Park rangers are generally on hand to provide information to visitors. Guided lighthouse tours are available by prior arrangement for a small fee. Day-of-tour passes are available on a first-come, first-served basis and must be reserved in person at the interpretive center no earlier than 10 a.m. on the day of the tour. Reservations are accepted up to 90 days in advance for a limited number of tours. To make an advance reservation, call (877) 444-6777.

The only downside to this spectacular area and the intriguing Cobble Beach is that it draws substantial crowds, especially during summer—to the point that parking anywhere near the stairwell down to the beach can be impossible. To get the most bang for your buck, get to the park when it opens at 8 a.m. on a day when the low tide bottoms out at about 9 a.m. A weekday morning minus-tide between May and July is prime because crowds are sparse, the tide pools are at their best, and seabird rookeries are active. Off-season minus-tides are also great, but the rookeries are not active, although a variety of wintering bird species are common, including various sea ducks and shorebirds.

Exploring tide pools at Yaquina Head. Photo by Bob Wick/BLM

Agate Beach

 Location: North end of Newport.

 Access: Short trail to the beach leads through a large tunnel under Oceanview Drive; large parking lot with room for trailers; additional access by trail leads to north end of beach (see below).

 Facilities: Restrooms, picnic tables.

 Amenities: Nearby Ossie's Surf Shop offers lessons, rentals, and local intel.

Within view of Yaquina Head and its historic lighthouse, Agate Beach is a popular spot for surfers; in fact, Ossie's Surf Shop, along Highway 101, 1 mile north from the state park access site for the beach, has been helping Oregon surfers (and kayakers) since 1998. The best surf breaks at the north end of this mile-long beach, so traditionally many surfers use the rip along Yaquina Head for quick transport out to the break. The headland also serves to block north winds, which otherwise tend to blow quite often along the Newport-area beaches. Surf reports are available online, and a webcam, with the view looking down on Agate Beach from Yaquina Head, is available at www.blm.gov/or/resources/recreation/yaquina/webcam.php.

Most surfers and a few other beachgoers use a secondary access point, much closer to the south side of Yaquina Head than the state park: just south of the intersection with the highway and the road to Yaquina Head, a long, narrow public parking lot sits alongside the highway in front of Agate Beach Motel (which is conveniently located for visitors to both Agate Beach and Yaquina Head Natural Area); at the south end of this parking lot, across the entrance on Northwest Gilbert Way, a small green sign announces "Trail to Beach," with an outhouse a few steps down the path.

Agate Beach is also fairly popular for surf fishing for redtail surfperch, but because the beach can be busy—and because surfperch bite best at low light—plan any fishing expedition for sunrise, preferably on an incoming tide. Compared to surfing and surf fishing, a simple stroll on the beach at dawn or dusk, or a picnic on the upper beach might seem pedestrian, but Agate Beach is ideal for both when the wind stays down. The beach here is wide but not always flat, as row upon row of ridgelike dunes often form, especially in summer, adding an exotic look to the sandy expanse.

The state park access to the southern end of Agate Beach is west of Highway 101, along Oceanview Drive. From the north, Oceanview Drive is a right

turn off the highway 0.7 miles south of the road to Yaquina Head, and then 0.4 miles south on Oceanview. From the south, turn left at the light at Northwest 20th Street across from the Fred Meyer store and then take an immediate right onto Edenview and follow it down to a right turn onto Oceanview, leading about 0.4 miles to the state park.

Agate Beach from the flank of Yaquina Head. Photo by John Shewey

Sunset at Nye Beach. Photo by Sasquatch1/CreativeCommons

Nye Beach

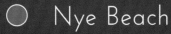

Location: Stretching along the Newport beachfront north of Yaquina Bay.

Access: Beachside parking areas at Nye Beach Turnaround and Don Davis Park; street side parking within easy walking distance in the neighborhood of Nye Beach.

Facilities: Restrooms, picnic tables, foot wash.

Amenities: The community of Nye Beach borders the beach and offers myriad choices in dining, shopping, and lodging.

Fronting Newport's eclectic, touristy district of the same name, ever-popular Nye Beach stretches for several miles, from the Yaquina Bay north jetty northward to Agate Beach. The entire beach is one long stretch of white sand, sometimes—especially in summer—smooth and soft, other times rippled by ridges and piles as sand is moved on and off the beach by the seasonal wave patterns. Although generally quiet by winter, Nye Beach—the beach and the community—spring to life as summer arrives, the wide, white beach providing the perfect playground for families, walkers, kite flyers, and more. Although it attracts plenty of visitors, the beach's sheer length assures plenty of room to

spread out, and except at its south and north ends, a respite from the frequent winds in the form of a bowl of chowder, a hot coffee, a cold drink, or an interesting shop is never far away. The two main access points to the beach proper are at Nye Beach Turnaround and at Don Davis Park. The turnaround includes a large parking area and is easy to reach from Highway 101: in Newport, turn west off the highway onto 2nd Street, West Olive Street, 3rd Street, or 6th Street, respectively. Continue a few blocks west to Northwest Coast Street. From 6th Street, turn left (south) and go one block to a right turn onto Northwest Beach Drive (the Turnaround); from the other three westbound streets, turn right

(north) on Northwest Beach Street and continue north to Northwest Beach Drive (the area is well signed). Don Davis Park, site of the city's Vietnam Veterans Memorial, has a gazebo with seating (a nice shelter from the weather) and sits at the west end of West Olive Street.

Nye Beach panoramic. Photo by James Schumacher/CreativeCommons

Yaquina Bay State Park

Location: Newport, at the north foot of the Yaquina Bay bridge.

Access: Moderate-difficulty trail downhill to the beach from large parking area, which can fill on summer weekends.

Facilities: Restrooms, picnic tables, historic lighthouse open to public.

Contact: Yaquina Bay State Park, (541) 265-5679, www.oregonstateparks.org.

The historic Yaquina Bay Lighthouse, built in 1871, is the star attraction at Yaquina Bay State Park, which occupies a high, conifer-clad bluff overlooking the north jetty of the bay. The lighthouse was recommissioned in 1996 as a navigation aid and today is open to the public (11 a.m. to 4 p.m. during summer, and noon to 4 p.m. the balance of the year, except closed Mondays and Tuesdays from November through February). Admittance is free, though donations are encouraged. Access requires a short, fairly steep walk up the access trails (a parking lot behind the lighthouse serves those who cannot make the walk).

Yaquina Bay jetties from the beach at Yaquina Bay State Park. Photo courtesy of Oregon Coast Visitors Association

This attractive but busy state park also provides ready access to the wide, wind-rippled sand beach abutting the Yaquina Bay north jetty. The jetty itself is dangerous because heavy seas slam strong waves up against the rocks, potentially imperiling anyone walking atop the structure (the inner section of the jetty is open to pedestrians and generally safe). The beach, however, is pleasant and spacious— technically it's the southern terminus of Nye Beach. Trails lead down from the parking lot at the state park, through a set of beach dunes and finally out onto the glistening white sand. The primary access is a formal walkway with stairs departing the south parking lot.

Yaquina Lighthouse. Photo by NOAA

Heavy winds hammer South Beach. Photo by Karen Hayungs

South Beach State Park

Location: South side of Yaquina bay in Newport, Highway 101, milepost 143.

Access: Trails leading from the campground to the beach range from 0.25 to 0.5 miles in length; large day-use parking lot adjacent to beach.

Facilities: Campground, restrooms, picnic tables, paved bike trail, interpretive trail, nature trail. Campground has 225 electrical/water sites, 60 tent sites, 27 yurts (two pet friendly), hiker/biker camp, three group camping areas, flush toilets and hot showers, RV dump station, firewood and ice for sale, five campsites/24 yurts with universal access. Reservations recommended via www.oregonstateparks.reserveamerica.com.

Fees: Camping fees apply; no fees for day-use area.

Amenities: Restaurants and hotels in the community of South Beach are within walking distance. Full marina and RV services, as well as charter fishing boats, are available at the Port of Newport's South Beach Marina.

Contact: South Beach State Park, (541) 867-4715, www.oregonstateparks.org.

South Beach stretches south several miles from the south jetty at Yaquina Bay, melding into Lost Creek Beach and then Ona Beach to form a contiguous 7-mile stretch of gleaming sand beach interrupted only by several creek deltas. South Beach State Park, with its sprawling campground and popular day-use area, is the hub of both access and activity at South Beach; further access is largely blocked by housing developments except on the north end of the beach where a short walk from the Yaquina Bay south jetty leads directly to the north end of this beautiful swath of sand. The state park offers a network of trails for hiking and biking, and beachgoers on horseback have become fairly common sights on South Beach. Just off the beach, winding through shore pine (lodgepole pine), alder thickets, wax myrtle, Sitka spruce, rhododendron, coastal marsh, vegetated dunes, and more, the Cooper Ridge Nature Trail encircles the campground; to the west, the Old Jetty Trail runs north–south through the upper beach dunes; and several east–west running paved trails connect the entire trail network.

○ South Beach State Park *(continued)*

South Beach is a surprisingly good beachcombing location—surprisingly because of the crowds it attracts for a variety of recreational activities. But during winter, few people walk the beach, and fewer still (at any time of year) hike a mile or more south from the campground to the solitude that usually rewards those who make the effort (especially first thing in the morning). South Beach is also popular for kite flying, picnicking, and surfing, with the break that wraps around the south jetty being especially popular, and best on a southwest swell (the location is called "the Box" by local surfers). When the surf sets up here, especially in summer, the Box can draw crowds; just beware of venturing too close to the jetty itself, where a nasty rip current tends to run alongside the rocks. The south jetty offers the closest access point for surfers, and is also prime real estate for birdwatching, especially between October and April when Yaquina Bay swells with migratory species, many of which overwinter here: less than half a mile south from the south end of the bay bridge, turn right onto Abalone Street and wrap around back to the north, then turn left on Southwest Jetty Way; drive to the end of the vehicle access and park in the wide gravel lot near the outhouses; walk south over the dunes to the beach. From the south, turn right off Highway 101 on SE Pacific Way before you reach the bay bridge; take the first left turn under the bridge and continue through the intersection straight onto Southwest Jetty Way.

South Beach offers fair prospects for anglers seeking surfperch, particularly during low-light incoming tides of mid- to late spring, and the south jetty of Yaquina Bay, bordering the beach's north end, is a fair bet for black rockfish, copper rockfish, and a few other species. The first quarter mile of the jetty top is easy to walk; after that it becomes an arduous rock-hopping endeavor best left to the highly adept (and the outer jetty is dangerous not only because of the brutal walking/scrambling needed to get there, but because of the propensity for massive, powerful breakers to crash up and over the rocks).

In the immediate neighborhood are two of Newport's must-see attractions, the Oregon Coast Aquarium (www.aquarium.org) and the Hatfield Marine Science Center (http://hmsc.oregonstate.edu). The South Beach side of Newport (meaning the section of town south of Yaquina Bay) is also home to Rogue brewery—or more correctly Rogue's Bayfront Pub—located in the large building between the bay bridge and the South Beach Marina (Rogue also has a pub on the north side, down on the historic Yaquina Bay waterfront). The pub serves Rogue's vast array of ales along with local seafood (lucky be the patron who arrives during the summer albacore season, when Rogue and other Newport restaurants serve this delicacy). Not far away, in a small shopping district just south of the aquarium and a block east of the highway, the formerly locals-secret Fishtails Café (www.fishtailscafe.com) has rapidly gained notoriety for its hearty homestyle meals, especially breakfasts.

South Beach. Photo by NicoleH/CreativeCommons

Lost Creek Beach. Photo by Kirt Edblom/Creative Commons

Holiday Beach/Lost Creek Beach

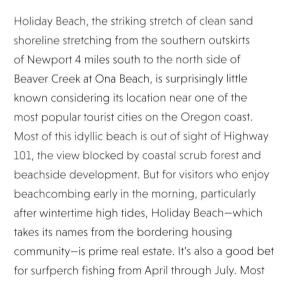

 Location: Lost Creek State Recreation Site, 5 miles south of Newport.

 Access: Short trail to the beach from the parking area at Lost Creek State Recreation Site; informal highway shoulder parking 1.5 miles south from the state park.

 Facilities: Restrooms, picnic tables.

 Contact: Lost Creek State Recreation Site, (541) 867-7451, www.oregonstateparks.org.

Holiday Beach, the striking stretch of clean sand shoreline stretching from the southern outskirts of Newport 4 miles south to the north side of Beaver Creek at Ona Beach, is surprisingly little known considering its location near one of the most popular tourist cities on the Oregon coast. Most of this idyllic beach is out of sight of Highway 101, the view blocked by coastal scrub forest and beachside development. But for visitors who enjoy beachcombing early in the morning, particularly after wintertime high tides, Holiday Beach—which takes its names from the bordering housing community—is prime real estate. It's also a good bet for surfperch fishing from April through July. Most

of this beach (sometimes called Lost Creek Beach because of the state parks access at Lost Creek) slopes gently into the surf, making for frequently safe conditions that allow anglers close approach to subtle troughs and holes where surfperch feed.

The primary access site for Holiday Beach is 5 miles south of the Yaquina Bay Bridge, at Lost Creek State Recreation Site. The parking lot is rarely full even on summer weekends, and even if it is, with several miles of beach, visitors willing to walk can almost always distance themselves from other beachgoers. In addition to the state park, this stretch of beach has several unmarked informal access sites: the

southernmost is 1.5 miles to the south, just north of the Ona Beach (Brian Booth State Park) parking lot: look for a wide highway pullout on the west shoulder north of Beaver Creek. From there, walk through the low dunes to the beach. Another unmarked access is almost 1 mile north of the state park, near milepost 146 just south of where the passing lane ends, at a wide gravel pullout along the southbound lane of the highway (you can also park along a narrower pullout along the northbound lane).

Ona Beach

Location: Brian Booth State Park, Highway 101, milepost 149, 5.5 miles south of South Beach State Park, 2 miles north of Seal Rock SRA.

Access: Trails lead to the beach from Brian Booth State Park.

Facilities: Picnic tables, restrooms, boat launch on Beaver Creek.

Contact: Brian Booth State Park, (541) 867-7451, www.oregonstateparks.org.

The state park formerly known as Ona Beach was renamed Brian Booth State Park in 2013 in honor of the first chairman of the Oregon State Parks and Recreation Commission formed in 1990. Ona Beach centers on the mouth of Beaver Creek, which flows out across a wide swath of sand to meet the ocean, and extends south down to the rocks at the north end of the Seal Rock Beach sea stacks. The entire beach is excellent for surfperch fishing on lowlight incoming tides, and beach walkers or runners looking for solitude can quickly outdistance any crowds by heading south. The state park comprises three distinct segments. Ona Beach day-use area, alongside Highway 101, provides access to the beach via a trail of about 300 yards, which crosses over the creek on a wooden footbridge. This forested park, often protected from the wind, is ideal for picnics.

Across the highway from the day-use area, a launch site (with parking) serves kayakers, canoeists, and other boaters who want to explore the tidal reach of Beaver Creek upstream (east) through the estuary. During summer, the state park offers guided kayak excursions (equipment included) via reservation at (541) 563-6413. Beaver Creek Road, leading east from the highway, skirts the tidal marsh, providing excellent prospects for birdwatching (but beware of traffic). The road forks after about a mile and the left fork, North Beaver Creek Road, leads a short distance uphill to a turn-in to the park headquarters, which includes interpretive displays and information, as well as a trail network leading down into the Beaver Creek glen.

The beach itself is also a good birding location. Shorebirds frequently stop here during migration. Western and least sandpipers, dunlin, and whimbrels are regular visitors; sanderlings sometimes show up in large flocks; black turnstones and black oystercatchers are common on the rocks on the south end of the beach. Heerman's gulls and brown pelicans are common in late summer and autumn, and pigeon guillemots occur year-round. Bald eagles hunt and scavenge the area and often land on the beach.

During winter, the rocks at the south end of the beach are increasingly exposed as sand is transported offshore by the waves, and intriguing, photogenic layers of bedrock sometimes emerge.

Ona Beach at Brian Booth State Park. Photo by John Koss

Photo by John Shewey

Curtis Street Beach (aka Seal Rock Beach North)

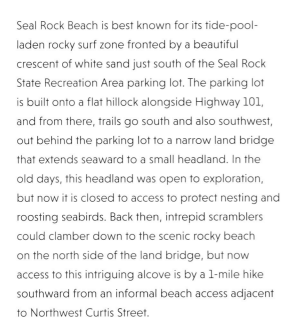

Location: Highway 101 milepost 150, 0.8 miles north of Seal Rock SRA and 1.1 miles south of Ona Beach (Brian Booth State Park).

Access: Gravel parking area and short trail to the beach across Highway 101 from Northwest Curtis Street.

Facilities: None.

Seal Rock Beach is best known for its tide-pool-laden rocky surf zone fronted by a beautiful crescent of white sand just south of the Seal Rock State Recreation Area parking lot. The parking lot is built onto a flat hillock alongside Highway 101, and from there, trails go south and also southwest, out behind the parking lot to a narrow land bridge that extends seaward to a small headland. In the old days, this headland was open to exploration, but now it is closed to access to protect nesting and roosting seabirds. Back then, intrepid scramblers could clamber down to the scenic rocky beach on the north side of the land bridge, but now access to this intriguing alcove is by a 1-mile hike southward from an informal beach access adjacent to Northwest Curtis Street.

From the aforementioned trail that provides a view of the land bridge dividing the south and north sides of Seal Rock Beach, you can look north to survey the rugged black basalt sea stacks that protect the inner beach and decide whether the area warrants close inspection before committing to the hike—for tide-poolers, the walk is well worthwhile. Pick a minus tide and head down the beach from Curtis Street about two hours ahead of the low tide. Though less extensive, the tide pools on this north extension of Seal Rock beach are every bit the equal of those at the popular state park access, but because of the hike, they attract few visitors. On incoming tides, this beach is a good bet for anglers seeking greenling and striped sea perch. On rare occasions during winter, enough sand is hauled offshore here to reveal ancient trees.

The parking area across from Curtis Street serves as an emergency-vehicle access to the beach, so don't block the roadway leading out onto the sand.

○ Seal Rock Beach

Location: Highway 101, milepost 151, 9 miles south of Newport, 5 miles north of Waldport.

Access: Fairly steep but easy trail down to the beach from state parks day-use site.

Facilities: Restrooms, picnic tables, overlook with benches.

Amenities: The adjacent community of Seal Rock offers a handful of eateries and shops.

Contact: Seal Rock State Recreation Site, (541) 867-7451, www.oregonstateparks.org.

One of the best and most popular tide pool beaches in Oregon, Seal Rock Beach at Seal Rock State Recreation Site benefits handsomely from an extensive row of small sea stacks and connecting basalt reefs that help shelter the beach from the heavy surf of the central coast. At low tides, all the bedrock outcroppings inside the outer rocks are exposed and usually easy and safe to explore, one reason the tide pools here are popular with families and school groups. The other reason is that Seal Rock is a fairly easy drive from the Willamette Valley.

The day-use area is perched on a bluff, the inland foot of a minor headland that divides Seal Rock Beach in half, with the north half accessible by hiking 1 mile south from Curtis Street (see previous entry). From the parking lot, a loop trail leads out to views of the adjacent headland and down to the beach as well as to a pleasant picnic site set back in the woods. The headland is closed to access to protect nesting birds, but from the beach, you can walk to the base of a huge basalt reef angling southward and explore tide pools at its base. Hidden behind this narrow spine of rock is long chasm—breakers surge up into the crevice,

Seal Rock Beach. Photo by Justin Pierron/Creative Commons

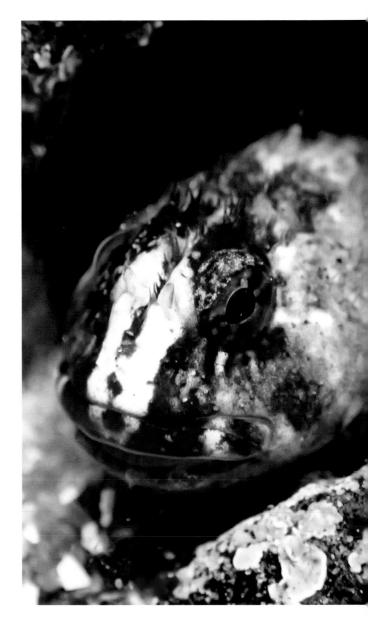

and often you can hear them crashing against the rocks and then draining back out. Under rough conditions at high tides, plumes of water shoot out the inland terminus of the chasm. To the south, a pretty, crescent-shaped beach is studded with rock outcroppings and their tide pools, and at minus tides you can walk right out to the base of the outer sea stacks.

The popular stretch of Seal Rock Beach stretches for more than a quarter mile south to a wall-like rock ridge that juts out from the mainland and extends into the surf zone. To the south of this escarpment, another quarter-mile stretch of clean, beautiful sand beach extends down to another rocky beach. This south end of the beach is far quieter, as you must scramble over rocks at low tide to get there, or hike north from the beach access at Quail Street on Holly Beach (see next entry).

In addition to its excellent tide pools, Seal Rock Beach is an excellent birdwatching location, with black oystercatchers appearing frequently, and a variety of other shorebirds being common during migration and winter: on the rocks, look for black turnstones, surfbirds, and wandering tattlers; on the sand, watch for flocks of small sandpipers, such as sanderlings, western sandpipers, and dunlin; on the headlands, look for common murres, pigeon guillemots, cormorants, and gulls; and in the surf, keep an eye peeled for harlequin ducks, scoters, and loons. Harbor seals frequent the area, and sea lions appear from time to time as well. Moreover, across the highway from the parking area, the little community of Seal Rock offers a variety of shops and eateries, including long-popular Yuzan Japanese Cuisine, a popular ice cream shop called Indulge Sweets, and a drive-up coffee shop—Seal Rock Bakery & Espresso—that offers its own excellent baked goods.

Tidepool sculpin at Seal Rock beach. Photo by Tara Silber/BLM

Holly Beach (aka Collins Creek Beach) and Driftwood Beach

 Location: 2 miles north of Waldport, and just south of Seal Rock, Highway 101 mileposts 153 to 151.5.

 Access: Short, easy trails to the beach from Driftwood State Park (south end of the beach), and Quail Street (north end of the beach).

Facilities: Paved parking lot, picnic tables, and restrooms at Driftwood State Park; no facilities at Quail Street.

Contact: Seal Rock State Recreation Site, (541) 867-7451, www.oregonstateparks.org.

Holly Beach, or Collins Creek Beach, is separated from the south end of Seal Rock Beach to the north by a cluster of rock outcroppings in the surf zone, although at low tides, with a little rock scrambling, you can walk between Holly Beach and Seal Rock Beach. From the north end of Holly Beach at Quail Street, nearly 1.5 miles of soft sand stretches down to Driftwood State Park and what the park calls "Driftwood Beach." The west end of Quail Street offers a hidden, unsigned access point; the short, gravel road turns west off Highway 101, 1 mile south of Seal Rock State Park and 1.5 miles north of Driftwood State Park. Quail Street has a two-car beach parking area at its west end a few yards from the beach, and a second pullout

The rocks at Holly Beach. Photo by Art Bromage/CreativeCommons closer to the highway for one or two vehicles. This is a residential area, so be quiet and courteous and don't block driveways.

The advantage to the Quail Street access is proximity to the great tide pools at the north end of Holly Beach: if ever-popular Seal Rock Beach just to the north is swarming with people on a minus tide, sneak down to Quail Street and explore what might be called "Seal Rock Lite" at the north extent of Holly Beach, where myriad bedrock reefs form tide pools that are the equal of those at Seal Rock, but not as extensive. Low tides allow beachgoers to wander down from Seal Rock, but few people realize this because the rock bluffs that neatly divide Seal Rock Beach into its north and south halves appear barrierlike, and even to reach the south end of this beach, you must scamper past this bluff. Reaching Holly Beach from there requires another third of a mile of beach walking, so few people bother. The rocks at the north end of Holly Beach aren't nearly as protected as the inner beachfront at Seal Rock's north half, but at minus tides they are well worth exploring.

Driftwood Beach at Driftwood State Park. Photo courtesy of Oregon Coast Visitors Association

Bayshore Beach/Bayshore Spit

Location: North from the Alsea River at Waldport.

Access: Four established and several informal access trails leading through narrow dunes to the beach behind a residential development.

Facilities: None.

Contact: Waldport Chamber of Commerce, (541) 563-2113, www.waldport-chamber.com.

Bayshore is a fairly sprawling bedroom community of Waldport, on the north side of the mouth of the Alsea River, composed largely of vacation rental homes, but also with lots of residents. The westernmost row of houses stretches for 2 miles along the upper dunes bordering a broad, clean, oft-windy sand beach, but the city made sure to create beach access throughout the neighborhood. Oceania Drive runs north–south at the west edge of Bayshore and the street's mile-long north half provides four access points to the beach. Three of them (Bayshore North, Bayshore Middle, and Bayshore South) are obvious: just look for white crosswalks stenciled with the words "Beach Access." Parking is limited at Bayshore North and Middle, so

be careful not to block driveways or impede street traffic; at Bayshore South, ample parking is available at adjacent Bayshore Park on Mackey Street. A fourth and northernmost beach access site, marked only by a small sign and trail between houses, is at the north end of Oceania Drive, where it meets a private and gated residential road.

The south end of Bayshore, which occupies Bayshore Spit, offers a few informal access trails to the beach through undeveloped lots, but parking is very limited and if you park along a road shoulder beware the soft sand that tends to drift across the road here, sometimes covering it, often filling the roadside margins (not to mention burying driveways

and yards, and at times nearly burying houses)—it's easy to get a vehicle stuck. A narrow strip of sand beach also stretches along the north bank of the bay from the Alsea bridge on Highway 101 west to Alsi Resort and is accessible from a parking lot at the south end of Bayshore Drive, adjacent to the resort.

To reach the Bayshore beaches from Highway 101 southbound, turn west onto NW Sandpiper Drive (1.2 miles south of Driftwood State Park) and follow it a winding 0.7 miles down to its intersection with Oceania. From Highway 101 northbound, cross the Alsea River at Waldport and continue 0.5 mile north to a west (left) turn onto NW Bayshore Drive (at the Baymart store); follow Bayshore 0.5 miles downhill to a west (right) turn onto Westward Ho Drive, which runs a short distance west to Oceania.

Bayshore Beach, stretching north from the Alsea River, typically offers good shell collecting and beachcombing, particularly in winter after heavy storms, and is also a popular beach for jogging, hiking, dog running, and kite flying. The white sand stretches northward nearly 4 miles, all the way to the north end of Holly Beach.

Bayshore Beach. Photo by John Shewey

Salmon anglers near Keady Wayside in Waldport. Photo by John Shewey

Keady Wayside

Location: Waldport.

Access: Shore access from Keady Wayside and from large parking area behind Alsea Bay Historic Interpretive Center at the south foot of the Alsea Bay bridge.

Facilities: Restrooms.

Amenities: Restaurants, shopping, lodging within walking distance.

Contact: Waldport Chamber of Commerce, (541) 563-2113, www.waldport-chamber.com.

William P. Keady State Wayside is a small park in Waldport overlooking Alsea Bay. In addition to the wayside itself, visitors can park in a larger lot behind the Alsea Bay Historic Interpretive Center at the south foot of the Alsea Bay bridge (from the north, turn right on NW Spring Street or NW Hemlock Street; from the south, turn left on SW Maple Street and drive north past Keady Wayside). The wayside and the short stretch of bayfront here is very popular with anglers targeting chinook salmon during later summer and early autumn, and also a good spot to look for birds between autumn and mid-spring.

Anglers can readily access the shoreline at the wayside and by parking behind the interpretive center. At low tides, the receding water reveals a narrow sandy beach extending from the bay bridge westward past Keady Wayside and out to Yaquina John Point, a great place for a stroll (stay up close to the upper beach to avoid gooey, muddy sand) or for clam digging and raking, as well as harvesting ghost shrimp. Alsea Bay is also popular with boaters targeting crabs and salmon, as well as other fish, but beware dangerous bar conditions.

Footwear available at the Alsea Bay Bridge Interpretive Center. Photo by PhotoAtelier/CreativeCommons

Wakonda/Tillicum Beach

Location: Along Highway 101, from Governor Patterson Memorial State Recreation Site 1 mile south of Waldport for 5 miles south to the north outskirts of Yachats.

Access: Short trails to the beach from multiple locations.

Facilities: Campground at Beachside State Recreation Site has 30 electrical sites with water (two universal access), 40 tent sites, hiker/biker camp, two yurts (both universal access), flush toilets and hot showers, and a day-use site. Tillicum Beach Campground has 60 campsites, water, and restrooms. Picnic tables and restrooms at Governor Patterson Memorial State Recreation Site.

Fees: Day-use fee or recreation pass required at Tillicum Beach Campground; camping fees at Tillicum Beach Campground and Beachside State Recreation Site. Waldport Chamber of Commerce, (541) 563-2113, www.waldport-chamber.com.

Contact: Beachside State Recreation Site, (541) 563-3220, www.oregonstateparks.org; Yachats Area Chamber of Commerce, (800) 929-0477, www.yachats.org.

The 6 miles of sand that stretches from Yaquina John Point in Waldport at the mouth of Alsea Bay down to the beginning of the rocky shoreline of Yachats goes by a variety of names: Wakonda Beach, Tillicum Beach, Beachside Beach, Big Creek Beach, and a few others, depending on specific location. They are contiguous, with no discernable borders, and served by both well-marked and hidden access points.

The northernmost access is a mile south of Waldport at Governor Patterson Memorial State Recreation Site, which allows an easy walk north up to the beach beneath Yaquina John Point along Alsea Bay. Named for Oregon's 18th governor, Isaac (Ike) L. Patterson, this 10-acre state park provides easy access to miles of sand beach ideal for beachcombing. Patterson (1859–1929) served from 1927 to 1929, dying of pneumonia while in office. He was an advocate of

parks and road-system development and appointed the state's first parks commission.

Just over one-half mile to the south, two narrow highway pullouts, across from Breakers Drive and Whitecap Drive, respectively, have short, steep trails down to the beach. The midpoint access to this stretch of coastline, 2.2 miles south of Patterson and 5 miles north of Yachats, just south of milepost 159,

is Beachside State Recreation Site, which offers an excellent beachfront campground set amid shore pines. Heading south, the next beach access is from U.S. Forest Service Tillicum Beach Campground, which has a day-use site.

South of Tillicum Beach Campground, access to this postcard-pretty beach is by way of unmarked trails with tiny parking areas within beachfront residential areas. These access points are at the west ends of Colorado Street, Idaho Street, and Oregon Street, respectively north to south, all located between Highway 101 mileposts 161 and 161.4. Be respectful of the residents, and don't block driveways. About a mile south of Oregon Street, directly across Highway 101 from NE Vingie Street (near milepost 162), a wide gravel pullout on the west side offers ample parking for a trail that leads through the coastal brush to the beach; wooden planks along the trail help keep your feet dry during the wet season. From this access site, you can walk less than a mile down to colloquially named Basalt Gateway—the north end of the rugged, rocky shorelines of Yachats.

Wakonda/Tillicum Beach at the Vingie Street access. Photo by John Shewey

Rocky shoreline and tide pools at Yachats. Photo by Scooter Lowrimore/CreativeCommons

Yachats Area & Smelt Sands State Recreation Site

Location: Yachats.

Access: Day-use site with trail paralleling the shore and providing access to pocket beaches.

Facilities: Restrooms, trails.

Amenities: Variety of shops, restaurants, and lodging options in Yachats, well within walking distance of shore access and beaches.

Contact: Yachats Area Chamber of Commerce, (800) 929-0477, www.yachats.org; Smelt Sands State Recreation Site/Yachats State Recreation Area/Yachats Ocean Road State Natural Site, (541) 867-7451, www.oregonstateparks.org.

The eclectic and scenic little community of Yachats is renowned for its highly photogenic, incredibly rugged rocky coastline composed largely of ocean-carved black basalt. Most of the commercial side of town, along with substantial residential development, sits on the north side of the diminutive Yachats River, which enters the Pacific through a triangular cove that forms the town's largest sand beach. On the south side of the river, the town continues southward another mile along Highway 101. Access to the rocky coastline and the Yachats River cove is preserved by three state parks: Smelt Sands State Recreation Site on the north end

of town; Yachats State Recreation Area on the north side of the Yachats River, overlooking the mouth of the river; and Yachats Ocean Road State Natural Area, which encompasses the shoreline south of the river along the west side of Yachats Ocean Road, a three-quarter-mile-long loop route west of Highway 101.

Parking for the Yachats Ocean Road State Recreation Area is in designated lots, and slots along the road. At low tide levels, a broad sand beach is revealed along the north end of Yachats Ocean Road, but the south half of the state park is dominated by

rugged, wave-battered bedrock. On the north side of the river, Ocean View Drive leads west from the highway and runs a short distance along the Yachats River delta to Yachats State Recreation Area, which has restrooms and an observation platform, which is sometimes staffed by volunteer whale-watching experts, as whales are often seen from Yachats. The beach area at the mouth attracts a few expert surfers and sea-kayakers, but beware the powerful currents and nearby viciously jagged rocks.

○ Yachats Area & Smelt Sands State Recreation Site *(continued)*

At the north end of Yachats, Smelt Sands State Recreation Site provides access to more scenic, rugged, rocky coastline complete with spouts and blowholes. During storms, massive breakers collide with the rocks, sending sheets of seawater high into the air, and on clear days, the setting sun casts vibrant light and colors across the rocks and ocean.

Named for tiny fish called smelt, which run up onto the beach with incoming waves to spawn, Smelt Sands State Recreation Site, on the north end of Yachats, is probably even better as a photographer's dreamscape. Anticipating prime ocean sunsets, photographers with tripods often gather here on summer evenings. The beach is mostly bedrock, but sand slot beaches cut in the gaps and channels make it a fine tide-pooling beach when low tides and surf conditions allow. It's also a popular spot to surf fish from the rocks for greenling, rockfish, sea perch, and other species.

However—and this is an important caution—don't explore the local tide pools or fish off the rocks on any but the calmest conditions: The *Oregonian*

Waiting for perfect light at Smelt Sands State Recreation Site in Yachats. Photo by Mason Marsh/www.masonmarsh.com

once characterized Smelt Sands as the "poster park for sneaker wave safety in Oregon," testimony punctuated by a memorial at the park erected after two teenagers were swept out to sea some years ago.

Smelt Sands, a small day-use site, sits at the end of a short access road at the Lemwick Lane turnoff from Highway 101 at milepost 163.5. From the parking area, the 804 Trail leads north along the low bluffs just above the beach, providing low-tide access as well as excellent vistas for whale watching, birding, photography, and wave watching—during high tides, especially storm-driven tides, crashing breakers form impressive spouting horns. The trail extends for nearly a mile, behind several hotels.

South of Smelt Sands, private property blocks access to the coastline for a short distance, but the city of Yachats has done an admirable job of maintaining egress to the shoreline, including the somewhat hidden-in-plain-site Ocean View Park, which offers a short trail down to a mesalike basalt bedrock outcropping cut by channels and pockets that form tide pools, which can be explored at low tide under

calm surf conditions. Moreover, this rugged but relatively flat exposed reef yields to a slightly elevated course-sand beach at its west edge, up against a low cliff, creating perhaps the best place in town to set up a chair and just watch the ocean—or set up a tripod with a camera ready for sunset photos or a spotting scope to look at birds and possibly whales. The trail down to Ocean View Park is easy to miss, but begins on the west side of Ocean View Drive across from West 7th Street and winds a short distance down to the beach.

Yachats, in fact, is a prime birdwatching spot because the rocky shoreline and surf zone routinely attracts black turnstones, wandering tattlers, surfbirds, black turnstones, common murres, rhinoceros auklets, marbled murrelets, scoters, loons, and a variety of other species, and occasionally even pelagic species, such as shearwaters and jaegers. The town itself offers a variety of excellent options for dining and lodging, as well as various and interesting shops.

Ocean View Park in Yachats. Photo by John Shewey

Cook's Chasm at Cape Perpetua. Photo by Rick Obst/CreativeCommons

Cape Perpetua Scenic Area

 Location: Along and near Highway 101, 3 miles south of Yachats, 22 miles north of Florence.

 Access: Comprehensive trail system provides access to various stretches of shoreline.

 Facilities: Interpretive visitors center with bookstore; restrooms; trails;
Cape Perpetua Campground has 39 campsites, water, restrooms, and picnic shelters.

 Fees: Day-use fee or recreation pass required (available at visitors center); camping fees required for campground.

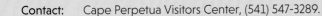 **Contact:** Cape Perpetua Visitors Center, (541) 547-3289.

The rugged, postcard-pretty shoreline of Cape Perpetua Scenic Area ranks among the state's better tide pool locations, primarily off the Captain Cook Trail. Near the bottom of the trail, a viewing platform provides a panorama of the benchlike rock outcroppings, which at low tides during periods of calm surf offer easily accessible tide pools, and from there a short stairwell trail leads down to the rocks. The trail departs from the visitors center, on the east side of Highway 101, crosses under the highway, and continues down to the shoreline, reaching the tide pool area after about 0.25 mile total. The hike can be shortened slightly by using a small parking lot on the west side of the highway, just north of the entrance road to the visitors center. A few hundred yards south by trail from the tide pool area, Captain Cook Trail reaches Cook's Chasm—a narrow, churning trench cut in the bedrock—and oft-photographed Thor's Well, a natural hole in the rocks that when washed over by breakers seems to drain seawater like a kitchen sink.

Captain Cook Trail is wheelchair accessible (moderately difficult) from the Cook's Chasm/Thor's Well trailhead just south of the turnoff to the visitors center. In fact, Cape Perpetua Scenic Area offers several wheelchair accessible locations, including the Devils Churn overlook, Cape Perpetua overlook, and the visitors center, as well as the 0.5-mile Whispering Spruce Trail.

The park's only accessible sand beach, Cape Cove Beach, is accessible by a steep stairwell trail near milepost 167, just south of Cape Perpetua Campground and just north of the visitors center turnoff. Parking for the beach is a narrow pullout along the west side of Highway 101 on the south side

○ Cape Perpetua Scenic Area (continued)

of the creek. This scenic pocket beach is bordered on both sides by rock escarpments with tide pools, the south end abutting the rocks at the downhill end of Captain Cook Trail.

Cape Perpetua Scenic Area also has a large, popular campground strung along Cape Creek east of Highway 101; during the busy summer season, make reservations to secure a site at this pleasant campground set amid lush, mature conifer forests dominated by Sitka spruce, Douglas fir, and western hemlock; for reservations, log on to www.recreation.gov or call (877) 444-6777. In addition to its beach and tide pool area, Cape Perpetua features 10 additional trails, including trails (and a road) that reaches the top of the cape, where a sunny day illuminates one of the grandest views on the Oregon coast. The visitors center itself is also well worth visiting, with interpretive displays, staff to answer questions, and a small bookstore and gift shop. Just north of Cape Perpetua, Devils Churn—a long, narrow chasm in the bedrock that surges violently with incoming breakers—is accessible via a long, steep stairwell trail at the U.S. Forest Service day-use site (day-use fee or recreation pass required).

Cape Cove Beach at Cape Perpetua. Photo by Doug Kerr/CreativeCommons

Devils Churn at Cape Perpetua. Photo by Peter Merholz/CreativeCommons

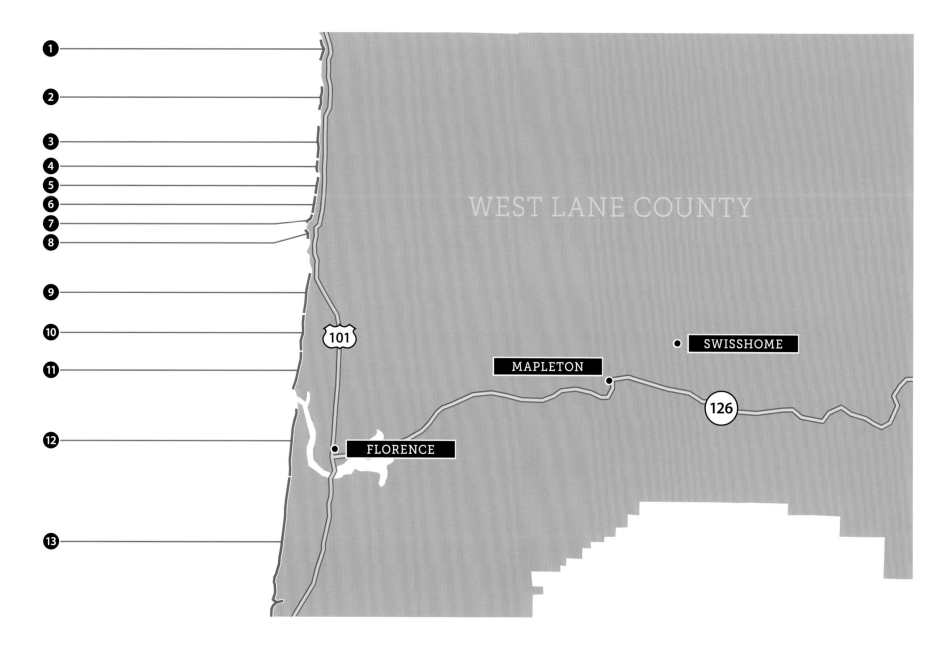

WEST LANE COUNTY

1

2

3

4

5

6

7

8

9

10

11

12

13

101

126

SWISSHOME

MAPLETON

FLORENCE

LANE COUNTY BEACHES

1. Neptune State Scenic Viewpoint Beaches
2. Stonefield Beach
3. Tokatee-Klootchman
4. Ocean Beach
5. Roosevelt Beach
6. Washburn Memorial State Park
7. Hobbit Beach
8. Cape Creek Beach
9. Baker Beach
10. Sutton Beach
11. Heceta & Florence North Jetty Beach
12. Siuslaw Spit
13. Siltcoos Beach

Neptune State Scenic Viewpoint Beaches

 Location: 5 miles south of Yachats along Highway 101.

 Access: Four state parks access sites with short trails to the beaches.

 Facilities: Restrooms at Neptune; picnic tables at Neptune North and Neptune.

Neptune State Park, south of Yachats, comprises 302 acres, 2 miles of rugged coastline, and several access points: Neptune North, Neptune, Strawberry Hill State Park, and Bob Creek Wayside. Neptune North sits adjacent to a narrow slot beach at the mouth of diminutive Gwynn Creek; this slice of sand, enclosed by low bluffs just west of and visible from Highway 101, is easily accessible at low tide, either by fighting through the brush on the north side of the paved parking lot for Neptune North (Highway 101, milepost 168.1), or taking one of the short trails out to the beach from the south side of the parking lot, then walking north over the bedrock reef. The extensive rocks here provide nice tide pools at low tide, and even produce a spouting horn at higher water levels.

Exploring the tide pools at Neptune North. Photo by David McClurg

To the south of the Neptune North parking lot, the main section of the beach is sprawling sand, studded with low rocks, stretching half a mile south to the next extensive onshore bedrock, passing the mouth of scenic Cummins Creek along the way. Just south of Cummins Creek, the next parking area (Neptune) has easy access to the sand beach leading north and the expansive tide pools in the rocks to the south, as well as both a small cave and a tiny sand pocket beach within those rocks. Neptune also has restrooms, picnic tables, and easy access to Cummins Creek, an idyllic little coastal creek flowing through verdant forest.

Another mile to the south, Strawberry Hill State Park (day use) has a short trail leading directly out onto the rocks and the many tide pools accessible at low tides. Harbor seals frequently haul out to bask on these rocks, usually on the outermost flat reef, but still close to shore. They often number several dozen or more. To the north, a beautiful sand pocket beach stretches nearly half a mile to another minor headland, and to the south a cobblestone/gravel beach reaches southward about the same distance, providing a good place to look for agates; on minus tides,

Neptune State Park and Cummins Creek Beach. Photo by Sam Beebe/CreativeCommons

○ Neptune State Scenic Viewpoint Beaches *(continued)*

extensive wave-carved bedrock at the south end of the beach offers myriad tide pools to explore.

A bit farther south, at milepost 170, Bob Creek Beach at Bob Creek Wayside is the southernmost access point to Neptune State Park, and a favorite haunt of agate hunters, as well as a good tide pool beach, with the north end being especially interesting. During the wet season, Bob Creek can carry too much water to safely cross, but otherwise it's an easy ford at most any mid to low tide level. The beach has extensive fields of gravel and cobble, making it a prime location to search for agates. The midsection of the beach is studded with extensive rock reefs, bordered above by cobble, and the south end features a sand beach with extensive gravel and cobble all the way down to the foot of Bray's Point and its hidden sea cave.

Neptune State Park is within a state-designated marine reserve. Clam and mussel harvest is allowed at the Neptune beaches, but not at the Strawberry Hill beaches, and in all areas no other marine life may be removed and fishing is not allowed. All of these beaches offer good prospects for finding agates and

The rocky beach at Strawberry Hill. Photo courtesy of Oregon Coast Visitors Association

other interesting rocks. During winter, with lots of sand hauled offshore by high-energy wave patterns, more cobble and gravel is exposed, improving the potential for finding agates. However, when rock-hounding the beach, never forget the sage advice: don't turn you back on the ocean.

Bob Creek Beach. Photo courtesy of Oregon State Parks

Stonefield Beach. Photo by John Shewey

Stonefield Beach

Location: Highway 101, milepost 171.5, 7 miles south of Yachats, 18 miles north of Florence.

Access: Two state parks access sites with trails to the beach.

Facilities: None.

Aptly named, Stonefield Beach, at the mouth of Tenmile Creek, features an upper beach composed of cobble, shingle, and gravel, a decent place to look for agates, especially during winter when more of the gravel is exposed (although the beach at Bob Creek a short distance north is better for agate hunting). Additionally, the beach has a minor outcropping of basalt within the surf zone north of the creek mouth that offers tide pools worth exploring. Perhaps best of all, Stonefield Beach State Recreation Site offers the only public access to the nearly mile-long stretch of gleaming sand along the unincorporated community of Searose Beach just to the north, where private property precludes access to the shoreline. From either of the two Stonefield Beach access points—Stonefield Beach on the south side of Tenmile Creek bridge and Stonefield Beach North on the north

side of the creek—you can hike north all the way to the base of Bray's Point (or south a quarter mile to the end of the beach at more onshore reefs). Shortly into the northward hike you must cross over the aforementioned bedrock, which can be impossible to do at big high tides, especially during winter.

The south access has a parking area at the top of the beach, reached by a 200-yard-long road leading west from the highway, but high tides and winter storms fill it with debris often enough that it is now closed most of the time, leaving visitors to vie for limited parking space at the turnoff. From there, walk down the closed roadway to the beach. Or use the much larger north access, a wedge-shaped gravel pullout across the highway from Tenmile Creek Road. From there, a trail leads west to the bank of Tenmile

Creek and on to the beach. However, during high flows anytime between mid-autumn and late spring, the creek delta is not safe to cross.

Tokatee-Klootchman State Natural Site

Location: Highway 101, milepost 172.5, 8 miles south of Yachats, 17 miles north of Florence.

Access: Short, steep trail to the beach.

Facilities: None.

Contact: Tokatee–Klootchman State Natural Site, (541) 547-3416, www.oregonstateparks.org.

With a half mile of sand beach bordered by sprawling wave-battered bedrock to the north and 1.5 miles of seldom-visited, narrow, bluff-guarded sand beach stretching south to the next public access at Ocean Beach Day Use site, the beach at Tokatee–Klootchman State Natural Site is one of the most appealing in the area. Far more people stop at the small parking area to gaze at the beach and ocean from above than actually descend the short trail to walk the sand. The rocky intertidal zone at the north end offers extensive tide pools at the lowest tides, but because of the nearly half-mile walk needed to get there, few visitors make the effort; hit this spot on a minus tide and you won't be disappointed. To the south, the beach wraps around several minor shoreline promontories before reaching the gleaming, wide expanse of sand in front of Ocean Beach Day Use site, but hiking around the last low headland is only possible at very low tides and not advisable under any conditions. The beach at Tokatee–Klootchman is a good bet for finding a variety of birds, and because the parking is slightly elevated, it's a good spot to look for whales. Though not particularly expansive, the sand beach stretching north from the access site is a good bet for beachcombing, especially in winter.

The information sign at Tokatee–Klootchman State Natural Site. Photo by John Shewey

Tokatee–Klootchman Beach. Photo by John Shewey

Ocean Beach. Photo by John Shewey

Ocean Beach Day Use Site

Location: Highway 101, milepost 171.5, 7 miles south of Yachats, 18 miles north of Florence.

Access: Short trail down to the beach from paved parking area.

Facilities: Restrooms, picnic tables.

Fees: Day-use fee or recreation pass required.

Contact: Siuslaw National Forest, (541) 563-8400.

Ocean Beach Day Use site is a pleasant, somewhat secluded little park with picnic tables set above one of the most alluring sand beaches on this part of the coast. The bright sand, considered part of Roosevelt Beach to the south, stretches northward about a mile, while the beach is scenically bordered to the south by a domelike headland 200 yards from the picnic area. At very low tides you can walk around the ocean side of the headland to Roosevelt Beach proper, but high tide will cut off your return journey, so watch the water levels; the base of the headland has some nice tide pools. If you get cut off, head south to Rock Creek and walk up to the highway. The headland, incidentally, is easy to climb (for the fit and agile) from a highway pullout at its base and the top provides a commanding panorama. Like Tokatee–Klootchman to the north, this extensive swath of sand is a good bet for beachcombing after winter high tides.

Wrentits are tiny songbirds that live in coastal scrub. Photo by John Shewey

Roosevelt Beach (aka Rock Creek Beach, including Big Creek Beach)

 Location: Highway 101, milepost 174.4 to 175.4, from Rock Creek Campground to Muriel O. Ponsler Memorial State Wayside.

 Access: Highway pullouts with short trails to the beach, and beach trail from Rock Creek Campground; direct beach access from Muriel O. Ponsler Memorial State Wayside.

 Facilities: Rock Creek Campground has 15 campsites, water, restrooms, day-use site. Muriel O. Ponsler Memorial State Wayside has picnic tables.

 Fees: Camping fees apply; day-use fee or recreation pass required for day-use parking at Rock Creek Campground.

Contact: Siuslaw National Forest, (541) 563-8400.

Roosevelt Beach, though little known by that name and sometimes called Rock Creek Beach, is a gorgeous, photogenic, mile-long, mostly-sand beach stretching from the headland just south of Ocean Beach Day Use Site south past Rock Creek and Big Creek, and down to the mouth of China Creek at Muriel O. Ponsler Memorial State Wayside. Along the way are occasional rock outcroppings, sandstone bluffs, and stream deltas. Despite the proximity of the small, wooded Rock Creek Campground, Roosevelt Beach is almost never crowded, with most visitors using the easy access at Muriel O. Ponsler Memorial

State Wayside. Roosevelt Beach is accessible at both ends as well as from a pair of small highway pullouts with short trails to the beach. The northernmost short trail is directly across the highway from the turnoff into Rock Creek Campground, with parking on the road shoulder at the base of the headland just to the north or at the shoulder of the campground road (be very careful crossing the highway); the next trail is at a small, triangular pullout along the southbound highway lane about 200 yards south of Rock Creek bridge. The next access is at Big Creek, 0.6 miles south of Rock Creek, where a gravel lot sits adjacent

to the northbound lanes just north of the Big Creek bridge; from there, walk carefully across the highway and look for a narrow trail through the brush at the north end of the guardrail on the southbound lane. However, for visiting the beach around the mouth of Big Creek, most people eschew the challenging parking near the creek and walk north a little more than a quarter mile up the sand from Ponsler Wayside.

Big Creek at Roosevelt Beach. Photo by John Shewey

The beach at Washburne Memorial State Park. Photo by Troy Smith

Carl G. Washburne Memorial State Park

Location: Highway 101, 16 miles south of Yachats, 14 miles north of Florence.

Access: Trails from state-parks day-use site and campground.

Facilities: Picnic sites, restrooms, RV dump station at day-use site; campground has 51 full-hookup sites, seven electrical sites with water, seven tent sites, two yurts, hiker/biker camp, hot showers, and flush toilets.

Fees: Camping fees apply.

Contact: Carl G. Washburne Memorial State Park, (541) 547-3416, www.oregonstateparks.org.

The expansive beach at Carl G. Washburne State Park, sometimes called Blowout Creek Beach, attracts lots of visitors during its busy summer season for its wide strip of bright sand, ideal for kids, kites, sports, and most any other activity. Hobbit Beach (see next entry) to the south, at the base of Heceta Head, is an easy walk down the beach from Washburne. On a clear day, the beach at Washburne provides excellent views in both direction—Heceta Head to the south and northward to Cape Perpetua. During the winter, when gravel and cobble beds are exposed all along the beach, this shoreline frequently offers interesting beachcombing early in the morning following a high tide.

The 1,211-acre state park here was a gift to the state on April 13, 1962, under the will of Narcissa J. Washburne in memory of her husband, Carl G. Washburne, a former State Highway Commissioner (1932–1935) and a Eugene investor and businessman. The day-use site sits on the west side of Highway 101, and the popular campground sits east of the highway. The entire state park is laced with hiking trails, and in addition to the beach, a pair of freshwater ponds south of the campground attract a variety of wildlife.

○ Hobbit Beach

 Location: Highway 101, milepost 177.3, 13 miles south of Yachats, 13 miles north of Florence.

Access: 0.4-mile trail to beach.

Facilities: None.

Contact: Heceta Head State Scenic Area, (541) 547-3416, www.oregonstateparks.org.

Hobbit Beach is a scenic little strip of sand abutting the north escarpment of Heceta Head; reaching it requires a half-mile hike through dense coastal forest from a small pullout on Highway 101: a quarter mile south of milepost 177 (1 mile south of the Carl G. Washburne day-use site and 1 mile north of the entrance for Heceta Head lighthouse) watch for the gravel pullout on the east side of the highway (look for a large sign declaring "No Overnight Parking"). This spot, with room for about six vehicles, sits at a junction for trails in the state park, and during summer, you can often readily identify the location by the vehicles parked there. To reach Hobbit Beach, walk to the north end of the pullout and carefully

Hobbit Beach looking north. Photo by Paige Hamm/CreativeCommons

cross the highway to the trailhead sign. Just inside the forest, take the signed right-hand fork and continue ever deeper into the darkening forest with its lush understory that crowds the trail. The end of the trail reveals a pristine sand beach leading south to the base of Heceta Head.

Well away from the highway, Hobbit Beach is a fine location to run dogs, but they must remain on-leash while on the trail; be exceptionally careful of the oft-busy highway: leash the dog in the vehicle and maintain a secure grip as you cross the road and head down the trail. The beach here is also great for beachcombing, particularly first thing in the morning on a low tide—before other visitors arrive. A 1-mile beach walk heading north takes you up to the day-use site at Washburne State Park. Beware that high tides, especially storm-driven winter high tides, can squeeze the beach down to a narrow strip of debris-littered sand—in stark contrast to the broad expanse of spotless sand during a summer low tide. Often during winter and spring, with lots of sand hauled offshore by scouring, parts of the beach are littered with cobble.

Hobbit Beach, looking south toward Heceta Head. Photo by Michael King

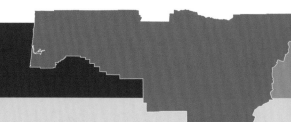

Cape Creek Beach at Heceta Head (Devils Elbow State Park)

 Location: Heceta Head Lighthouse State Park, Highway 101 milepost 178.2, 14 miles south of Yachats, 12 miles north of Florence.

 Access: Large paved parking at the top of the beach.

 Facilities: Restrooms, picnic tables.

 Fees: Day-use permit, state parks pass, or valid state park camping receipt required; onsite kiosk for purchasing daily permits.

 Contact: Heceta Head State Scenic Area, (541) 547-3416, www.oregonstateparks.org.

Heceta Head Lighthouse State Scenic Viewpoint (formerly Devils Elbow State Park) encompasses the 1,000-foot-high headland itself, on which stands Heceta Head Lighthouse, as well as the scenic little cove below at the mouth of Cape Creek, the Devils Elbow headland to the south, and 7 miles of hiking trails. A sandy pocket beach set deep between two precipitous headlands, Cape Creek Beach is a popular attraction during the summer tourism season and inevitably draws crowds. Well protected by the headlands, the cove is a great place for a picnic on the beach—easily accomplished with the parking lot just a few steps away. The 56-foot lighthouse began

operation in 1894, and the nearby keeper's house (Heceta House), built in 1893, now serves as a bed-and-breakfast, operated by a concessionaire of the U.S. Forest Service (visit www.hecetalighthouse.com). High above Cape Creek where it enters the beach, the 619-foot Cape Creek Bridge, designed by Conde McCollough and opened in 1932, suspends Highway 101 as it passes through verdant coastal forest.

Heceta Head takes its name from the Basque explorer, Bruno de Hezeta (1744–1807), a Spanish naval officer who commanded an exploratory expedition to the Pacific Northwest in 1775. The

expedition, launched from Mexico, comprised two ships, the *Santiago*, commanded by Hezeta, and the *Sonora*, commanded Bodega y Quadro. The explorers made numerous discoveries, and ultimately claimed the Northwest for Spain after Hezeta, with a small company of men, steered a landing craft to shore at what is now Grenville Bay, Washington. They didn't stay long and the next day, Bodega sent a launch to shore with seven men to collect fresh water and cut firewood, but they were attacked and killed by Quinault warriors, who then paddled out to attack the *Sonora*. The Natives were beaten back, with casualties, by gunfire. Bodega named the place *Punta de los Martires*, Point of the Martyrs; located on the Quinault Indian Reservation, it's now rather unromantically called Grenville Point. Hezeta's diaries were translated and published as *For Honor and Country: The Diary of Bruno de Hezeta* (Oregon Historical Society Press, 1985).

Cape Creek Beach at Heceta Head. Photo courtesy of Oregon State Parks

Baker Beach/Sutton Beach

Location: Highway 101, milepost 182.2, 18 miles south of Yachats, 9 miles north of the Siuslaw River bridge in Florence.

Access: Trail from Baker Beach Campground to the south end of the beach; steep roadside trail to north end of beach.

Facilities: Five rustic campsites with fire rings, vault toilet, small parking area at Baker Beach Campground (no water).

Fees: Camping fees apply at Baker Beach Campground; day-use permit or recreation pass required for Baker Beach Trail.

Contact: Siuslaw National Forest, Central Coast Ranger District, 1130 Forestry Lane, Waldport, (541) 563-8449; C&M Stables (beach rides), (541) 997-7540, www.oregonhorsebackriding.com.

Four-mile-long Baker Beach (the south end is often called Sutton Beach) is popular with horse riders and the area includes a variety of interconnected riding/hiking trails, but the direct route to the beach for hikers is a 0.4-mile trail taking off from the west end of the parking area at Baker Beach Campground. Baker Beach is a vast stretch of sand stretching from Cox Rock (just south of Sea Lion Caves) south to the mouth of Sutton Creek. Visitors wanting to see the area by horseback can hire the services of highly-reputed C&M Stables, (541) 997-7540, www.oregonhorsebackriding.com, located on Highway 101 just south of Baker Beach Road.

Alder Dune Campground, set amid dense coastal forest, sits just west of Highway 101, 1.5 miles south from Baker Beach Road, and offers two day-use parking areas (daily fee applies) with trails to the beach. The trail from Baker Beach Campground is much shorter, however. Still, Alder Dune is a pleasant campground and good base for exploring the area.

The best part of Baker Beach is the north end, and for the reasonably fit, getting there requires only a 250-yard descent along a seldom-used trail from a paved Highway 101 pullout at milepost 181 (the second

pullout south from the entrance to the well-signed Southview housing area). Park at the south end of the short pullout to leave room from for other vehicles (few people use the trail, as it requires a steep hike back up from the beach, but people often pull in to enjoy the view). Be careful on this trail during the wet season, as it tends to be muddy and slippery.

This pleasant stretch of sand beach, with steep fore-dunes (especially in winter), is fairly popular with horse riders, who typically ride up from Baker Creek Campground, but pedestrian visitation is

sparse. Beachcombing for shells and interesting rocks can be quite good, and at very low tides, the terminal north end of the beach, up against the base of the Cox Rock headland, offers nice tide pools. Baker Beach is under snowy plover restrictions from March 15 to September 15, meaning motorized and nonmotorized vehicles, kites, drones, and dogs (even on leash) are not allowed in both the dry- and wet-sand portions of the beach, and that visitors must stay off the dry-sand portions of the beach.

Baker Beach equestrians. Photo by Pat Benjamins/C&M Stables

Heceta Beach and Florence North Jetty Beach

Location: Florence area, north of the Siuslaw River estuary.

Access: Variety of small access sites with short trails to the beach.

Facilities: Restrooms.

Amenities: The Florence area offers a variety of attractive lodging and dining options, including the eclectic and oft-busy old town district at the north foot of the Highway 101 bridge across the Siuslaw River.

Contact: Florence Area Chamber of Commerce & Visitors Center, (541) 997-3128, www.florencechamber.com.

Much of Heceta Beach, along with the interconnected Florence North Jetty Beach, is composed of firm, well-packed sand that when even slightly wet is great for jogging, mountain-biking, horse riding, and more. The popular beach runs for 2 miles, from the Siuslaw River north jetty north to the mouth of Sutton Creek near the north end of the community of Heceta Beach, and while oft-visited, this spacious swath of sand seldom seems crowded. Heceta Beach is a great place to run well-behaved dogs off leash. Lane County Parks administers much of the above-beach shoreline, including a nice

county park access on the north side Driftwood Shores Resort, which has a posted leash requirement. However, the beach itself is state property and is a designated off-leash site for dogs from the Siuslaw north jetty north to the mouth of Sutton Creek. Beyond Sutton Creek (Baker Beach/Sutton Beach), the next 4 miles of beach and fore-dunes are under snowy plover restrictions and dogs are not allowed between March 15 and September 15. State law requires dogs to be under firm voice command, and this is especially important at Heceta Beach because the area is popular with equestrians.

Heceta Beach South, an Oregon State Parks access, offers a small parking lot and short trail to the beach on the south side of Driftwood Shores Resort: from Highway 101 north of Florence, just south of milepost 187, turn west onto Heceta Beach Road and follow it northwesterly 2 miles, then turn north (right) onto 1st Avenue. Follow 1st Avenue a short distance north to the signed beach access sites on both the south and north sides of Driftwood Shores Resort. The county site (Heceta Beach North), on the north side of the hotel, has an onsite pay kiosk and requires a nominal day-use fee. A third access site, with very limited

parking, allows you to escape the bustling summer crowds at the access points on 1st Avenue: in front of Driftwood Shores, drive east one block on Falcon Street, then turn left on 4th Avenue and follow until it ends at Joshua Street. Turn left and follow Joshua to a left (south) turn onto 3rd Avenue, and then a right turn on Ocean Way, and look for the beach trail at the corner of Ocean Way and 2nd Avenue. Parking is limited to the road shoulder, but don't block the fire hydrant or driveways.

A mile of sand beach stretches south from the Heceta Beach South access site and the only other public access site is at the south end, at the Siuslaw north jetty: from Heceta Beach at the Driftwood Shores Resort area, follow 1st Avenue south to Heceta Beach Road (called Kiwanda Street on it westernmost one block) and go east one block to a left (south) turn on Rhododendron Drive. Follow Rhododendron 1.2 miles to the signed right turn at North Jetty Road. From Highway 101 northbound in Florence, turn left (west) on 35th Street and follow it 1 mile to a right on Rhododendron, then go 1.2 miles to the signed left turn onto North Jetty Road (35th Street is 2.2 miles north of the Highway 101 bridge over the Siuslaw River in Florence). North Jetty Road leads 1 mile down to the state parks access site for the jetty and the adjacent beach. Along the way are two narrow sand lagoons squeezed between the jetty and the adjacent shore-pine scrub woodlands, and these shallow wetlands are excellent birding sites, particularly during spring and fall migration. Parking is roadside at several places, with a large dirt parking lot between the two lagoons, 0.4 miles down North Jetty Road. The lagoons are fringed by a narrow sand beach, so walking along the edges is easy.

Java ready to play ball at Heceta Beach. Photo by John Shewey

○ Siuslaw Spit

 Location: South side of the Siuslaw River west of Florence.

 Access: Road access to several day-use sites with short trails to the beach.

 Facilities: Restrooms.

 Contact: Florence Area Chamber of Commerce, (541) 997-3128, www.florencechamber.com;
Oregon Dunes National Recreation Area, (541) 271-6000, www.fs.usda.gov/recarea/siuslaw/recarea/?recid=42465.

An intriguing area offering a variety of beach activities, the Siuslaw Spit frames the west edge of the Siuslaw River as this fertile stream turns northward at Florence on its final leg to the Pacific Ocean. The spit stretches for more than 3 miles, its entire length fronted on the ocean side by a bright, beautiful, oft-wind-battered sand beach. Vegetated dunes back the beach and the inland portion of the spit hides a variety of mostly seasonal freshwater wetlands.

Sand Dunes Road, which heads west from Highway 101, 0.6 miles south from the Siuslaw River bridge at Florence, runs south–north along the spit for 4 miles, providing excellent access to the ocean side of the spit. After turning off Highway 101, Sand Dune Road passes by two large off-road-vehicle staging areas used by dune buggy and ATV enthusiasts who have acres and acres of sand dunes to ride through. The dunes and staging locations include spacious sand-camping areas. West from the sand-driving staging areas, Sand Dunes Road swings north to head up Siuslaw Spit and along the way are five small, well-spaced, day-use parking areas. The beach is hidden behind steep fore-dunes, but easy to reach via short trails from these parking areas. This section of the beach is closed to off-road vehicles and is great for early-morning beachcombing, hiking, running, and playing with the dog.

The Siuslaw River south jetty forms the north end of the spit, and the jetty structure extends inland, southward, along the edge of the bay to a small cove at South Jetty County Park. The cove is partially enclosed by a finger jetty, and an adjacent crabbing dock can accommodate plenty of visitors. Parking is available near the foot of the crabbing dock and across Sand Dunes Road from the aforementioned cove. From this latter parking area, a sand trail leads westward 250 yards through vegetated dunes to the beach. Sand Dunes Road continues northward along the jetty for another half mile, with one large gravel parking area and road shoulder parking as far west as a set of large boulders that block further driving. The beach is a short walk from anywhere along the road.

The jetty itself is popular with anglers fishing for bottomfish, such as black rockfish, and the low-tide mud, sand, and gravel flats along the inland side of the spit attract clam diggers. The broad beach on the south side of the jetty is a well-known surfing spot that can kick up a surprisingly large and consistent break. Even more popular with skilled surfers is the big break that rolls up the bay itself, along the south jetty: large waves roll into the bay mouth and begin to break as they approach the jetty. This break is best left to experienced boarders, largely because the jetty rocks themselves can present a substantial hazard to those who inadvertently venture too close.

The entire Siuslaw Spit area is excellent for birdwatching, with a variety of habitat types. During migration and winter, the jetties attract black turnstones and surfbirds, while the mudflats and sandflats attract a variety of other shorebirds. Ducks are common, as are cormorants and other seabirds. Freshwater ponds in the center of the spit are hotspots as well.

The beach on Siuslaw Spit. Photo by Martin Bishop/CreativeCommons

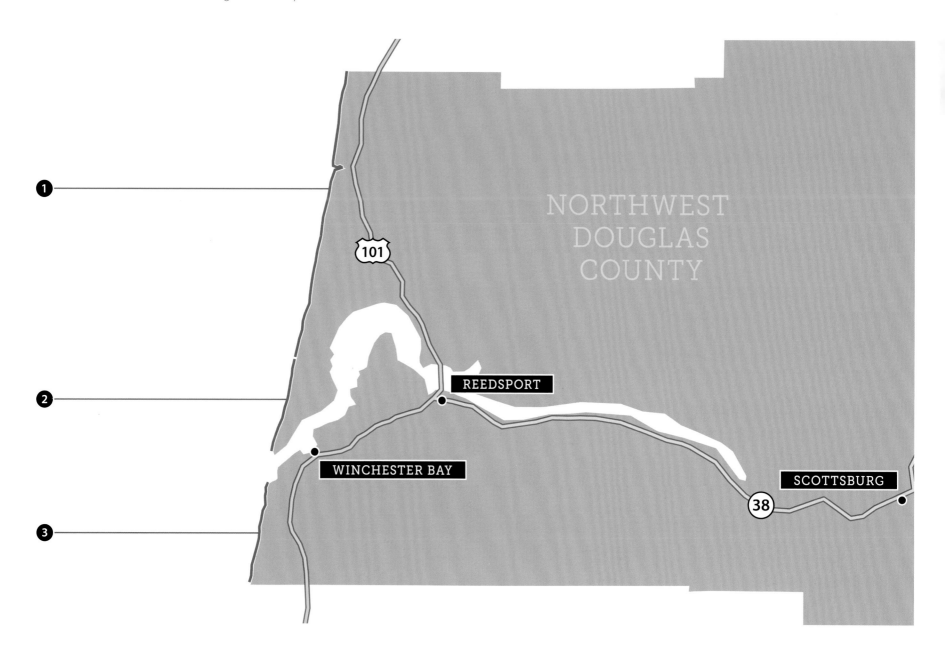

NORTHWEST
DOUGLAS
COUNTY

101

1

REEDSPORT

2

WINCHESTER BAY

SCOTTSBURG

3

38

DOUGLAS COUNTY BEACHES

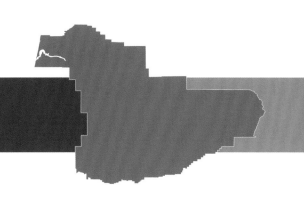

1. Siltcoos Beach & Oregon Dunes National Recreation Area

2. Sparrow Park Beach

3. Umpqua Lighthouse State Park & Ziolkouski Beach

The Oregon Dunes Loop Trail approaches the beach. Photo by Paige Hamm/CreativeCommons

Siltcoos Beach and Oregon Dunes National Recreation Area

 Location: 7 miles south of Florence.

 Access: Trails over/through dunes to beach, ranging from 100 yards to 2.5 miles.

 Facilities: Various campgrounds and day-use sites.

 Fees: Day-use fee or recreation pass required.

 Contact: Oregon Dunes National Recreation Area, (541) 271-6000, www.fs.usda.gov/recarea/siuslaw/recarea/?recid=42465; Florence Area Chamber of Commerce, (541) 997-3128, www.florencechamber.com.

Siltcoos Beach takes its name from the Siltcoos River, which meanders for just 3 miles from its source at 3,164-acre Siltcoos Lake to the ocean, providing a popular venue for canoeists and kayakers. This beautiful stretch of wide-open, windswept sand beach is part of the Oregon Dunes National Recreation Area (NRA), a 40-mile-long stretch of coastline replete with sprawling sand dunes. The mouth of the Umpqua River at Reedsport largely divides the NRA into north and south halves, the north half extending north to the Siuslaw River, and the south half stretching down to Horsfall Beach near North Bend. Many sections of the dunes are open to off-road vehicles, and dune driving is one of the most popular activities in the Oregon Dunes NRA. But other sections of the dunes, as well as interwoven stretches of forest, are closed to vehicles, leaving many appealing options for hikers, and a number of trails that lead to the beach.

The most direct access to Siltcoos Beach is from the Siltcoos Beach day-use and off-road vehicle staging area, 1.5 miles west of Highway 101 via Forest Road 1070 (Siltcoos Beach Access Road). Here, a large parking area sits just above the beach, north from the mouth of the Siltcoos River, with a vehicle and pedestrian access trail down to the beach. To reach the beach south of the Siltcoos River, use the Waxmyrtle Trail from Waxmyrtle Campground, back down Siltcoos Beach Access Road about a half mile east from the day-use site. The trail leads southwest about 0.75 miles to the beach. One-half mile south of the Siltcoos Beach Road, 7.5 miles south of Florence, Taylor Dunes Trailhead day-use site sits just off Highway 101, but the same road leads a short distance farther down to Carter Dunes Trail

○ Siltcoos Beach and Oregon Dunes National Recreation Area *(continued)*

(and Carter Lake Campground), which offers a more direct 0.6-mile route to the beach. Two miles farther south on Highway 101, the Oregon Dunes Loop Trail begins at Oregon Dunes day-use site (10 miles south of Florence, 9 miles north of Gardiner). It leads westerly about 0.75 miles through the dunes to the beach. You can also link to the southern end of the Oregon Dunes Loop Trail to access the beach from the Tahkenitch Creek Trail, a 5-mile round-trip hike that begins at the Tahkenitch Creek Trailhead, 1.5 miles south of Oregon Dunes day-use site.

These trails lead through a variety of habitat types, including expansive sand dunes, coastal lodgepole pine and deciduous forest, marshes, deflation planes, and riparian zones. Wildlife abounds, especially for visitors who hike the trails early in the morning. Significant stretches of the beach here are regulated to protect nesting western snowy plovers. From March 15 to September 15, the dry-sand beach (upper beach) is closed to access as per signage. The wet-sand beach is open to hiking and horseback riding, but closed to vehicles, bicycles, dogs, camping, and kite-flying. Be sure to check current regulations, which are prominently posted

throughout the area. The beaches within the Oregon Dunes NRA tend to offer intriguing beachcombing following big storms, and the same beach-access trails that are busy during summer tend to be largely deserted in winter.

The Oregon Dunes NRA has a number of campgrounds. Reservations are advisable, especially from late spring through mid-autumn. The area is riddled with freshwater lakes of all sizes, from small, shallow ponds, to sprawling lakes such as Siltcoos Lake, the largest lake on the Oregon coast. Many are stocked with trout and others hold populations of warm-water gamefish such as largemouth bass and yellow perch. Many of the campgrounds provide ready access to lakes.

In addition to Siltcoos Beach, the Oregon Dunes NRA beaches sometimes go by a variety of local names, depending on location, such as "Tahkenitch Beach." But the beach here is largely contiguous from the Siuslaw River Spit near Florence down to the north jetty at the mouth of the Umpqua River, interrupted only twice, by the Siltcoos River and by Tahkenitch Creek. South from the jetty compound

at Winchester, the beach is once again largely continuous, interrupted only by Tenmile Creek. The NRA includes the next two beaches described in this chapter—Sparrow Park Beach and Ziolkouski Beach—and Horsfall Beach and North Beach described in chapter 4.

Sometimes called Tahkenitch Beach, this stretch of beach is accessible via a short hike through the sand dunes from Oregon Dunes day-use site.
Photo by Paige Hamm/CreativeCommons

Sparrow Park Beach. Photo by Dan Portman

Sparrow Park Beach

Location: North side of Winchester Bay, at the end of Sparrow Park Lane west of Gardiner.

Access: Drive or walk onto the beach from the end of Sparrow Park Lane west of Gardiner.

Facilities: None.

Sparrow Park Beach stretches north from the north jetty of Winchester Bay. Gleaming sand, open to driving, the beach is popular among anglers fishing for redtail surfperch. The access to this beach, Sparrow Park Road, is west of Gardiner, the small town on the north shore of the bay, across the Winchester Bay bridge from Reedsport. Sparrow Park Road turns west off Highway 101 about 2 miles northwest of downtown, then winds its way westward for 4 miles to the beach. The gravel road is narrow, with little room to turn around, and thus not suited for RVs. From where the road reaches the beach, vehicles can drive southward but not northward on the sand, and it's 5 miles down to the north jetty—plenty of room for anglers, beachcombers, dogs and owners, and other beachgoers to spread out.

Surfperch fishermen at Sparrow Park Beach. Photo by John Shewey

Umpqua Lighthouse State Park/Ziolkouski Beach

Location: 6 miles southwest of Reedsport.

Access: Short trails to beach from parking areas off Salmon Harbor Drive.

Facilities: State park campground has 10 full hookup sites, nine electrical sites with water, 20 tent sites, eight yurts (three pet friendly, one with universal access), hiker/biker camp, two log cabins (one pet friendly), hot showers, flush toilets.

Contact: Umpqua Lighthouse State Park, (541) 271-4118, www.oregonstateparks.org; Oregon Dunes National Recreation Area, (541) 271-6000, www.fs.usda.gov/recarea/siuslaw/recarea/?recid=42465.

Just south of the Umpqua River's mouth, Umpqua Lighthouse State Park, with freshwater Lake Marie as its centerpiece, sits inland from an archetypal Oregon sand beach, often called Ziolkouski Beach, which is served by large day-use parking areas along Salmon Harbor Drive. This area is immensely popular with dune buggy enthusiasts because of the extensive sand dunes that stretch south for 15 miles, nearly to North Bend, but the beach itself is actually off limits to motorized vehicles and is often nearly deserted, especially during winter.

Come summertime, however, the dunes, campgrounds, and beaches are bustling with activity. In fact, the little town of Winchester hosts the annual Dune Fest in late July, a massively popular event that draws so many participants and onlookers that people visiting this part of the coast for other reasons and caught unaware of the festival, won't find a single room for rent anywhere in the area. Dune Fest (www.dunefest.com) stretches across four to five days and attracts sand-driving enthusiasts from all over. Naturally, the towns of Winchester and Reedsport cater expertly to the dune-buggy crowd; rentals

Riding the Winchester dunes, with Ziolkouski Beach in the background. Photo courtesy of Oregon Coast Visitors Association

are available locally from several outfits, including Spinreel Dune Buggy and ATV Rental, (541) 759-3313, www.ridetheoregondunes.com, and Steve's ATV Rentals, (844) 278-3837, www.stevesatvrentals.com

This entire stretch of dunes, the Umpqua Dunes Area, is part of the Oregon Dunes National Recreation Area, administered by Siuslaw National Forest, which maintains the Oregon Dunes Visitor Center nearby at 855 Highway Avenue in Reedsport. The visitor center offers a variety of map and information resources, as well as knowledgeable and helpful staff.

Umpqua Lighthouse. Photo by Kirt Edblom/Creative Commons

CHAPTER

5

Photogenic beauty of Oregon's south coast. Photo By Mason Marsh/www.masonmarsh.com

SOUTH COAST BEACHES: COOS AND CURRY COUNTIES

Oregon's south coast might just be the most dramatically scenic coastline in the Unites States, highlighted by rugged, precipitous headlands and sea cliffs, its beaches studded with bedrock, boulders, and basalt monoliths, and its near-shore waters bristling with sea stacks and islands. All of this geological wonder collides with the powerful Pacific to forge postcard-pretty scenes at every fold in a shoreline that, from above, looks like the edge of an unfinished jigsaw puzzle.

All along the southern Oregon coastline, verdant forests reach out onto headlands and creep down to rocky shores that hide tiny sand pocket beaches, and for every well-known, easy-to-reach beach in Coos and Curry Counties, another hidden beach awaits visitors who revel in exploration. Each stretch of sand, no matter how lengthy, ultimately ends at rocky, wave-blasted headlands where breakers send white plumes of water high into the air and where low tides reveal some of the best tidepools in the Pacific Northwest. Such resplendent natural beauty should draw throngs of tourists, yet the beaches of southern Oregon offer solitude aplenty thanks to the region's relative isolation from major

population centers: Portland is four hours by car, nonstop, from Coos Bay and six hours from Brookings; even from seemingly nearby Medford, the drive westerly to Brookings takes nearly three hours.

The south coast is also known for its temperate climate, so much so that the Curry County coast, from Langlois and Port Orford south to Brookings, is colloquially known as Oregon's Banana Belt. Though the climate is not quite warm enough to grow bananas, many visitors are surprised to discover that Oregon's south coast agriculture specializes in cranberries and Easter lilies. In fact, most all of the lilies grown for the potted Easter lily market come from a short stretch of the coast from the Brookings area south to California's Smith River; and the region is the fourth-largest cranberry producer in the nation.

Coos Bay and North Bend, conjoined towns with about 28,000 residents, comprise the largest community on the south coast. Coos Bay–North Bend is a working town, rich in the history and traditions of timber harvest, shipping, and dairy farming, but it offers everything a visitor needs and many surprises. Otherwise, small, eclectic towns, strung along this 130-mile-long coastline, beckon visitors: Charleston, Bandon, Port Orford, Gold Beach, and Brookings all thrive, in part, on tourism, and each offers unheralded excellent restaurants, myriad lodging options, quirky and eclectic shops, waterfront bars, charter fishing fleets, and more.

China Beach. Photo by John Shewey

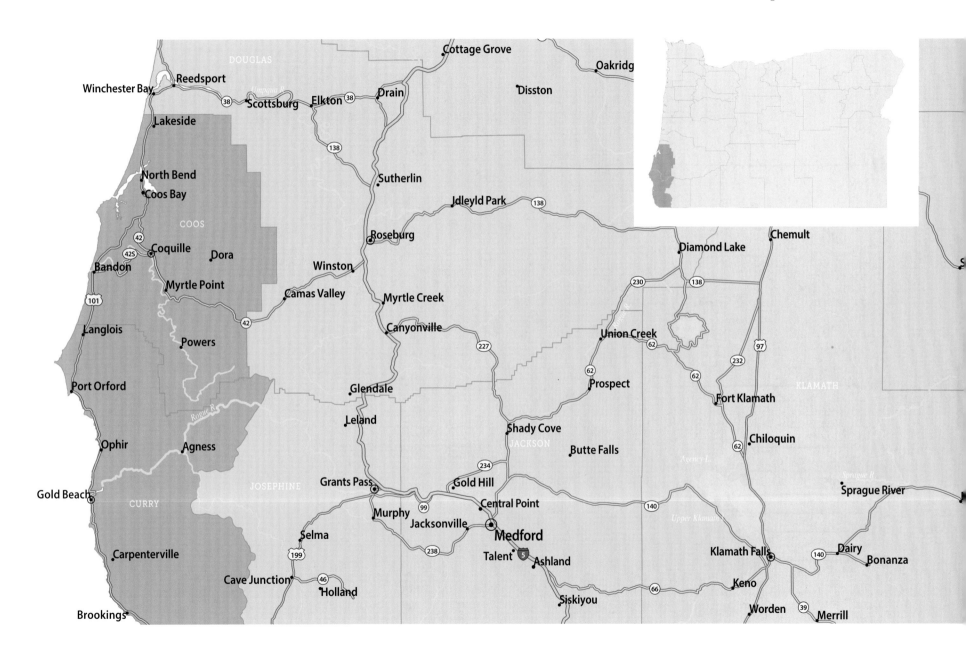

LAKESIDE

101

NORTH
COOS COUNTY

NORTH BEND

COOS BAY

1

2

3

4

5

6

7

8

NORTH COOS COUNTY BEACHES

1. Horsfall Beach

2. North Spit Beach

3. Bastendorff Beach

4. Yoakam Beach

5. Lighthouse Beach

6. Sunset Bay State Park

7. Simpson Beach & Shore Acres State Park

8. Cape Arago State Park

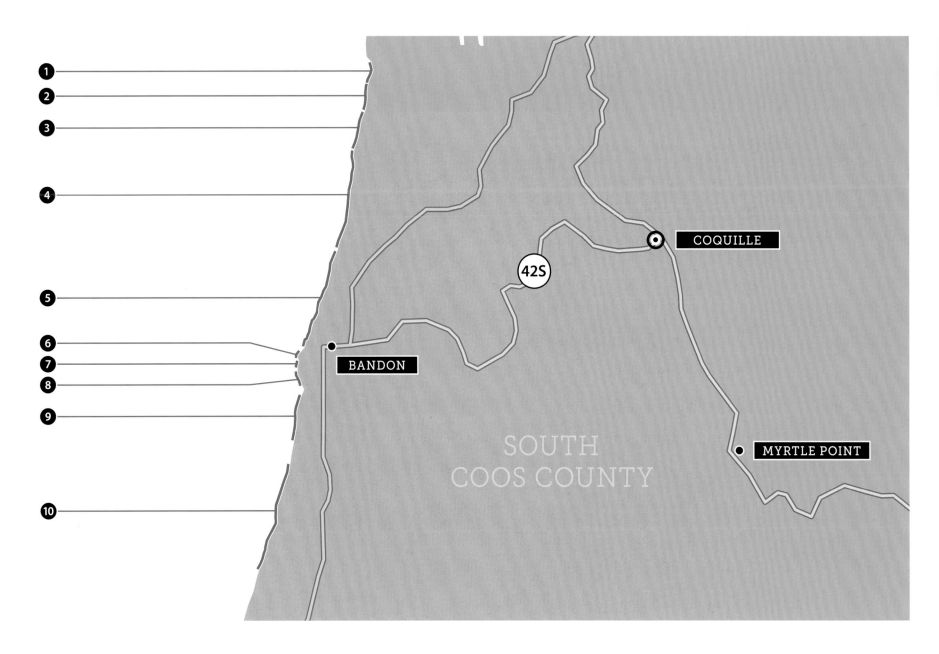

SOUTH COOS COUNTY BEACHES

1. Sacchi Beach
2. Agate Beach
3. Merchants Beach
4. Whisky Run Beach
5. Bullards Beach
6. Bandon South Jetty
7. Coquille Point Beach
8. Face Rock Beach
9. Haystack Rock & Devil's Kitchen
10. China Creek Beach

Horsfall Beach and North Spit/North Beach

 Location: Coos Bay–North Bend, north from the Coos Bay north jetty.

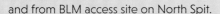 **Access:** Vehicle and pedestrian access to the beach from Horsfall Beach day-use area at the west end of Horsfall Road, and from BLM access site on North Spit.

 Facilities: Horsfall Campground has 34 nonelectric RV/car sites (two with universal access), restrooms, water.

 Fees: Camping fees apply; daily fee or recreation pass required for Horsfall day-use site.

 Contact: Horsfall Beach, Siuslaw National Forest, (541) 271-6000; Bureau of Land Management, Coos Bay District, (541)756-0100, www.blm.gov/or/districts/coosbay.

The North Spit of Coos Bay is the southern extent of more than 20 miles of contiguous sand beach and coastal dunes stretching north all the way to Winchester at the mouth of the Umpqua River. Most of this vast swath of sand attracts off-road-driving enthusiasts by the droves, and access to the south end of this section of coastline is readily available at Horsfall Beach, which melds southward into what is often called North Beach, out on the ocean side of North Spit. But, while a top activity in this area is beach and dunes driving, North and Horsfall Beaches are regulated by restrictions to minimize disturbances to nesting western

snowy plovers, so throughout the summer season, when snowy plover restrictions apply (typically May 1 to September 30 here, but check current regulations), vehicles are not allowed on the beach from approximately 500 feet north of the Horsfall Beach access south to the southern boundary of the Oregon Dunes NRA—a stretch of just over 1 mile.

The access road for both beach sections—Trans Pacific Lane—turns west from Highway 101 in the middle of the Haynes Inlet causeway at milepost 232.7. Signs indicate Horsfall Campground, which is popular with

off-road-vehicle enthusiasts, largely designed for RV parking, and packs campers into fairly tight quarters, neighbors not far away when it's crowded. At the west end of the Trans Pacific Lane causeway, turn right (north) onto Horsfall Beach Road; the campground is just up the road, and the day-use site, right above the beach, is 2.5 miles farther west.

To reach the BLM access site for North Spit/North Beach, follow Trans Pacifc Lane past the turnoff to Horsfall Beach, and continue 3 miles to the BLM North Spit boat launch on the bay side of North Spit. This is the only developed public access site on the spit, and has ample parking within walking distance of a sand hiking/off-road-vehicle trail, located a short distance farther down the road.

North and Horsfall Beaches are typically productive fishing locations for redtail surfperch, and at times can produce razor clams (check regulations and seasons with Oregon Department of Fish and Wildlife), and this entire stretch of beach is well-known among the locals for it beachcombing potential following big Pacific storms. It's also a nice place to exercise dogs except during the snowy plover closure from September 15 to March 15. On the bay side, mud and sand flats are popular for harvesting clams and sand shrimp, and anglers fish for perch and bottom fish off the rocks. Though striped bass populations are not what they were during that fishery's heyday decades ago, anglers still catch them, as well as a few salmon from the banks here.

Horsfall Beach. Photo by BLM

Vehicle tracks on the beach at North Beach. Photo by BLM

Bastendorff Beach

Location: Extending south from the Coos Bay south jetty near Charleston.

Access: Pedestrian access and parking areas along Bastendorf Beach Road and from Bastendorff Beach Park.

Facilities: Bastendorff County Park campground has 74 water/electric sites, 25 tent sites, two cabins, hiker/biker camp, hot showers, restrooms; large day-use area has numerous amenities, including a large playground.

Fees: Camping fees apply.

Contact: BLM Coos Bay, (541) 756-0100; Bastendorff Beach County Park, (541) 888-5353.

Especially popular with residents of the Coos Bay/ North Bend area, Bastendorff Beach routinely attracts summertime crowds and likewise blossoms with visitors any time the sun pops out during the balance of the year. Built of firm sand, and absorbing picturesque surf, this mile-long crescent-shaped beach is framed by the Coos Bay south jetty on the northeast and the jagged rocks of ever-scenic Yoakam Point on the southwest. The primary access is Bastendorff Beach Road, a right-hand turn 1.5 miles from Charleston as you head southwest along the Cape Arago Highway. The road passes by Bastendorff County Park and then descends to beach level; parking is available along the shoulder and at several large pullouts.

Bastendorff Beach attracts visitors of all kinds. Families with children frequent the beach, building sand castles, flying kites, and splashing in the shallows; runners and joggers, sometimes with dogs alongside, enjoy the firm sand; surfers and boogie boarders arrive en masse when conditions are ideal; anglers

Bastendorff Beach looking southwest. Photo by BLM

fish the surf for redtail surfperch and from the jetty for perch and bottomfish. Picnickers abound, and revelers range from teenage to middle age. The one thing Bastendorff seldom provides is solitude; instead a social atmosphere prevails. Depending on where you park, the jetty is easy to reach for the price of a short walk (be very careful on the jetty rocks, which are no place for children and dogs), and the little cove at the base of Yoakam Point is less than half a mile down the sand from where Bastendorff Beach Road first reaches the beach.

The county-park campground is popular and pleasant, set amid verdant forest. Nearby, on Cape Arago Highway just southwest of Bastendorff Beach Road, RVers can enjoy easy beach access by renting space at Oceanside Beachfront RV Resort, (541) 888-2598, which also offers rental cabins and, significantly for beachgoers in need of lunch, a little walk-up restaurant called The Crab Shack.

Bastendorff Beach. Photo by John Shewey

Lighthouse Beach. Photo by John Shewey

Lighthouse Beach and Yoakam Beach

 Location: Cape Arago Highway, 2 miles west of Charleston.

 Access: Two unmarked trail access points, one at Lighthouse Beach and one at Yoakam Beach.

 Facilities: None.

Two of the most scenic beaches in the Charleston area, interconnected Lighthouse Beach and Yoakam Beach stretch from the northeast foot of Chief's Island—home of Cape Arago Lighthouse—northeast to Yoakam Point and its golden spines of sandstone. The beach runs for more than half a mile, but its easternmost end, Yoakam Beach, is largely separate except at very low tides, when you can scamper around a ridge of rock extending out from the 50-foot-high bluff that guards this beach. This small fortresslike beach is the part of beautiful Yoakam Point State Natural Area, composed of two tiny pockets of sand incised into the sandstone and composite-stone cliffs and the bedrock reefs of Yoakam Point that reach well out into the surf.

On a warm summer day, these tiny pockets of golden sand at Yoakam Beach, framed by dramatic outcroppings of colorful stone, are mesmerizing places to enjoy a morning cup of coffee or afternoon picnic. Late-afternoon sunlight plays kaleidoscopically on the colorful rocks, creating a photographer's dream. The only indication of beach access here is a small sign announcing "Day Use Only" set back in a narrow pullout 0.3 miles west from the entrance road to Bastendorff Beach. From here, a 300-yard trail heads back through verdant coastal forest to a steep trail leading down a narrow arroyo to the beach—makeshift stairs and a guide rope help mitigate for the steep, oft-slippery path. Just to the left of the bottom of the access trail, intriguing layered composite bedrock, turned on its side by geologic forces, marks the

path around a narrow ridge at low tide to lengthy Lighthouse Beach, which is backed by a low cliff with houses atop that seem perilously close to the edge should the ocean ever decide to eat away more of the sandstone.

Access to Lighthouse Beach is even more covert, gained via a secret trail leading off the Cape Arago Highway 0.9 miles south from the entrance to Bastendorff Beach and a few yards south of Lighthouse Way. Look for a narrow gravel pullout along the southbound lane just before you reach a small sign announcing Sunset Beach State Park. From the middle of this pullout, an easy-to-miss trail leads back through the trees, crosses Lighthouse Way just above the beach, and drops down a narrow, oft-muddy path between two houses,

273

○ Lighthouse Beach and Yoakam Beach *(continued)*

with a guide-rope to help. Local surfers use this path and are routinely respectful of the property owners, coming and going quietly. Follow their example. Emerging on the beach, you'll see Cape Arago Lighthouse on Chief's Island just a scant quarter mile distant, and at very low tides, you can walk toward it to explore tide pools at the terminal west end of Lighthouse Beach. The other direction, back to the east, the beach stretches for half a mile, skirting two minor ridges that extend into the surf at high tide, to reach the rock spine that separates it from the pocket beaches at Yoakam Point.

Traditionally Lighthouse Beach has been the haunt of anglers seeking surfperch, but in recent years, more and more surfers have discovered the seclusion of this hidden stretch of sand, which is typically deserted or nearly so even while Bastendorff Beach, a mile to the east, and Sunset Bay, literally right around the corner to the west, swarms with visitors. Under ideal conditions, Lighthouse Beach offers a big, clean, curling break that attracts expert surfers—sometimes by the dozen—and even beginners can find great waves here. Experienced kayakers

Yoakam Beach. Photo by John Shewey

sometimes show up just off Lighthouse Beach,
typically launching at Sunset Bay and enjoying
the scenic paddle out around Qochyax Island
and Gregory Point on calm days. Beware, however,
that these are rocky waters and calm oceans
can turn rough quickly—only veteran paddlers
should navigate beyond the mouth of Sunset Bay.
Lighthouse Beach also offers good birdwatching
and early-morning beachcombing.

Yoakam Beach. Photo by John Shewey

Sunset Bay. Photo by Mason Marsh/www.masonmarsh.com

Sunset Bay State Park

Location: Cape Arago Highway, 3 miles west of Charleston.

Access: Large day-use area directly above the beach; trail to beach from campground.

Facilities: Sunset Bay State Park campground has 29 full-hookup sites, 34 electrical/water sites, three universal access sites, 66 tent sites, hiker/biker camp, eight yurts (one pet friendly, three with universal access), hot showers, restrooms; day-use area has picnic tables, restrooms, and small-boat launch site.

Fees: Camping fees apply.

Contact: Sunset Bay State Park, (541) 888-3778, www.oregonstateparks.org.

Justifiably popular, ever-scenic Sunset Bay is so well protected by its enclosing headlands that on calm days the surf barely makes a ripple, lapping gently at the crescent-shaped sand beach. Shallow reefs outside the mouth of this quarter-mile-wide cove block the incoming waves so effectively that breakers simply don't make it through this natural bay's narrow entrance, especially at low tide.

Sunset Bay draws throngs of people daily during summer and just about any sunny day the balance of the year. Voluminous parking is just steps from the sand, and restrooms, along with two recreational-type beach volleyball courts (non-regulation) are located just off the south end of the beach. At low tide, the rocky north end of the bay is easy to explore. Photographers should come prepared with a tripod and linger until sunset, as the rocks here can serve to frame some beautiful evening images.

The lightly used boat launch at the north end of the sand part of the beach is ideal for launching a kayak, and while the parking lot is close enough to simply carry gear down to the shoreline, a four-wheel-drive vehicle can navigate the launch area. Kayakers can enjoy superb sightseeing as well as excellent fishing around the rock structure in and outside both ends of the bay, especially to the north out around Baltimore Rock. At times, Sunset Bay is home to a kayak angling contest held in August. The inner bay is ideal for learning how to kayak the ocean, and once adept at these calm waters, paddlers can venture out a little farther to the broad mouth of the bay.

Simpson Beach and Shore Acres State Park

Location: Shore Acres State Park, 4 miles southwest of Charleston via Cape Arago Highway.

Access: Short trail through gardens and down to small, secluded pocket beach.

Facilities: Restrooms, interpretive displays, observation shelter overlooking ocean.

Fees: Day-use fee or recreation pass required.

Contact: Shore Acres State Park, (541) 888-3732, www.oregonstateparks.org.

Louis J. Simpson (1877–1949) moved to the Coos Bay area in 1899 at the behest of his wealthy father, timber baron and shipping magnate Asa Meade Simpson. Historians Richard and Judy Wagner, in *The Oregon Encyclopedia*, explain that the elder Simpson sent Louis to the family's North Western Lumber Company in Hoquiam, Washington, where "Simpson rebelled by drinking, gambling, and incurring debts. Yet, his artistic nature flourished, and he wrote short stories, acted in local theatre, sang, and orated. He also fell in love with Cassandra Stearns, who divorced her husband in 1899 to marry him. The forbearing elder Simpson, Asa, gave the young couple a new

start at his company town of North Bend, north of Marshfield, today's City of Coos Bay."

Simpson soon became a tremendous advocate for the region, lobbying diligently for bringing railroads to the area, and also travelling the West Coast during World War I to drum up support for the Military Highway, later Highway 101. In 1906, he began work on a luxurious seaside home that he would name Shore Acres. The estate included a spacious mansion, heated indoor swimming pool, ballroom, tennis courts, and verdant, spectacular gardens. Cassandra died in 1921, six years after the couple had made

Shore Acres their permanent residence, and a few months later, the mansion burned. The next year, Simpson remarried and lived for the next few years in the gardener's cottage until the mansion could be rebuilt even larger.

Sadly The Great Depression spelled the beginning of the end for Simpson's beautiful home and gardens, which fell into disrepair, and finally in 1942, the state of Oregon bought the property for use as a state park. The Wagners' biography of Simpson, *L.J.: The Uncommon Life of Louis Jerome Simpson*, tells his story in great detail. Today, Shore Acres State Park preserves the restored gardens of the property, even though the mansion had to be razed after World War II. The park hosts a variety of events during the year, one of the most popular being the incredible Holiday Lights display ongoing from Thanksgiving Day through New Years. The gardens bloom spectacularly from March through summer.

The tiny, secluded pocket beach—Simpson Beach— below the Shore Acres gardens is a footnote to the park grounds, but nonetheless dramatically beautiful. It occupies a narrow, 150-yard-wide cove, walled on both sides by tree-topped cliffs and during heavy seas offers excellent views of breakers crashing violently into the rocky spires. A short trail leads past the south end of the gardens to descend to the sandy beach, also accessible from a gravel pullout a third of a mile south of the state park entrance.

Simpson Beach at Shore Acres State Park. Photo by Pat Steeb

Middle Cove at Cape Arago. Photo by John Shewey

Cape Arago State Park

 Location: 5 miles southwest of Charleston via Cape Arago Highway.

 Access: Developed trails to two major beaches; steep, informal trails to third beach.

 Facilities: Restrooms, observation platform, picnic tables, picnic shelter.

 **Contact:** Cape Arago State Park, (541) 888-3778, www.oregonstateparks.org.

Cape Arago juts out into the Pacific about 5 miles southwest of Charleston at the end of the Cape Arago Highway. This incredibly scenic cape provides a panoramic view and is one of the best places in Oregon to see marine mammals, including countless sea lions, occasional northern elephant seals, and gray whales. The whales often come in close to the offshore rocks, sometimes lingering to feed for hours, and an observation platform atop Cape Arago a few steps from the parking area is ideally located for watching them. The wind can blow ferociously on the cape, so dress for the weather. The parklike setting on top of Cape Arago also offers restrooms and picnic tables.

Just to the north, the rocks at Simpson Reef and Shell Island serve as a major haul-out site for one of Oregon's largest concentrations of Steller's and California sea lions. From anywhere in the area, their barking and baying is incessant and ubiquitous, though actually following the sound to see the animals can be an exercise in futility and a lesson in acoustics: the myriad rocks and cliffs form echo chambers and the wind carries the sound. Sometimes the sea lions are easier to hear from a distance than from close by. The best observation point is the Simpson Reef Overlook (bring binoculars), located alongside Cape Arago Highway 0.4 miles north from the top of Cape Arago and 3.5 mile southwest from the entrance to Bastendorff Beach.

Cape Arago offers access to three different beaches, two on the south side of the cape, and one on the north side. The North Cove, as the latter is called, is closed seasonally from March 1 to June 30 to protect seal pups. Otherwise, this beach is accessible by a signed trail leading off the northwest side of the main parking area at Cape Arago, and is a great place for birdwatching and tide-pooling. North Cove's shoreline is fringed by verdant coastal forest and the narrow, rocky south end of the beach is well protected, tucked behind the north ridgeline of Cape Arago. The beach curves northward, transitioning to sand, and then back to rock as it stretches about a third of a mile up toward Simpson Reef Overlook. The signed South Cove trail departs the south end of

Cape Arago State Park *(continued)*

the short loop road on top of the cape and zigzags down the steep hillside to emerge on a narrow strip of sand and bedrock. The cove here is well protected by precipitous Drake Point, a narrow ridge jutting southward off the cape. Low tide reveals excellent tide pools at the base of Drake Point. As South Cove's shoreline curves around to the south, away from Drake Point, the beach is quickly reduced to a narrow jumble of rocks at the base of a steep mountainside. On very low tides, the rocks are accessible for a considerable distance, but the very real threats of rocks tumbling down from the cliffs above and of rising tides cutting off any escape suggest extreme caution. The inner cove here is so protected that its makes for good kayaking on calm summer days; in years gone by, boats would seek anchorage here—Sir Francis Drake may have even anchored here in 1579.

The third beach, Middle Cove, is dramatically scenic and intriguing, occupying the tiny cove beneath the observation deck on top of the south side of Cape Arago. Access is for the intrepid only, and is available from two places: the easiest route descends a badly eroded informal trail down the arroyo across the

View of Middle Cove from the observation deck at Cape Arago. Photo by John Shewey road from the picnic area along the south side of the loop road. It is a short, difficult, physically demanding descent and slippery when wet. The more difficult and inadvisable route dives very steeply off the ridge adjacent to the steps leading up to the observation platform; this route is essentially for mountain goats only, and is impossible when wet, and hence the short walk up to the aforementioned easier route is wise. For fit and hardy explorers, the beach here, easy to see from above, is sheltered by small, nearshore basalt sea stacks. The short part of the beach that appears from above to be sand is actually composed mostly of shell fragments, and the lengthier rocky shoreline beyond has many large round cobbles as well many rocks bearing fossilized clam shells. Minus tides reveal incredible tide pools.

South Cove at Cape Arago. Photo courtesy of Oregon State Parks

⦿ Sacchi Beach and Agate Beach

◎ **Location:** Seven Devils State Recreation Site, about 14 miles north of Bandon and 20 miles southwest of Coos Bay.

🚗 **Access:** Hike-in only from Merchants Beach to the south.

👫 **Facilities:** None.

📞 **Contact:** Seven Devils State Recreation Area, (800) 551-6949, www.oregonstateparks.org.

Seven Devils State Recreation Site takes its name from a ridgeline that ends abruptly in cliffs above the Pacific shore south of Cape Arago. At the southwest end of Seven Devils, the sea cliffs of this forested ridge yield to sand beach that runs southward, interrupted by minor points, all the way to the mouth of the Coquille River at Bandon—a distance of about 10 miles. The northernmost 5 miles of this coastline comprises four named beaches: Sacchi, Agate, Merchants, and Whiskey Run, from north to south respectively, all of them part of Seven Devils State Recreation Site. Only Merchants Beach and Whiskey Run Beach have immediate access; the roads and land fronting Agate and Sacchi are entirely private and inaccessible, leaving these two scenic stretches of sand to those willing to hike north from Merchants Beach.

Merchants Beach (see next entry) has a large paved parking lot just a short walk from the sand and from there, the hike north to Agate Beach covers about 1 mile. A minor bluff, scattered with odd boulders, marks the north end of Merchants Beach and the beginning of Agate Beach, which stretches northward for about one-half mile. True to its name, Agate Beach is an excellent location to search for the colorful, ocean-smoothed stones, but mostly during winter when gravel beds are exposed as sand is

Sacchi Beach ends at spectacular rocks formations meeting the sea. Photo by Richard O'Neill

Agate Beach. Photo by Richard O'Neill

○ Sacchi Beach and Agate Beach *(continued)*

hauled off the beach by winter wave patterns. The agate prospects continue on Sacchi Beach, which is separated from Agate Beach by an unnamed point that reaches out into the surf zone. At high tide, passing this point can be difficult or impossible, depending on water levels, so low tide is the best time to visit Sacchi Beach.

The looming cliffs of Seven Devils rise from the north end of Sacchi Beach, preventing any further northward exploration, although the base of the cliffs are fun to explore for intertidal organisms at low tides. Sacchi Beach has a variety of interesting rocks, including Lady Sansaria, whose top, viewed from the right angle, looks something like a woman staring out at the ocean (the rock is named for the adjacent Sansaria subdivision).

In addition to the wintertime agate hunting prospects, Agate and Sacchi Beaches offer excellent and oft-interesting beachcombing and wildlife watching. The beachcombing, of course, is best after winter high tides, but can be good any time during the year, particularly for those who arrive at dawn to

Sacchi Beach, looking north toward Cape Arago. Photo by Richard O'Neill

beat the crowds, so to speak. However, these two beaches seldom attract more than a few people at a time. Local residents who live in the gated developments above these beaches enjoy easy access from private sites, but are seldom numerous. An excellent beachcombing strategy is to hike north from Merchants beach 3 or 4 hours after high tide, walk the 2.5 miles north to the cliffs at the north end of Sacchi Beach, then make the return hike at peak low tide, taking time to explore the tide pools at the cliffs before turning back south. See direction in the next entry for Merchants Beach.

A low-tide passage through the rocks connect Agate Beach to the south with Sacchi Beach. Photo by Richard O'Neill

○ Merchants Beach

Location: Seven Devils State Recreation Site, about 12 miles north of Bandon and 20 miles southwest of Coos Bay.

Access: Paved parking area with short trail to the beach.

Facilities: Picnic tables and restrooms.

Contact: Seven Devils State Recreation Area, (800) 551-6949, www.oregonstateparks.org.

When the wind is down, broad, scenic Merchants Beach is a great place for an oceanside picnic on a summer day, and come winter, when few people venture to the beaches of Seven Devils State Rec Area, this 2-mile-long beach is terrific for beachcombing, especially after big storms. A short walk north—about a mile—leads to Agate Beach, which is aptly named in winter, when sand being sloughed off the beach reveals agate-bearing gravel beds. Merchants Beach is also the start point for hiking north past Agate Beach to Sacchi Beach, and walking 1 mile south along Merchants Beach leads down to rocky Fivemile Point, a great place to look for birds. At low tide, you can walk the beach around Fivemile Point; at high tide, the point is passable via a trail leading over the rocks.

As for the name of Merchants beach, the Oregon State Parks information sign at the site explains, "Merchants Beach was named for one of Coos County's pioneer families. Born in 1838, Charles Merchant left his New York home as a boy and made his way west on his own, with little money or education. After a time in the California goldfields, he arrived here in 1860. An intelligent and hardworking man, he successfully established himself in mercantile, shipbuilding, and timber, eventually becoming one of the county's foremost

Merchants Beach. Photo by John Shewey

financiers and landowners. In 1862, he married Mary Lincoln Gunn and they had 16 children, most of them living to adulthood. Descendants of the Merchant family still live in the area today."

From Coos Bay, follow Highway 101 south about 14 miles, past milepost 252, and turn west (right) onto West Beaver Hill Road. Go 1.7 miles and turn left onto East Humphreys Road/Whiskey Run Road and follow it 2.5 miles to a right (north) turn onto Seven Devils Road, which leads 2 miles to the signed entry to Seven Devils State Rec Site and the parking area for Merchants Beach. From Bandon, follow Highway 101 north about 4 miles, past toward milepost 257, and turn left onto Seven Devils Road and follow it north 4.5 miles to the parking area.

Merchants Beach. Photo by John Shewey

Whiskey Run Beach

Location: Seven Devils State Recreation Site, about 20 miles southwest of Coos Bay, and about 10 miles north of Bandon.

Access: Small paved parking area with short trail to the beach.

Facilities: Restrooms, vehicle access.

Contact: Seven Devils State Recreation Area, (800) 551-6949, www.oregonstateparks.org.

The southernmost of the four beaches of the Seven Devils State Recreation Site north of Bandon, Whiskey Run Beach is a wide, flat swatch of sand that continues uninterrupted southward, melding with Bullards Beach. To the north, Whiskey Run Beach extends north from its access site for nearly a mile up to Fivemile Point. At low tide, the short, rocky section of beach at Fivemile Point is passable; at high tide, hikers must use a trail over the rocks above the beach.

Like Sacchi, Agate, and Merchants Beaches to the north, Whiskey Run Beach is seldom crowded, and on weekdays outside the summer season, frequently deserted. It's a fine spot for beachcombing, riding horses, running the dog, kite flying, or just playing in the sand.

Whiskey Run also attracts a few windsurfers and surfers, and along with part of Bullards Beach to the south, it is open to vehicles, from Fivemile Point down to the northernmost beach access at Bullards Beach State Park. The vehicle entry road down onto the beach, at the end of Whiskey Run Road, is steep and rocky, and usually muddy, requiring four-wheel-drive vehicles with high clearance. Visitors not wishing or equipped to drive on the beach park along the edges of the turnaround area at the end of the road and walk the short trail down to the sand.

Whiskey Run Beach. Photo by John Shewey

From Coos Bay, take Highway 101 south about 14 miles, past milepost 252, and turn west (right) onto West Beaver Hill Road. Go 1.7 miles and turn left onto East Humphreys Road/Whiskey Run Road and follow it west 4 miles to the parking lot for Whiskey Run Beach. From Bandon, follow Highway 101 north about 4 miles, and turn left onto Seven Devils Road, following it north 2.8 miles to a left turn onto Whiskey Run Road, which leads about 1.3 miles to the beach.

Fivemile Point divides Whiskey Run Beach from Merchants Beach to the north. The beach at the point is only passable at low tide, though a trail leads over the inland side of the rocks. Photo by Richard O'Neill

◎ Bullards Beach

Location: 2 miles north of Bandon, on the north side of the Coquille River estuary; turnoff at Highway 101 milepost 259.

Access: Easy trail from day-use area to beach; mile-long trails from campground to beach.

Facilities: Large state park campground with 103 full-hookup sites, 82 electrical sites with water, universal access campsites, hiker/biker camp, 12 yurts (three pet friendly, three universal access), horse camp with eight primitive sites, flush toilets and hot showers; RV dump station; day-use area with restrooms.

Fees: Camping fees apply.

Contact: Bullards Beach State Park, (541) 347-2209, www.oregonstateparks.org.

Bullards Beach State Park features one of the largest campgrounds on the Oregon coast, with trails networking throughout the park's 1,289 acres. It's also among the busiest coastal state parks, with an annual day-use attendance of more than a half million visits—and for good reason: Bullards Beach itself is postcard pretty, a long stretch of clean, tan sand stretching about 4 miles, terminating at the Coquille River north jetty on the south end and melding seamlessly into Whiskey Run Beach to the north; together, Bullards Beach and Whiskey Run Beach total about 5 miles.

The Bullards Beach day-use site sits just above the beach, with short trails leading through a narrow band of vegetated low dunes. From there, a 1.5 mile hike south on the beach reaches the Coquille River north jetty and historic Coquille River Lighthouse. Paralleling the beach and running along Coquille Spit between that separates the ocean from the lower Coquille River, Bullards Beach Road, heading south from the Bullards Beach day-use site, also reaches the lighthouse and its day-use parking area. The lighthouse was built in 1896 and operated until 1939,

and is now staffed from mid-May through September from 11 a.m. to 5 p.m. The main campground at Bullards Beach sits a little more than half a mile off the beach and is largely sheltered from the coastal winds. From the campground, two different trails lead to the broad, sandy beach. The Beach Trail, part pavement and part bark chips, runs for 1.25 miles, and is suitable for bicycles; 0.75-mile Pearl's Trail, named for a member of the Bullard Family, crosses through the coastal dunes.

Bullards Beach attracts lots of people, particularly on summer days, but this broad swatch of coastline offers ample room to spread out. From mid-autumn through spring, however, Bullards Beach is often surprisingly quiet, even deserted, making it a good beachcombing location, especially if you walk north toward Whiskey Run Beach on an early morning falling tide. Bullards Beach is also popular with dog owners, but be watchful for baby seals and other wildlife. Equestrians also frequent Bullards Beach. The southern portion of the beach is closed to vehicle access, while the northern portion, north from the day-use parking area is open to vehicles, which sometimes drive down from Whiskey Run Beach.

Top: Mew gulls on Bullards Beach. Photo by John Shewey
Bottom: Bullards Beach. Photo by KKendall/CreativeCommons

Bandon South Jetty & Children's Beach

 Location: Bandon.

 Access: Easy foot access from parking area at Bandon South Jetty Park.

 Facilities: Restrooms.

 Amenities: Nearby old town Bandon offers numerous excellent restaurants, along with charter fishing services and other amenities.

Contact: Bandon Chamber of Commerce, (541) 347-9616, www.bandon.com; Port of Bandon, (541) 347-3206, www.portofbandon.com.

One of the south coast's most popular tourist towns, Bandon nonetheless remains relatively quaint and quiet except on busy summer weekends. Its downtown boardwalk district attracts most of the attention from visitors, while its clean, dramatically scenic beaches tend to be surprisingly uncrowded. The town occupies the south side of the mouth of the Coquille River and supports a small charter-fishing fleet that enjoys ready access to ocean fishing and crabbing.

The old town area, location of what is dubbed the boardwalk district, sits nearly 1 mile inland from the

Bandon South Jetty beach. Photo by John Shewey

nearest ocean beach, usually referred to as South Jetty Beach because it begins at the Coquille River south jetty and extends southward to meld with the Coquille Point Beach; First Street leads through old town Bandon (west of Highway 101) and then curves south to become Edison Avenue; about 100 yards down Edison, a west turn on Jetty Road leads to Bandon South Jetty Park, where a large gravel parking lot provides ready access to the beach and the jetty. Highly scenic with looming sea stacks just offshore, the beach is a great place for an early morning or evening walk. It's also a good bet for surfperch fishing, and a nice place to run the dog.

Before reaching the park, Jetty Road skirts a cove in the bay that is bordered by a narrow sand beach called Children's Beach. Protected by partial jetties from the full force of waves surging into the mouth of the Coquille River, Children's Beach tends to be calm, and adjacent to the sand strip, a rocky intertidal zone invites exploration—by children and adults alike—at low tides. Children's Beach is a short walk from South Jetty Park, or you can park at a wide pullout along Jetty Road adjacent to the beach.

Agate hunting at Bandon South Jetty Beach. Photo by David McClurg

Coquille Point Beach (aka Kronenberg Beach)

Location: Off Beach Loop Road in Bandon, with access at the west ends of 8th Street and 11th Street.

Access: Short, fairly steep trails/stairwells down to beach.

Facilities: Interpretive trail on the headland above the beach.

Contact: Bandon Chamber of Commerce, (541) 347-9616, www.bandon.com.

Coquille Point hangs out over the coastline, providing expansive views of the seastacks guarding the sandy beaches extending to the north and south; the beaches meet at a narrow neck of sand just below the westernmost extent of the point, allowing visitors to walk from one beach to the next. At minus-tides, tidepools are exposed and accessible along the bases of the nearest rocks, and these monoliths—collectively called the Bandon Needles—provide habitat for a variety of seabirds, including cormorants, common murres, tufted puffins, black oystercatchers, and black turnstones. Harbor seals often haul out at the base of the rocks on low tides.

Atop Coquille Point, Kronenberg Park includes a short interpretive trail system stretching between the two access points (8th Street and 11th Street) and looping out to the edges of the point; signs discuss wildlife and natural history. The lightly-used 8th Street parking area is a small cul-de-sac with room for maybe 10 vehicles; the 11th Street access can accommodate about twice that number. Beach Loop Road, which provides access to Bandon's beaches, runs north–south about a mile west of Highway 101; to reach Beach Loop Road and Coquille Point from old town Bandon, follow 1st Street west until it swings south and becomes Edison Street, then follow Edison 0.3 miles and turn right

Coquille Point Beach below north entrance. Photo by John Shewey

(west) on 8th Street and go 0.6 miles to Beach Loop Road (continue a short distance to the end of 8th Street to park at the Coquille Point Beach access). The 11th Street access is three blocks south on Beach Loop Road. To reach Beach Loop Road from Highway 101 to the east, turn west on 11th Street (milepost 274.5), Seabird Drive (milepost 275.5), or the Beach Loop Road/Highway 101 intersection (milepost 277.5), north to south respectively,

Bandon's beaches are entirely interconnected, allowing for uninterrupted hiking; the northern most access is the south jetty (see previous entry) and the southernmost access is China Creek Beach. Coquille Point's 11th Street access makes an ideal base for beach hikers walking a mile north to the south jetty or a mile south to Face Rock. At the highest tides, egress between the beaches on the north and south faces of Coquille Point is limited to a narrow dune at the foot of the cliff; at the lowest tides, you can walk behind (on the ocean side) the 200-foot-long rock directly below the terminus of Coquille Point.

Top: South end of Coquille Point Beach. Photo by John Shewey
Bottom: Coquille Point Beach from Kronenberg Park. Photo by John Shewey

Face Rock State Scenic Viewpoint

Location: Off Beach Loop Road in Bandon, 0.6 miles south of 11th Street, and 0.6 miles north of Seabird Lane.

Access: Short, steep stairway trail down to beach from large parking area.

Facilities: Restrooms.

Contact: Bandon Chamber of Commerce, (541) 347-9616, www.bandon.com.

Face Rock sits just offshore from a minor headland named Gravel Point, and beyond it, to the northwest are the smattering of small sea stacks called Cat and Kitten Rocks. Closer, within the surf zone, another huge rock is accessible at low tides. The viewpoint, a state parks day-use site with a large parking lot and bathrooms, features a trail that follows along the edge of the cliff, providing excellent views of the beaches and sea stacks. At the south edge of the parking lot, a trail with stairs descends to the beach, and the little strip of sand at the foot of this trail often escapes the wind, being protected by the adjacent cliff; about 200 yards down the beach, a smattering of large rocks are accessible at low tide. During summer, volunteers for the Oregon Department of Fish and Wildlife sometimes set up spotting scopes at this viewpoint so visitors can see tufted puffins and other seabirds on Face Rock and the other sea stacks nearby, and each late April, Shoreline Education for Awareness (www.sea-edu.org) holds its annual Puffin Party at Face Rock (sometimes at Coquille Point), with members of the nonprofit on hand with spotting scopes and information.

The beach south of Face Rock viewpoint. Photo by John Shewey

Looking north from Face Rock viewpoint. Photo by John Shewey

Beach access at Mars Lane in Bandon. Photo by John Shewey

Haystack Rock & Devils Kitchen (Bandon State Natural Area)

 Location: Off Beach Loop Road in Bandon.

 Access: Short, easy trails from each of two access points.

 Facilities: Restrooms.

 Contact: Bandon Chamber of Commerce, (541) 347-9616, www.bandon.com.

Haystack Rock (one of three on the Oregon Coast) is a modest monolith buried in the sandy surf, with Bird Rock in front of it and other unnamed rocks that are close enough to be accessible at low tides. Most beachgoers who visit the Haystack Rock area walk the beach from Face Rock to the north or Devils Kitchen Day Use area to the south, but a direct access is available at the end of Mars Lane. Hardly ever used because it lacks signage of any kind other than at the trail itself, and is virtually hidden in a residential area off Bandon's Beach Loop Road, Mars Lane access has room for three or four cars, parked respectfully to avoid interfering with residents. Typically yours will be the only vehicle parked here.

Devils Kitchen access, with ample parking and restrooms, is just to the south, the next west turn south of Saturn Lane. About one-half mile south of the Devils Kitchen access, Bandon Wayside sits within the coastal forest and provides picnic tables sheltered from wind; a little-used, badly overgrown informal trail leads to the beach, but access is much easier at Mars Lane and Devils Kitchen. Like the entire stretch of beach south from the south jetty at Bandon, these beaches are composed of clean, windswept sand with scattered rocks and sea stacks to add variety and intrigue.

Yellow monkeyflowers. Photo by John Shewey

301

China Creek Beach. Photo by John Shewey

China Creek Beach

Location: South end of Beach Loop Road south of Bandon; from Highway 101, milepost 277.5, turn west onto Beach Loop Road and go 1 mile to the left turn into the access site; or travel south down Beach Loop Road 2.3 miles from Face Rock State Scenic Viewpoint.

Access: Large parking lot with short trails to the beach; snowy plover closures of dry-sand beach in effect March 15–September 15.

Facilities: None.

The last of the easily accessible beaches along Coast Loop Road in Bandon's southern outskirts, China Creek Beach is actually much quieter than the beaches just a short distance to the north. Adjacent to and south from the parking lot, the beach is fronted by vegetated dunes, and is a designated western snowy plover nesting area, with signs indicating where you can and cannot tread. For beach hikers, this parking area anchors one end of the 3-mile trek to or from Coquille Point or a bit farther, to or from the south jetty at Bandon. You can also hike south, but restrictions during the plover nesting season require beachgoers to stay on the wet sand (which is easier walking than up on the dry sand anyway). South of China Creek Beach, extensive private property, and the New River, which runs parallel to the beach, leave no public egress to almost 9 miles of sand beach. The only access is by foot, either south from China Creek Beach or north from the beach adjacent to Floras Lake, although you can also cross the New River via kayak. This entire stretch is managed to protect nesting western snowy plovers, with restrictions in place from March 15 to September 15. Hikers on this stretch of beach need to dress for high winds, which blow frequently, usually from the north during summer, making the southbound hike (China Creek Beach to Flores Lake) much easier than bracing the wind and driving sand by hiking north.

Volunteer "plover hosts" help explain the plight of western snowy plovers to beachgoers. Photo by John Shewey

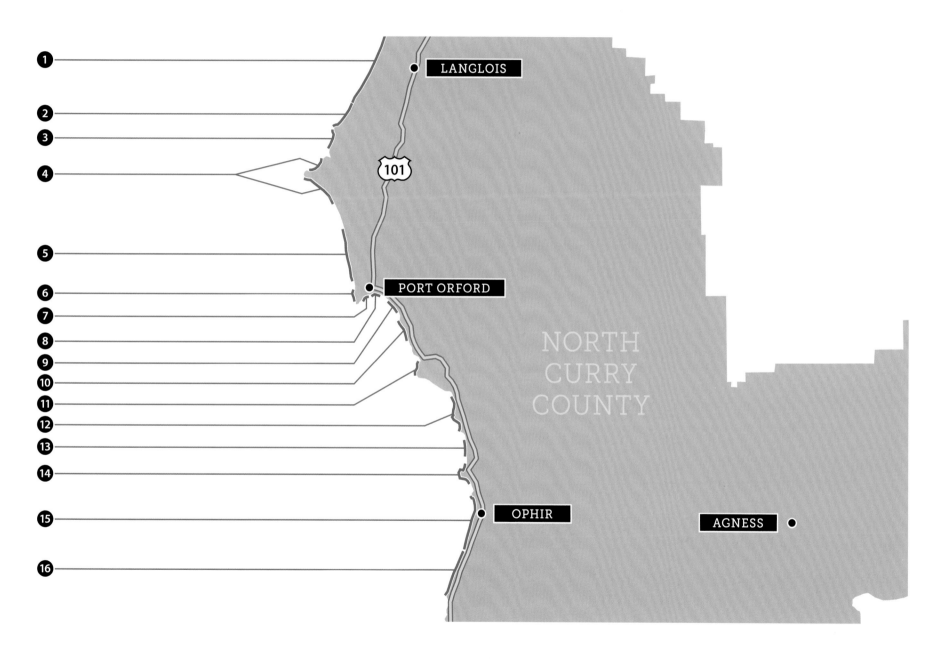

1

2

3

4

101

5

6 — PORT ORFORD

7

8

9

10

11

12

13

14

15 — OPHIR

16

LANGLOIS

NORTH
CURRY
COUNTY

AGNESS

NORTH CURRY COUNTY BEACHES

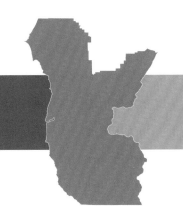

1 Floras Lake Beach

2 South Beach

3 Blacklock Point Beach

4 Cape Blanco State Park

5 Paradise Point

6 Agate Beach

7 Dock Beach

8 Battle Rock Beach

9 Hubbard Creek Beach

10 Rocky Point Beach

11 Humbug Mountain State Park

12 Humbug Mountain South

13 Beach

14 Arizona Beach

15 Sisters Rock State Park

16 Ophir Beach & Nesika Beach

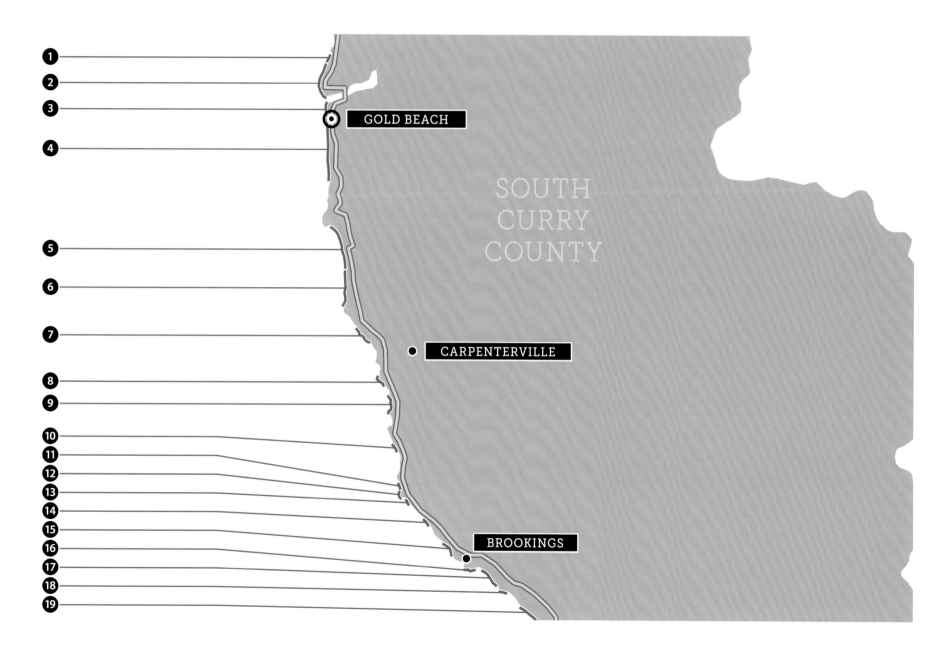

SOUTH
CURRY
COUNTY

GOLD BEACH

CARPENTERVILLE

BROOKINGS

SOUTH CURRY COUNTY BEACHES

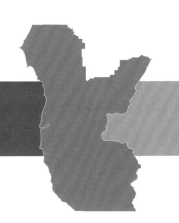

1. Agate Beach
2. Bailey Beach
3. Airport Beach
4. South Beach
5. Meyers Creek Beach
6. Pistol River State Park Beach
7. Hooskanaden Beach
8. Secret Beach
9. China Beach
10. Whaleshead Beach
11. House Rock Beach
12. Cape Ferrelo Beach
13. Lone Ranch Beach
14. Rainbow Rock Beach
15. Harris Beach
16. Mill Beach
17. Sporthaven Beach
18. McVay Rock State Recreational Area
19. Crissey Field Beach

○ Floras Lake Beach/South Beach

Location: Floras Lake, 4 miles southwest of Langlois.

Access: Parking lot at Boice Cope County Park on northeast corner of Floras Lake with sand trail leading 0.25 miles to beach.

Facilities: Campground with electric/water and water-only RV sites, tent sites.

Fees: Camping and day-use fees apply.

Contact: Boice Cope County Park, (541) 373-1555, www.co.curry.or.us/Departments/Parks/Boice-Cope-Park.

Floras Lake, covering 236 surface acres, is best known as a destination for kiteboarding and windsurfing, with lessons and rentals for both sports available through Floras Lake Windsurfing (www.floraslake.com/flw2.html). This freshwater lake is separated from the Pacific Ocean by a narrow strip of vegetated dunes above Floras Lake Beach, which stretches, uninterrupted, for miles. The north sector of the beach is under western snowy plover restrictions between March 15 and September 15, and the same incessant howling wind that makes Floras Lake such an attraction to kiteboarders and windsurfers also elicits awe for the tiny plovers that nest out in the open on the upper beach.

By far the best part of Floras Lake Beach is the south end, sometimes called South Beach, where multihued 100-foot-high cliffs—the "Orange Bluffs" or "Blacklock Bluffs"—rise straight up off the beach. It is unique among Oregon beaches and well worth the 5-mile round-trip hike down the beach from Boice Cope County Park. The cliffs begin as low bluffs about a mile into the hike, but are much taller and more dramatic farther down, near the southern

Blacklock Bluffs. Photo by Richard O'Neill

terminus of the beach. Avoid this beach during full-moon and new-moon high tides and powerful storm-driven tides because at such times, the breakers can reach up to the base of the cliffs.

Dogs are allowed off-leash at this southern extent of the beach, but leashes are required a short distance north on the beach across the dunes from Floras Lake; north of Floras Lake, dogs are not allowed on the beach. During the early morning calm, on the first two hours of an incoming tide, surf anglers can sometimes find good fishing for redtail surfperch at the south end of the beach, where it forms a small cove. But be sure to select a quarter-moon tide (minimal water exchange between high and low tides) during periods of calm seas because this beach takes a pounding; it tends to be fairly steep, too, so forget about wading the surf and stay on the sand above the water line.

The Oregon Coast Trail weaves through the Floras Lake area, and provides a nice viewpoint atop the South Beach cliffs, with this location easiest to reach (by foot or mountain bike) from the trailhead for

Blacklock Point at the Cape Blanco State Airport (see next entry). From that trailhead, you will hike to two signed trail junctions. At the first junction, bear left toward Blacklock Point, and at the second junction, go right to reach both viewpoints. The southern viewpoint provides the best panoramic view, but farther north, you can climb down through the bluffs to reach the beach.

Adjacent to Floras Lake, the beach is somewhat monotonous, but nonetheless dramatic and lightly trodden, composed of course tan sand, and often carved into low bluffs and dunes by the frequent powerful winds. When those winds are moderate, this beach is great for kite flying, though heed the plover advisory signs.

Floras Lake Beach. Photo by John Shewey

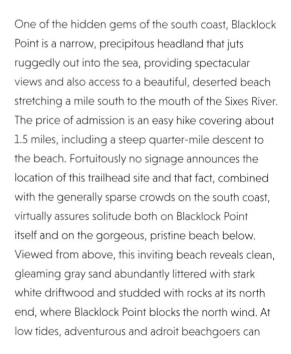

Blacklock Point Beach

 Location: Floras Lake State Natural Area, 8.5 miles southwest of Langlois, via Airport Road.

 Access: 1.5-mile trail, mostly level until steep 0.25-mile descent to the beach.

 Facilities: None.

One of the hidden gems of the south coast, Blacklock Point is a narrow, precipitous headland that juts ruggedly out into the sea, providing spectacular views and also access to a beautiful, deserted beach stretching a mile south to the mouth of the Sixes River. The price of admission is an easy hike covering about 1.5 miles, including a steep quarter-mile descent to the beach. Fortuitously no signage announces the location of this trailhead site and that fact, combined with the generally sparse crowds on the south coast, virtually assures solitude both on Blacklock Point itself and on the gorgeous, pristine beach below. Viewed from above, this inviting beach reveals clean, gleaming gray sand abundantly littered with stark white driftwood and studded with rocks at its north end, where Blacklock Point blocks the north wind. At low tides, adventurous and adroit beachgoers can

clamber northward along the base of the point and explore excellent tidepools formed by copious rocks.

The turnoff to the trailhead, Airport Road, is directly opposite Pacific High School at Highway 101 milepost 293.5. From there, follow Airport Road west 2.8 miles to its terminus at the Cape Blanco State Airport, which is seldom used. Park near the cement barriers in the gravel pull-off between the airport gate and a big green warehouse-type building to the east. The trail, great for mountain biking, is located near the south side of the gate, across the road from the parking area (a second parking area is available in a dirt cul-de-sac adjacent to the trailhead). Follow the trail westerly, bearing left and two signed forks for Blacklock Point. After the second fork, narrow boardwalks provide dry footing over boggy ground until it dries out in

summer; after the second fork, the trail heads through shore pine/spruce forest until topping out in a shaded parklike setting at the end of the woods and then emerging out onto the headland.

A short distance further, the trail to the beach departs downhill to the south and the headland trail continues west, heading well out toward the narrow tip of Blacklock Point, crossing a knife-edge ridge along the way that can be dangerous during the frequent high winds that batter this section of the coast. The trail to the beach is easy, but steep, and fine for kids, but the trail out onto the point is potentially perilous for anyone other than intrepid hikers with sure footing. If you bike out to the beach trail, carry a chain long enough to lock your bike to a tree where the main trail emerges from the woods.

Left: The beach south of Blacklock Point. Photo by John Shewey
Right: Blacklock Point. Photo by John Shewey

The beach south of Cape Blanco. Photo by Troy Smith

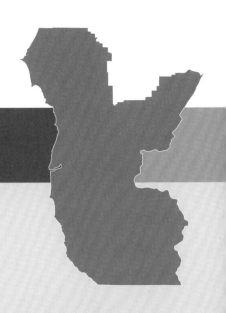

Cape Blanco State Park

Location: 4.5 miles north of Port Orford; Cape Blanco Road heads west 5 miles from Highway 101 (milepost 296.5) to the key facilities of the state park.

Access: Trails to the beaches on both sides of Cape Blanco; foot, horse, and vehicle access to the beach south of the cape near the state-park campground.

Facilities: Campground with 52 electrical sites with water (available first come, first served; seven sites with universal access); four reservable cabins (one pet friendly; one with universal access); reservable horse camp with eight primitive sites; group camp; hiker/biker camp; tours of historic Cape Blanco lighthouse available April–October, call (541) 332-2207 for schedule and information; tours of historic Hughes House available April–October, call (541) 332-0248 for schedule and information.

Contact: Cape Blanco State Park, (541) 332-6774, www.oregonstateparks.org.

Cape Blanco State Park is best known for its historic lighthouse, opened in 1870, and ferocious winds—during the infamous Columbus Day Storm of October 12, 1962, the wind hit an astonishing 179 miles per hour at the cape, and hardly a day goes by that it doesn't blow about 20 miles per hour or more.

South Beach, the beach below the south side of the cape, is punctuated by towering Needle Rock and is accessible by trail, with a parking lot located south of the campground (take the road to the horse camp to avoid the slow drive through the busy main campground). Vehicles are allowed on the beach from this point south to Port Orford, where Paradise Point (see next entry) provides the access site for vehicles, but you aren't likely to see rigs on the sand at South Beach because to get there, drivers must cross the Elk River mouth about a mile to the south, or face a rugged drop down to the beach from the vehicle access at the state park. The river runs northward behind the beach, forming Tituna Spit and the entire section of beach here is beautiful and generally void of people except during the late-summer/fall salmon runs. During late summer and early fall, the mouth of the Elk is easy to wade across at low tide. If you drive this stretch of beach, you'll need a four-wheel-drive beach-capable vehicle and plenty of common sense.

The cape itself, a massive headland and the westernmost point in Oregon, has hidden arches and sea caves at its base, accessible at very low tides from South Beach, but get out before the tide turns and beware powerful sneaker waves. The cape and

313

○ Cape Blanco State Park (continued)

the sea stacks in the area, as well as the beaches and inland portions of the park, are home to myriad birds, including peregrine falcons. It's a great place to look for seabirds, though a spotting scope is handy, and occasionally even pelagic species, such as sooty and pink-footed shearwaters, are seen from the cape.

North of Cape Blanco, and accessible by trail (or kayak) through the state park, the beach stretches northward to the mouth of the Sixes River. One steep trail leads down from the large gravel parking lot just east of the lighthouse complex. Two others depart from a day-use parking lot on the south bank of the Sixes River north of the Hughes House inland from the main part of the state park: 4 miles west of Highway 101, watch for the state park signs pointing north to the Hughes House and turn right; follow this road toward the house but take the right-hand fork when the road splits and continue to the day-use parking lot at the end of the road. From there follow the trail west through the scrub about 0.75 miles to the beach, or follow the trail along the Sixes River to the beach. Kayakers can launch here and paddle either direction.

The beach below the north slope of Cape Blanco. Photo by James MacIndoe/CreativeCommons

The river reaches the ocean in front of stately Castle Rock, a sea stack that divides the incoming breakers and creates dramatic cross currents in the surf at the delta. During summer and early fall, the mouth of the river is easy to ford at low tide (and is sometimes barbound), and hikers can continue up the beach about a mile to Blacklock Point. Generally you'll have this entire beach to yourself.

Looking north from Cape Blanco. Photo by BLM

Garrison Beach at Paradise Point State Recreation Site. Photo by John Shewey

Paradise Point State Recreation Site (aka Garrison Beach)

 Location: Port Orford.

 Access: Short trail to the beach from gravel parking lot, and rugged beach-access road for 4-wheel-drive vehicles.

 Facilities: None.

 Contact: Port Orford Chamber of Commerce, (541) 366-8319, www.portorfordchamber.com; City of Port Orford, (541) 332-3681, www.portorford.org.

Hidden in an out-of-the-way corner of Port Orford, Paradise Point Beach—also called Garrison Beach because of nearby Garrison Lake—is accessible via the Paradise Point State Recreation Area, and is a decidedly pleasant location for a lonely beach walk or even a substantial beach hike north about 3 miles to the mouth of the Elk River. This deceptively rugged beach tends to absorb a punishing shore break, so be wary and don't wander too close to the surf line on steep sections of the beach or anywhere during periods of rough ocean conditions. This heavy surf makes Paradise Point Beach a good beachcombing location, particularly following big storms. Early morning is the best time to avoid the frequent high winds that sweep this beach. To reach the state park access site, turn west onto Paradise Point Road from Highway 101 about 1 mile north of Port Orford (watch for the turn lanes near milepost 300).

A whimbrel feeds along the surf line. Photo by Mike's Birds/Creative Commons

Agate Beach/Tseriadun State Recreation Site

Location: Port Orford.

Access: Easy gravel-then-sand trail from state park to the beach.

Facilities: Picnic area and restrooms.

Contact: Port Orford Chamber of Commerce, (541) 366-8319, www.portorfordchamber.com; City of Port Orford, (541) 332-3681, www.portorford.org.

The hidden gem of Port Orford, Agate Beach and Tseridun State Recreation Site benefit handsomely from a simple lack of signage, for if more visitors knew about the beach and the pleasant day-use park, the area would likely draw substantial crowds: Agate Beach is composed of coarse sand and gravel, earning its moniker by yielding agates to astute rock-hounding beachcombers, especially during winter. Tseriadun (pronounced serry-AH-dun) features tree-sheltered picnicking sites and a small parking area for the beach trail. From the end of the 200-yard trail, the beach stretches about a mile south to Paradise Point State Recreation Site and along the way runs parallel to the west shore of 130-acre Garrison Lake, which sits just over the upper dunes and provides fishing for rainbow and cutthroat trout. To the north, the beach leads a short distance to the rocky escarpments at the foot of Port Orford Heads, a great place for the sure of foot to explore, especially at low tides, which provide access to a small cove with a tiny gravel beach tucked up against the headland. Be sure to keep an eye on the time and the tide level and get in and out of the cove quickly (and make the scamper down to this enclave only at the lowest tides and calmest surf conditions).

Fresh mussels boiled and ready to eat. Photo by John Shewey

Agate Beach at Tseriadun State Recreation Site. Photo by John Shewey

Battle Rock Beach at Port Orford. Photo by John Shewey

Dock Beach & Battle Rock Beach

 Location: Port Orford.

 Access: Short, easy trails leading from designated parking areas in Port Orford.

 Facilities: Port Orford offers a handful of lodging and dining options.

 Contact: Port Orford Chamber of Commerce, (541) 366-8319, www.portorfordchamber.com; City of Port Orford, (541) 332-3681, www.portorford.org.

Dock Beach is pragmatically named for its proximity to the Port Orford docks, but is sometimes mistakenly called Dog Beach, perhaps because visitors often run their dogs on this 1,500-foot strip of gray sand bracketed by the dock facilities on the west end and Fort Point on the east end. On the other side of Fort Point is the steep headland called Battle Rock and the adjacent beach at Battle Rock City Park. The city park beach offers stunning scenery, facing south into the broad, sea stack-studded cove that is protected from the full force of the Pacific by the massive headland at Port Orford. At times, these fertile waters adjacent to Dock and Battle Rock Beaches are so calm that waves do little more than lap at the shoreline.

Battle Rock is named for a skirmish between would-be white settlers and native people of the Quatoma Band, which had its roots in the Oregon Donation Land Act of 1850, passed by the US Congress, which allowed settlers to claim Indian lands in western Oregon without regard for or input from the indigenous people. So on June 9, 1851, Captain William Tichenor piloted the steamship Seagull north from San Francisco and dropped off nine men at what would become Port Orford, and then returned to sea to resupply in San Francisco, promising to return in two weeks. The men were lightly armed, but did haul ashore a small canon. Immediately the local band of natives made their displeasure obvious, and the nine men retreated from the

beach to form a defensive—and easily defended—perimeter on the adjacent sea stack; the only egress to the rock was by way of a narrow ridge. When a large contingent of natives attacked, they were repulsed by the canon fire, suffering numerous casualties; two of Tichenor's men were injured by arrows. According to *Encyclopedia of Indian Wars: Western Battles and Skirmishes, 1850-1890*, "The Indians retreated, but kept the whites under siege for two weeks. When Tichenor did not return on the promised date, the stranded colonists abandoned their rock [under cover of darkness] and fled north, eventually finding safety among friendly Indians at Coos Bay."

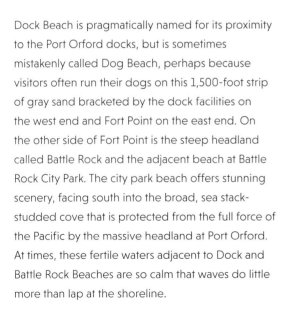

○ Dock Beach & Battle Rock Beach *(continued)*

Tichenor, in fact, did not make it back until July, but then disembarked with a force of 70 well-armed men; they built a fort and dwellings that were the beginnings of Port Orford. Today, Battle Rock provides a scenic backdrop to the city park and frames the south end a long, contiguous stretch of beach curving gracefully southward.

The beach at Battle Rock, and the viewpoint from the parking lot above, provides a great location for photographing the rugged coastline extending south: because of its orientation north-by-northwest of the shoreline stretching several miles down to Humbug Mountain, the park area allows photographers to catch evening summer sun illuminating the sea stacks in the expansive cove. Moreover, even better views are available for the price of a short hike out to the viewpoints at nearby Port Orford Heads State Park (use the Towers Trail and the Nellie's Cove Trail to reach the two viewpoints looking southward). The beach at Battle Rock is also popular with surfers, primarily when heavy winter storms create a well-formed break (at other times, the surf here tends to be too flat, but when a

consistent break sets up, surfers seem to appear out of nowhere). Windsurfers and kite-boarders can take advantage of the oft-windy days at Port Orford.

Battle Rock Park sits alongside Highway 101 on the south end of Port Orford. Trails lead to the beach and out onto Battle Rock; adjacent Fort Point is private property, but a miniature beach squeezed between Battle Rock and Fort Point is accessible, and at low tides, visitors can scramble west around the point to Dock Beach. The port facility and Dock Beach are located at the end of Harbor Drive, which swings south from the highway as it curves eastward through town. Kayakers revel in the oft-calm waters just off Port Orford and can launch at the harbor (or from the beach on calm days). Fishing and crabbing by kayak is somewhat popular here—and should probably be more popular considering not only the calm water inside the headland at Port Orford, but also the productivity of these waters (note that a short distance south, the Redfish Rocks Marine Reserve is off limits to the taking of any marine species).

The Port Orford Docks. Photo by Ray Gilden, Pacific Fisheries Management Council/Creative Commons

Beach at Port Orford. Photo by John Shewey

323

Hubbard Creek Beach. Photo by John Shewey

Hubbard Creek Beach

 Location: South end of Port Orford, just past the city limits.

 Access: Short trail under highway and down to beach from wide highway-pullout parking area.

 Facilities: Nearby Port Orford offers a handful of dining and lodging options.

Contact: Port Orford Chamber of Commerce, (541) 366-8319, www.portorfordchamber.com; City of Port Orford, (541) 332-3681, www.portorford.org.

Hubbard Creek Beach is the next beach south from Battle Rock City Park beach in Port Orford, but in reality this entire stretch of the coastline comprises a more-or-less contiguous 4-mile-long beach. Hubbard Creek, however, offers an alternate access point about 1 mile down-coast from popular Battle Rock. On weekends between May and October, the Hubbard Creek access is often busy, but the balance of the year it tends to be quiet. Locals and visitors alike sometimes run their dogs at Hubbard Creek Beach, and the wide swath of sand is also popular with early-morning beach walkers, beachcombers, kite fliers. Moreover, the beach here sometimes offers a consistent if modest break that draws quite a few surfers and boogie-boarders, and during heavy winter surf, a big full-curl break always seems to attract at least a few expert boarders. Parking is limited to a gravel pullout alongside the northbound lane of Highway 101 (near milepost 302) on the south side of Hubbard Creek. From there, follow the dirt trail down under the small highway bridge, along the creek, and about 200 yards down to the beach.

Surfing at Hubbard Creek Beach. Photo by Pat Kight, Oregon Sea Grant/CreativeCommons

○ Rocky Point Beach (aka Retz Creek Beach)

Location: Highway 101 milepost 304.5, 3 miles south of Port Orford.

Access: Short trail from small gravel parking area.

Facilities: None.

Largely composed of cobblestone—gray when dry, shiny black when wet—Rocky Point Beach (also known as Retz Creek Beach) forms the shoreline border of the 2.6-square-mile Redfish Rocks Marine Reserve. The reserve is designed to protect the near-shore marine ecosystem; taking of any marine organisms is prohibited, meaning no fishing, clamming, crabbing, or other harvest. The beach here is dynamic and fascinating, especially during heavy surf conditions, when the draining waves cause the cobble to clatter loudly and rhythmically, almost soothingly. Negative tides are especially intriguing here, allowing visitors to find interesting intertidal species (observe, but don't remove organisms from the water, as all life is protected here). Just a few yards wide at high tide, this beach varies substantially in character with the shifting seasons: scouring events, especially in winter strip away sand, sometimes leaving cobble atop reefs of bedrock. The uppermost beach is littered with driftwood of all sizes and shapes.

The parking area is somewhat hidden and easy to miss. About halfway between Highway 101 mileposts 304 and 305, watch for a sharp west turn, with a stop sign marking the spot, that hairpins to the north and downhill to the secluded parking lot (and beach information sign). From there, a short trail leads through shrubbery to emerge on the beach. If you'd rather not leave your vehicle hidden from view, a wide gravel pullout across the highway (adjacent to the northbound lane) offers plenty of room (naturally, be careful walking back across the highway).

Rocky Point Beach. Photo by Oregon State Parks

Rocky Point Beach. Photo by John Shewey

The beach at Humbug Mountain State Park. Photo by John Shewey

Humbug Mountain State Park Beach

Location: 6 miles south of Port Orford.

Access: Trail from Humbug Mountain State Park Campground leads about 0.5 mile to the beach.

Facilities: Large campground with 40 electrical sites with water (two universal-access sites), and 55 tent sites; hiker/biker camp; hot showers; restrooms with flush toilets; trailhead for Humbug Mountain.

Contact: Humbug Mountain State Park, (541) 332-6774, www.oregonstateparks.org.

A scenic, crescent-shaped sand beach fronts the base of precipitous 1,756-foot-high Humbug Mountain, and is easy to reach by foot from nearby Humbug Mountain State Park campground. The trail departs the west end of the campground, but there is no day-use parking; the day-use area (and thus the day-use parking) is at the far east end of the campground, so many beach visitors park about midway between those two points, across the highway from the campground, at the Humbug Mountain trailhead parking area. From there, take the tunnel under the highway, cross Brush Creek on a wooden footbridge, and walk west through the campground to the beach trail. Alternately, some people park in the narrow gravel pullout on the southbound highway shoulder just past the guard rail south of the Brush Creek crossing, and then walk down under the highway and follow the creek to the beach. Humbug Mountain State Park campground occupies a wooded ravine and is largely protected from the wind, making it a nice base of operations for exploring the area. The beach is a scenic crescent of gray sand, narrowing quickly at its terminal south end directly below the mountain.

Trillium in bloom. Photo by Greg Shine, BLM/Creative Commons

Humbug Mountain South Beach

Location: South side of Humbug Mountain, 10 miles south of Port Orford.

Access: Short but difficult hike through heavy coastal scrub, ending in a potentially perilous scramble over shoreline rocks.

Facilities: None.

Fighting through stands of old-growth buckbrush ranks about a zero on the fun-factor scale, and that's the least of the difficulties faced by explorers wishing to gain access to what may be the least-visited foot-accessible beach in Oregon—the narrow, mile-long strip of gleaming sand extending south from south escarpment of Humbug Mountain about 10 miles south of Port Orford. At least buckbrush doesn't bite back: in addition to prodigious buckbrush, however, the more-or-less cross-country route to this pristine ribbon of beach leads through copious stands of poison oak, prickly trailing blackberries, and even pricklier gooseberry. Other than these verdant inconveniences, the hike down to this hidden-in-plain-sight secret beach is actually fairly short and relatively easy for intrepid hikers.

The route begins at a wide gravel pullout on the west shoulder of Highway 101, milepost 310.6, at the south end of a long guardrail along the southbound lanes. Park here, then walk north behind the guardrail for about 200 yards, along a brushy bench-land and past a plastic survey marker, and watch on the left for a scramble trail leading about 10 feet down the gravel embankment. Look for faint trails through the brush leading west (stay out of the deep ravine to the immediate north) and head that direction until you can turn north and pick your way down the grassy, brushy slope facing the beach, which you can see to the north. Remain to the south of the nearby ravine, but bear north down the slope toward the big black rocks that guard the beach's south terminus. Generally you can follow faint trails made by previous visitors

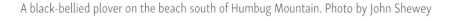

A black-bellied plover on the beach south of Humbug Mountain. Photo by John Shewey

and/or deer and elk. When the terrain flattens as you approach the rocks, aim for the largest of them, which when viewed from the route down, is surprisingly similar in profile to Humbug Mountain itself, which looms in the background. To the right (east) of this monolith, you can scramble down through the rocks to the beach; naturally, be very careful doing so. From the moment you depart the highway shoulder for the hike down, remain ever vigilant to poison oak and diligently avoid it.

Once on the beach itself, you can explore a mile of beach heading north, but be sure to avoid high tides—this narrow beach all but disappears on big high tides—full-moon and new-moon high tides can leave you no room to retreat because the headland is too steep to climb. Be especially wary of winter high tides, when the beach can completely disappear as surf hammers at the base of the precipice. Lucky visitors may spy elk or even black bear on this beach; usually, however, the only signs of their presence are footprints left in the sand. If you enjoy surf fishing for redtail surfperch, bring along some tackle. During summer, the surf here can be relatively calm on early morning neap tides, thanks to partial protection from Humbug Mountain, and mole crabs—favorite food of surfperch—are plentiful.

Be equally careful climbing back out of this beach, remembering every step of the way to watch for poison oak. At times, beach explorers here have attached an assist rope to heavy brush trunks in the south corner of the beach, a few yards inland from the big rocks. You can—very carefully—climb up the bluff here if the dirt has not been eroded out in a way to make the short climb dangerous. Otherwise, carefully negotiating the edge of the rocks is safer.

Humbug Mountain South Beach. Photo by John Shewey

Arizona Beach

Location: Highway 101, 12 miles south of Port Orford, 16 miles north of Gold Beach.

Access: Exit Highway 101 on the east, drive through Arizona Beach State Recreation Site picnic area, and under the highway to the beach parking lot that sits on the upper beach.

Facilities: None.

Arizona Beach stretches for almost a mile between two headlands that help shield this pretty swath of sand from fierce winds, reputedly explaining the beach's name: in the absence of wind, temperatures tend to be warmer here than on the exposed beaches. The truth, however, is that the wind can blow rather wickedly here at times and the beach takes its name from the home state of Captain Frank Friant, who bought the property now occupied by a state park in 1910.

Visible from adjacent Highway 101 and accessible by driving through a state park property on the east side of the highway, Arizona Beach attracts plenty of visitors during summer; when winds stay down, it's a fine stretch of sand for a picnic or just a pleasant stroll. When the wind blows, Arizona Beach is great for kite flying, and any time of year it's a fairly good bet for finding fun shells and other curiosities on the ebb tide. During winter, when sand is sloughed offshore, lots of rocks are exposed, especially at the already-rocky north and south ends of the beach—both places being well worth the short walk for tide-pooling at minus tides.

The 68-acre state recreation site, formerly a private campground, was purchased by the state using lottery funds in 2008. A small freshwater pond at this day-use park is open to angling for kids 17 and under only and is stocked with rainbow trout by the Oregon Department of Fish and Wildlife; the pond is open to fishing all year, but is drawn down in autumn to control aquatic weeds (best fishing is in spring and early summer when the pond is stocked). Otherwise, the park is limited to nice picnic sites, but it's also a fairly well-known birdwatching area because two creeks—Myrtle and Mussel Creeks, which merge to empty into ocean at Arizona Beach—run through the grounds, their courses marked by dense riparian shrubbery. A camp host is usually onsite during summers.

The scenic, rock-studded south end of Arizona Beach wraps around a minor headland, and then yields to an unnamed beach that forms the north end of the beach at Sisters Rocks State Park (see next entry). The beach hike from Arizona Beach down to Sisters Rocks covers little more than 1.5 miles and hardly anyone undertakes it—typical of south coast beaches. The middle section of the hike is well removed from the highway, which courses around the small headland. Low tide is best for this walk, with the high-tide trouble spot being the rocky stretch of beach about a half mile north of the parking area for Sisters Rocks. Pick a minus tide and you can explore myriad tide pools along the way.

Immediately south of Arizona Beach on the west side of Highway 101, one of the Oregon coast's quirkiest, most idiosyncratic tourist attractions, the Prehistoric Gardens, www.prehistoricgardens.com, is well worth a visit. This decades-old attraction features life-sized artistically rendered model dinosaurs displayed in a coastal rainforest setting; the park was the vision and accomplishment of the late E.V. "Ernie" Nelson, artist, sculptor, entrepreneur, and dinosaur enthusiast. It opened in 1955; children love it, and adults will find it interesting, educational, and pleasantly unique, all for a modest entry fee.

Arizona Beach. Photo by Oregon State Parks

Sisters Rocks State Park/Frankport Beach

Location: Highway 101 milepost 314.5, 13 miles south of Port Orford, 14 miles north of Gold Beach.

Access: Steep 0.25-mile-plus trail (a gated gravel road) leads down to the land bridge between beaches to the north and south, which are accessible by easy side trails.

Facilities: None.

For exploration-minded beach enthusiasts, Sisters Rock State Park is truly among the unheralded gems of the Oregon Coast, despite being hidden in plain sight of adjacent Highway 101. Three massive, wave-pounded, wind-hammered sea stacks, two of them connected to the mainland, dominate the scene—the Three Sisters for which the park is named. Fortunately for those who'd like to keep this complex and dramatic beach quiet, signage is limited to a single little Oregon State Parks shield sign along the highway.

Among the many dramatic surprises at Sisters Rocks is a gaping sea cave savagely churning with ocean water: the large land-side opening is hidden from view until you climb up a low bluff, easily found by looking for the various scramble trails, at the foot of the large central sea stack and peer into the maw of the cave. Be careful. Around the sea stack to the south, through a gap of densely packed boulders, are the two ocean-side openings of the cave. The cave is awesome at high tides, but also very interesting at low tides. The narrow rocky beachhead here, between the two onshore sea stacks, offers good tide-pooling at the lowest tides, but use extreme caution: the rocks are very slippery and this small cove, which provides an excellent view of the offshore sister, typically absorbs a heavy surf with frequent sneaker waves. The smaller sister that walls off the south side of this cove is notorious for falling rocks from high above, so stay away from the cliff. Informal trails lead up each of

Stonecrop in bloom at Sisters Rocks State Park. Photo by John Shewey

the escarpments to some extent, but beware loose footing and high winds.

On the south side of the park, Frankport Beach is marked by metal remnants from long ago: in the 1860s, the S.H. Frank Company tannery established a small port here, naming it the harbor of Frankport. Hides and tanbark were principal products originally, and as late as the 1950s, the port served lumber shipments as well. All of it is gone, now, however, save some implements of metal and the obvious signs of a rock quarry. A bit farther south, this attractive beach is studded with huge rocks within the surf zone and is accessible by a very steep informal trail diving off the hillside just before the main park trail passes alongside a rock escarpment on its way west; or you can wait until low tide, drop down to Frankport Beach via the main trail (west of the aforementioned rock escarpment), and then walk along the beach, skirting the first rock barrier, and explore the rocky shoreline extending about half a mile southward. To the north, the lightly trodden gray-sand beach, easily accessible, includes additional rocks studding the surf zone with geological wonders in the form of small arches and

sea caves. These features are easiest to explore at low tide, and intriguing at minus-tides.

The entire beach area offers excellent wildlife and wildflower viewing in addition to the tide-pooling. Birds frequent the area, including peregrine falcons. During spring and fall migration and during winter, the rocks and beaches attract a variety of shorebirds. Marine mammals are common, and—surprisingly—if you keep your eyes open while walking across the rocky flat leading toward the big sea cave, you may well spy western fence lizards during summer. Better known as an arid-country species found east of the Cascades, the lizards also inhabit coastal southern Oregon.

Parking for Sisters Rocks State Park is at an easy-to-miss gravel/dirt road entrance somewhat hidden by a low bluff on the west side of Highway 101 at milepost 314.5 (watch for the small state park sign). Pull in and park off to one side so other visitors have ample room as well. Follow the old road downhill to the south, around the locked gate, and down to the central area in front of the two onshore sea stacks.

The beach on the south side of Sisters Rocks State Park. Photo by John Shewey

◯ Ophir & Nesika Beaches

◎ **Location:** Along Highway 101, 17 miles south of Port Orford, 8 miles north of Gold Beach.

🚗 **Access:** State wayside with ample parking.

👫 **Facilities:** Restrooms.

Best known as Curry County's best surfperch fishing locations, Ophir and Nesika Beaches comprise nearly 6 miles of gorgeous white sand, from a minor headland called Devils Backbone south to the small community of Nesika. Technically the entire beach is Ophir Beach and the community at the south end is Nesika Beach, but the south end of the sand expanse is frequently called Nesika Beach. This amazing stretch of uncrowded beach offers ample room for surf anglers to spread out, and also plenty of great territory for beachcombers; even surfers sometimes put in an appearance here, particularly on the south end (Nesika Beach) during southerly winds.

Three primary access points and several secondary access points serve these beaches: Ophir Wayside (aka Ophir Rest Area) sits near Highway 101 milepost 319, providing immediate access down to the beach, along with restrooms and picnic tables. About 1 mile to the north, a wide gravel pullout provides plenty of parking room and a trail down to the beach at the mouth of Gregg's Creek. Two miles south of Ophir Wayside, almost to milepost 321, a west turn onto Nesika Road and then an immediate right (north) turn onto Old Highway 101 leads about 0.4 miles north to a popular parking area and trail down to the beach. In addition to those three access points, sharp eyes can pick out a couple more trails leading to the beach from small pull-outs along the highway, and about 0.25 miles north of the aforementioned wide gravel pullout at the mouth of Gregg's Creek, a fairly obvious trail leads west through the low dunes to reach the mouth

Nesika Beach. Photo by Reed Shipley

of Euchre Creek (which is easy to ford in summer, and which draws a run of winter steelhead).

North of the trail down to the mouth of Euchre Creek, most of the land between the highway and the beach dunes is private, but once you are on the beach from any of the access points, you can hike as far as you like—a valuable consideration for surf fishers if the wind blows hard from the north, because the sandy cove at the south foot of Devils Backbone is superbly sheltered and productive for surfperch. Make the hike as the tide ebbs and return before the tide gets too high to make the Euchre Creek ford as easy as possible (the creek is not fordable at high winter flows).

Late spring-through-mid-summer surfperch tides attract the most attention to Ophir and Nesika Beaches, but even when fishing is at its best, the beach is never crowded. Summer picnickers, beachcombers, joggers, and hikers are commonplace but never numerous, although in 2015, Ophir Beach did in fact draw quite a crowd when a deceased 78-foot blue whale washed up on the sand—an extreme rarity on the Northwest coast.

Ultimately scientists from the Marine Science Center in Newport stripped the carcass for its bones to study and ultimately display at the center.

Surf anglers from beyond the local area often stay at the private Honey Bear Campground and RV Resort, (800) 822-4444, www.honeybearrv.com, which conveniently sits alongside Ophir Road (parallel to Highway 101) about 0.25 miles east of Ophir Wayside, and includes the charming Black Forest Kitchen German restaurant and deli. Groceries, including a surprisingly robust selection of beers, are available at Nesika Beach Market, located about halfway along Nesika Road, 2.6 miles south of Nesika Wayside (Nesika Road loops west to and from Highway 101).

Ophir Beach. Photo by John Shewey

○ Otter Point & Agate Beach

Location: Otter Point State Recreation Site off Old Coast Road, at Highway 101 milepost 324, 2.5 miles north of the Rogue River bridge at Gold Beach.

Access: Designated trail leads out onto Otter Point; informal, short, steep trail leads down to Agate Beach on the north side of the point.

Facilities: None.

Contact: Otter Point State Recreation Site, (541) 332-6774, www.oregonstateparks.org.

Otter Point is a rugged headland that juts out into the rocky, rugged surf, providing superb views of the ocean and of the beautiful beaches to the north and south. Unlike most headlands along the coast, Otter Point's upper levels are composed of hard, sandy clay, crumbling in places, which yields to intriguing sedimentary rock down closer to the water. From the south end of a small parking lot (on the left as you enter the lot), two trails depart, with the right-hand fork leading out onto Otter Point, and the left-hand branch (the Oregon Coast Trail) heading south for about 0.4 miles before plunging a steep but easy quarter mile down to the spectacular, seldom-visited, north end of Bailey Beach (see next entry).

The trail out onto Otter Point is short, first passing through coastal shrubbery, and then leading out onto the barren sandstone. Once out on the headland, you can explore at will—however, there are no fences or signs to warn visitors not to approach the cliff edges too closely, for the crumbling soil can easily give way and far below the powerful surf slams relentlessly at jagged rocks. At lower tide levels, the rocks in the ocean far below reveal literal forests of sea palms (*postelsia palmaeformis*), a type of seaweed that thrives in the roughest, rockiest, wave-hammered intertidal areas. The rocks below are also home to black oystercatchers year-round, and other shorebirds, such as black turnstones, from fall through

early spring. Also from atop Otter Point, watch for seabirds, sea lions, and even whales. The headland's vegetated margins display an array of wildflowers during spring and summer.

Gazing off to the north from Otter Point, you can see a ruggedly scenic, rocky, gravelly beach extending off the foot of the point. This is Agate Beach (one of several "Agate Beaches" in Oregon) and its trail is hidden at the north end of the parking lot for Otter Point, where the informal path dives off into the trees. This narrow, winding trail—muddy and slippery when wet—leads little more than 100 yards to the beach. Along the way you'll cross a narrow wood-plank bridge hanging 8 feet above a small creek. Once you emerge on this wildly scenic beach you'll feel like you're stranded on your own deserted island, with abundant bird life, surf crashing against the rocks, tide pools teeming with critters—fortress like shelters built from driftwood, erected by previous visitors, only enhance the feeling. Agate Beach is aptly named—explore its gravel fields at low tide for agates and other interesting rocks.

This small state park is seldom visited because few people know of its existence. There are no signs for it on Highway 101. Near milepost 324, turn west off Highway 101 onto Old Coast Road and go almost a quarter mile to a right-hand turn at the sign for Otter Point State Recreation Site. This narrow dirt road (no room for trailers or RVs) leads about a quarter mile west to the parking area, which is elevated above the ocean, providing a limited but excellent view. The point is no place for dogs or small children (there are no fences or warning signs about the cliffs). The wind often howls across this exposed headland, so an early morning visit, before the wind comes up, is advantageous.

Agate Beach just north of Otter Point. Photo by John Shewey

The north end of Bailey Beach as seen from Otter Point. Photo by John Shewey

Bailey Beach

Location: From the north jetty at Gold Beach north approximately 3 miles to Otter Point.

Access: Designated and informal access sites along Old Coast Road and at north jetty in Gold Beach.

Facilities: None.

Contact: Gold Beach Chamber of Commerce, (541) 247-0923, www.goldbeachchamber.com.

Stretching for nearly 3 miles, from scenic Otter Point south to the mouth of the Rogue River at the north jetty in Gold Beach, Bailey Beach presents two different personalities: the south end is popular, with obvious access, while the north end is almost always deserted, happily benefitting from lack of signage on Highway 101 and access points off a road primarily used by local residents—Old Coast Road (aka Old Coast Highway), which roughly parallels the highway. Old Coast Road loops off Highway 101, with the north end at milepost 324 and the south end at a well-marked interchange near milepost 326, 1 mile north from the north foot of the Rogue River bridge. At the midway point, near Highway 101 milepost 325, a short spur (the street sign says "OLD COAST RD")

leads about 100 yards to Old Coast Road. From there, follow Old Coast Road 0.6 miles south (or 1 mile north from the south entrance to Old Coast Road) to where the road dips into a shallow ravine; park at the gravel pullout, and follow the trail that leads down the ravine to the beach.

This is the "Bailey Beach North" access, which leads out onto open, wind-carved sand, and the hike north along the beach to the foot of Otter Point covers an easy mile and almost always delivers you to complete solitude and excellent scenery, including a sea cave at the base of the point. You can also reach this section of the beach from the parking lot for Otter Point (see previous entry): take

the obvious trail off the south side of the parking lot, and after a few yards turn left on the Oregon Coast Trail. From there it's about 0.4 miles to a side trail that leads steeply down to the beach.

Bailey Beach's north half is great for a simple beach walk away from just about anybody, as well as for beachcombing, birding (especially fall, winter, and spring), and even digging for razor clams. Though it attracts more people, the south half of the beach, from the Rogue River south jetty north past the housing development of Rogue Shores, ranks among the south coast's popular clamming beaches. Except for its north end, Bailey Beach is open to street-legal vehicles, with four-wheel-drive strongly

○ Bailey Beach *(continued)*

recommended, with the vehicle access at the south jetty via several sand/dirt roads that lead through the low dunes. Luckily, few people drive the beach here, helping to preserve the uncrowded atmosphere. The jetty itself, incidentally, is popular with anglers, but also subject to hammering by strong swell that creates dangerous breakers—be very careful. This end of the beach is also a great place to let dogs stretch their legs and romp in the sand.

The north jetty, incidentally, is home to one of the south coast's quirkier, though certainly well-intentioned institutions: the North Jetty Cats Sanctuary, aka Fort Feline, a haven for feral cats in the form of numerous miniature cat houses, cared for by local residents, who bring food to the cats. The fort, near the inland base of the jetty, was started because the local animal shelter had no further space to take in cats, which are numerous along the jetty.

The south end of Bailey Beach is easy to access from several places (Bailey Beach North access is north of the beach's midpoint, but it's easy hiking in either direction from there). Wedderburn Loop Road turns

west just off the north foot of the Rogue River bridge; follow it 0.6 miles to the gravel/sand road that leads west, paralleling the jetty. Several undeveloped spur roads turn off this road and lead northwest to the beach. Wedderburn Loop Road swings northward, past a set of sewage settling ponds, and then meets Old Coast Road; follow Old Coast Road north to an unmarked beach access opposite Knox Lane (a wide pullout and sand road through the low dunes). Another informal access site sits just to the north, but reputedly the residents of the adjacent housing community of Rogue Shores have not been thrilled with the behaviors of beachgoers using these access sites, so tread lightly and unobtrusively.

The beach takes its name from the Bailey Ranch, which included much of the land along this strip of the coastline. Charles H. Bailey (1820–1902) emigrated from Ireland, settling for a time in Pennsylvania, but arriving in Curry County sometime in the late 1850s and establishing the ranch in Curry County. His son, Charles Bailey, Jr., (1864–1939), served as a county assessor, then as county sheriff from 1913 to 1917, then as Curry County judge for 12

Sunset at South Bailey Beach. Photo by John Shewey

years; during that time he also served as president of the local bank for 20 years. At age 75, a horse he was riding knocked him against the barn wall on the ranch, fracturing his hip, and he died thereafter from complications from the injury.

Entrance to Bailey Beach North. Photo by John Shewey

Airport Beach at Gold Beach. Photo by John Shewey

Airport Beach and South Beach (aka Hunter Creek Beach)

Location: Gold Beach.

Access: Secondary roads in Gold Beach lead to access for the Rogue River south jetty, Airport Beach, and the north end of South Beach; wide gravel pullout and short trails lead to the middle section of South Beach (Hunter Creek/Kissing Rock); south half of South Beach primarily accessible only by beach hiking.

Facilities: RV parking and restrooms at Gold Beach Visitors Center.

Amenities: Restaurants, lodging, and services available in Gold Beach.

Contact: Gold Beach Chamber of Commerce, (541) 247-0923, www.goldbeachchamber.com.

Stretching for 2 miles from the Rogue River south jetty south to the mouth of Hunter Creek, Airport Beach and then South Beach reign as the most popular beaches in the immediate vicinity of this attractive town of about 2,500 residents. But this oft-busy and attractive beach is only half the story because South Beach, south of Hunter Creek, continues uninterrupted for another 3 miles down to Cape Sebastian. However, south of Kissing Rock, an onshore monolith on the beach alongside Highway 101 where it crosses Hunter Creek, access is soon blocked by private property as the highway begins the climb south up to the cape; hence, the southerly 2.5 miles of South Beach is the lonely haunt of beach hikers, joggers, and the occasional rider. A large gravel pullout (Buena Vista Ocean Wayside, aka Kissing Rock wayside, at milepost 330.5) serves visitors to the Kissing Rock section near Hunter Creek, and another pullout with beach access is located 0.5 miles south. Thereafter, the highway swings inland out of sight of the beach and heads uphill.

However, the secluded southern end of the beach is accessible by two little-used interconnected trails, one from Cape Sebastian and an easier (relatively speaking) route from milepost 333, 1.9 miles south of Cape Sebastian: known as the 333 Trail, this route leads a fairly direct mile to the beach, but loses several hundred feet of elevation along the way, passing through alder bogs. Just south of milepost 333, and across Highway 101 from Eighty Acre Road, a wooden Oregon Coast Trail (OCT) post marks the trail; parking is in the gravel pullout a few yards to the

○ Airport Beach and South Beach (aka Hunter Creek Beach) *(continued)*

south. The trail leads west through alder and spruce woodlands. This is a loop route, so when you reach the first signed trail junction not far from the highway, you can go either way, though most people go left. The beach here is largely gray sand, with scattered gravel beds, which are more prominent in winter, an excellent time for agate hunting.

Back in Gold Beach, the north section of the beach is easily accessible in town. The northernmost access reaches the south jetty: from Highway 101, 0.3 miles southwest from the south end of the Rogue River bridge, turn north onto Harbor Way, go 0.3 miles and turn right on South Jetty Road/Oceanside Drive, which wraps around the north end of the local airport and then runs along the beach, providing numerous parking spots, trails, and vehicle entry points. Farther south from the highway in Gold Beach, 5th Place leads west to Oceanside Drive at the south end of the airport, and about 1 mile south of 5th Place, the Gold Beach Visitors Center also provides beach access via an easy, short trail from the parking lot. In addition to so-called Airport Beach (the stretch of beach fronting the town),

South Beach just north of Cape Sebastian, accessed via the 333 Trailhead. Photo by Barbara Sletmoe

a small beach sits within the jetties of the Rogue River's mouth—inside the jaws, so to speak. This beach is accessible from the south jetty at the north end of Airport Beach, and is popular with salmon anglers during late summer and fall, and with surfers when a big break forms.

The beach inside the jaws at Gold Beach. Photo by John Shewey

Meyers Creek Beach. Photo by John Shewey

Meyers Creek Beach

Location: Highway 101 mileposts 336–338, 6.5 miles south of Gold Beach and 19 miles north of Brookings.

Access: Easy, short trails to the beach from several highway pull-out parking areas.

Facilities: Outhouse at milepost 338.

Contact: Pistol River State Park, (800) 551-6949, www.oregonstateparks.org.

Beautiful Meyers Creek Beach (aka Myers Creek Beach and Meyers Beach), 6.5 miles south of Gold Beach, stretches for 2 spectacularly scenic miles, from its sheltered terminus at Hunters Cove, south toward the mouth of the Pistol River. The highly photogenic beach, composed of light gray sand, is studded with near-shore sea stacks, including two with caves, the best-known being aptly named Cave Rock just out from the highway at milepost 336.5, south of the main parking area for Myers Beach North (a large, partially paved parking lot sits on the west side of the highway after you come down the hill from the north). At extremely low tides, the cave is approachable on foot, and during calm ocean conditions, intrepid sea-kayakers can paddle through it.

To the north, Hunters Cove tucks up against Cape Sebastian, and from the aforementioned parking area, a hike of just under 1 mile takes you right up to the end of the sand beach; at low tide, the short stretch of rocky beach along the escarpment beyond the sand offers excellent tidepools. To the south of the north access parking area, the highway crosses Myers Creek, with another large parking area 200 yards south of the creek. Less than half a mile south is the third large parking pull-off, called the Myers Creek Beach Pistol River State Scenic Viewpoint. From here, trails lead down to a section of beach dominated by huge onshore/near-shore sea stacks that are fun to explore on low tides, particularly

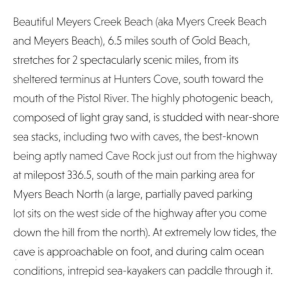

Sunset at Meyers Creek Beach. Photo by Pat Kight, Oregon Sea Grant/CreativeCommons

○ Meyers Creek Beach *(continued)*

Left: Meyers Creek Beach North. Photo by John Shewey
Right: Windsurfing competition at Meyers Creek Beach. Photo by Kevin Pritchard

minus-tides. Two more large parking areas serve the south end of the beach a short distance farther; the second and southernmost of them, at milepost 338, usually has an outhouse in service. Just out from this last southernmost parking area for Meyers Creek Beach, a massive onshore sea stack (simply called "The Rock") forms the north end of an inshore lagoon that stretches along the highway for the next mile down to the Pistol River.

Meyers Creek Beach is the south coast's most popular windsurfer's beach, even serving as the site for windsurfing competitions—the Pistol River Wave Bash—organized by the American Windsurfing Tour; the wind-blasted beach here attracts surfers as well. They usually use the southernmost access point at The Rock (milepost 338) because the access points a bit further south at the Pistol River require hiking through the dunes to get to the water.

Meyers Creek Beach is also a worthwhile stop for both beachcombers and birdwatchers. Beachcombers should arrive early in the morning, ahead of the modest crowds that can converge on Meyers Beach on summer days. Birding is best between late July and April, when shorebirds that breed in Canada and Alaska migrate through or overwinter; however, local peregrine falcons hunt seabirds here throughout the year, and Hunters Island, just beyond the surf zone at the north end of the beach, is an important breeding site for several seabirds, including Leach's storm-petrel.

The cave at Meyers Creek Beach. Photo by John Shewey

The beach south of the Pistol River. Photo by John Shewey

Pistol River State Park Beach

Location: Highway 101 milepost 339, 10 miles south of Gold Beach, 18 miles north of Brookings.

Access: Walk-in access via short, informal trails through vegetated dunes, departing from parking area west of highway.

Facilities: None.

Contact: Pistol River State Park, (800) 551-6949, www.oregonstateparks.org.

A gorgeous, though oft-wind-battered, sand expanse awaits visitor who take the time to hike a short distance through partially vegetated sand dunes to the beach near the mouth of the Pistol River. Routinely the wind blows so fiercely here that this beach, stretching up to Meyers Creek Beach on the north side of the Pistol River, ranks among the Oregon coast's most popular windsurfing sites and is even home to the annual Pistol River Wave Bash, a competition that is part of the American Windsurfing Tour, held each summer. The competition headquarters is set up at "The Rock" at the south end of Meyers Creek Beach, almost 1 mile north from the Pistol River South access site, located off the west side of Highway 101, 200 yards south of the Pistol River bridge, near milepost 339.

Pistol River South is the best access for this entire beach. If you hike north, you'll come to the mouth of the Pistol River, but it's often bar-bound from summer through mid-autumn, so presents no problem; otherwise, it's not fordable, so the southernmost access for Meyers Creek Beach (see previous entry) offers the only access down to the mouth of the river. The seldom-trodden south end of the beach at Pistol River terminates at Crook Point, a low headland and great place to check out at low tides, nearly 1.6 miles south from the Pistol River South access. Near the end of the beach, pretty little Sand Creek reaches the ocean, spilling out from the dunes beneath a pile of driftwood. Crook Point itself—the headland and surrounding rock spires and

stacks—are off limits because they are part of the Oregon Islands National Wildlife Refuge, but the end of the beach and the base of the colorful rocks are all well worth exploring on a low tide, and are superbly photographic in early morning or evening light.

The easiest walking to the south is on the beach itself, but from mid-summer until the rains begin in autumn, the easiest walking to get out to the beach is actually southward through a lengthy deflation plain within the dunes: from the west end of the parking area, strike off west through the first dune, and when you walk down into the low-lying deflation plain (from which you can see the sea stacks at Crook Point), look to the south to see a quarter-mile-long pond (called

○ Pistol River State Park Beach (continued)

Lola Lake by local residents); hike down along the pond, and once beyond it, bear southwesterly over to the beach. During the rainy season, Lola Lake often swells enough in size to make a direct-west path from the parking lot to the beach just as easy. Also, within the dunes, an interior trail leads westerly from a wide sandy highway pullout 0.4 miles south of the Pistol River South parking area (opposite the Frontage Road turnoff). The trail swings past the south end of Lola Lake and from there you can strike off west to the beach.

In addition, a direct mile-long trail route to the south end of the beach, at Crook Point, begins at an inconspicuous unsigned pullout on the west side of Highway 101, 1.7 miles south of Pistol River bridge and 3.9 miles north of Arch Rock Viewpoint. The pullout sits just south of a southbound-lane guard rail on a slight bend in the highway, with a steep sand bank on the east side of the road. It comes up fast and is easy to miss. From here, a segment of the Oregon Coast Trail heads northwesterly toward the beach north of Crook Point, first through pine/spruce forest and then breaking out into rolling vegetated dunes. Part of the route is a seldom-used horse trail, marked by white-topped wooden posts; at the only

trail junction, out in the dunes, the horse trail leads to the south end of the beach and the right-hand fork leads north through the dunes (you can get to the beach anywhere within the dunes by heading west).

On the north side of the Pistol River bridge, a mile-long shallow lagoon stretches alongside Highway 101. During summer and fall, you can park at the pullout on the north side of the bridge and scamper down to the river, and follow it west past the south end of the lagoon to reach the beach. This lagoon, and Lola Lake, are great birdwatching spots during the fall and spring shorebird migrations, and also during winter for overwintering species. The fall migration actually begins in late July and continues through October, and these two spots can produce a variety of shorebird species, including semipalmated plover, western sandpiper, least sandpiper, dunlin, red-necked phalarope, dowitchers, and others. Thanks to surrounding dunes at Lola Lake, intrepid photographers with long lenses can creep up quite close to birds without disturbing them.

Pistol River, traditionally highly regarded for its historically robust runs of fall chinook salmon and

winter steelhead, is so named because pioneer and militia volunteer James Mace lost his pistol in the river in 1853. Reputedly, a few years later, on June 17, 1856, the 80-man militia engaged the local band of the Chetco tribe, called Chetl-Essentan, and killed and captured enough of their members to force them to surrender. The Oregon State Archives records a slightly expanded account, noting that "According to an 1854 report from Indian agent J.L. Parrish, the river also bore the name of the Chetl-essentan Indians, who had a village near its mouth. In March, 1856, during the Rogue River wars, a company of volunteer troops was caught offguard and placed on the defensive by Indians at Pistol River. The volunteers held out, with a loss of one man, until their eventual rescue by regular troops [presumably on June 17]."

Like many bands of coastal natives, the Chetl-Essentans were few in number; the aforementioned agent, Parrish, counted 45 of them in total in 1854. The village sat just north of the river's mouth and the band claimed a home territory totaling about 8 miles of coastline.

Dunlin and a short-billed dowitcher feeding on the beach south of the Pistol River. Photo by John Shewey

Hooskanaden Beach

 Location: Samuel H. Boardman State Scenic Corridor, 13 miles south of Gold Beach.

 Access: Undeveloped trail down to beach.

 Facilities: None.

Contact: Samuel H. Boardman State Scenic Corridor, (800) 551-6949, www.oregonstateparks.org.

Hooskanaden Beach—the name, fittingly, means "gravel place" in the Tututni (Athabaskan) tongue—stretches three-quarters of a mile, and at low tide (by far the best time, and sometimes the only time to visit) essentially presents two different beaches in one incredible and seldom-visited package. The south half of the beach is a long, narrow crescent of sand leading down to a small, rugged headland; the north end of the beach is a jumble of rocks, challenging to walk, but intriguing, also eventually ending at a jagged headland. This gorgeous beach is one of the least known on the Oregon coast, even though the access trail is quite short, only about 300 yards, from a small pullout on Highway 101. But like many of Oregon's best beaches, no signage indicates the spot, and other than maintaining a short stretch of the Oregon Coast Trail that passes just above the north end of Hooskanaden Beach, Oregon State Parks has let this gem remain undeveloped in every way.

The nearshore rocks attract various birds, including some small nesting colonies, and harbor seals use the rocks as haul-out sites. A family of river otters inhabits the area, and lucky visitors, early in the morning, may spy the gregarious creatures scavenging along the beach and in the nearshore surf. The tide pools at both ends of the beach are fun, but visit them during summer, when weather and waves are calm—they are exposed to the open surf; Hooskanaden Beach can be dangerous during winter, or any time during periods of rough seas, and during the highest tides can completely disappear as breakers reach the bluffs above the beach. This strip of rock-studded beach is one of numerous southern Oregon beaches that holds promise for agate hunters—another activity that is best at low tide, but here (and everywhere), keep a close eye on the breakers and keep an escape route in mind. Agate hunting is best during winter when more gravel is exposed.

Access to the beach is surprisingly easy, but unmarked, via an undeveloped trail that leads downhill to the shore from a small pullout along the southbound lane of Highway 101, just past the entrance sign for Samuel H. Boardman State Scenic

Corridor at milepost 344. From the center of the pullout, drop straight down the hill to the wooden-post Oregon Coast Trail marker. From there, turn left and then right around a switchback to continue northwesterly down the slope, through a few pine trees, and down to a modest ravine with a trail junction; turn left to reach the beach. The trail leads about 300 yards down to the beach.

Two huge drainage pipes at the south end of Hooskanaden Beach testify to landslides below the highway just south of the trail that proved troublesome to repair. But otherwise there is little evidence of humanity on this wonderful beach, despite the easy access. Waves crashing against the rocks echo through the cove here, and it's easy to simply get lost in the natural wonder of it all. Opportunities to have a beach to yourself are rare, so put your cell phone back in your pocket and just look around and gather in the rugged beauty of Hooskanaden—this beach is a stark and addicting reminder that the Oregon coast offers many majestic landscapes that remain unaltered by mankind.

Top: Hoosekanaden Beach. Photo by John Shewey
Bottom: Hooskanaden Beach. Photo by Oregon Coast Visitors Association

Secret Beach

Location: Highway 101, milepost 345.3.

Access: Rough, steep trail to beach at low tide.

Facilities: None.

Contact: Samuel H. Boardman State Scenic Corridor, (800) 551-6949, www.oregonstateparks.org.

Not nearly as secret as it once was, diminutive, postcard-pretty Secret Beach has been described in major newspapers across the state, as well as various web sites, and while rarely crowded and often deserted, it is probably better known than other nearby and longer beaches, such as China Beach just to the south and Hooskanaden Beach just to the north. Although you can approach it at any tide level, Secret Beach is most accessible at low tide, which reveals a short stretch of sand—about 200 yards—with several small, incredibly scenic tree-topped sea stacks sitting just off the beach, creating an exotic and mysterious panorama. If you can time your Secret Beach trip for a sunset at low tide, be sure to bring a camera.

Early morning at Secret Beach. Photo by John Shewey

In the north corner of the beach, near the access trail, Minor Creek spills over a scenic little waterfall to drop onto the sand. The trail from the informal highway-side parking area runs about 300 yards through deep, dark woods, down to the beach. At the end, the trail spills out onto a spine of basalt, from which you carefully descend to the sand. Be especially careful when the rock is wet and wear hiking shoes, not flip-flops. Also be especially careful with children. At low tide, a gap between rock escarpments opens up on the south end of the beach and you can walk through to explore another small, sandy cove where Wridge Creek flows across the sand.

The trail to Secret Beach begins at a small, easy-to-miss pullout behind the north end of the guard rail on the southbound lane of Highway 101 at milepost 345.3, about 0.5 miles south of Arch Rock Viewpoint, and just north of Wilderness Drive.

Waterfall at Secret Beach. Photo by John Shewey

China Beach. Photo by Claudia Kuenkel

China Beach

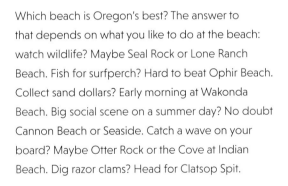

 Location: Samuel H. Boardman State Scenic Corridor, Highway 101 near milepost 347, 10 miles north of Brookings and 18 miles south of Gold Beach.

 Access: Steep, 0.75-mile trails from two locations along Highway 101.

Facilities: None.

 Contact: Samuel H. Boardman State Scenic Corridor, (800) 551-6949, www.oregonstateparks.org.

Which beach is Oregon's best? The answer to that depends on what you like to do at the beach: watch wildlife? Maybe Seal Rock or Lone Ranch Beach. Fish for surfperch? Hard to beat Ophir Beach. Collect sand dollars? Early morning at Wakonda Beach. Big social scene on a summer day? No doubt Cannon Beach or Seaside. Catch a wave on your board? Maybe Otter Rock or the Cove at Indian Beach. Dig razor clams? Head for Clatsop Spit.

But if your idea of the ultimate beach experience is finding a gorgeous, deserted strip of sand and wave-carved basalt that offers natural wonders and scenic splendor in every direction and requires a price of admission in the form of hiking steep, rather lengthy trails, then little-known China Beach is your Nirvana. In fact, just to the north, beautiful little Secret Beach, its name notwithstanding, is better known than China Beach.

Its churning surf zone magnificently studded with rock spires, mile-long, seldom-visited China Beach is among the most scenic beaches in Oregon, its gray sand stretching between Thomas Point to the south and Spruce Creek Point to the north. Though less than a mile one way, the two trails to China Beach are steep, dropping 350 vertical feet (remember that fact on your way down to the beach because you will need to hike back up). This lonely beach is supreme at low tide when you can explore it from end to end, so plan the 20- to 30-minute hike down to coincide with the last hour or two of the falling tide. Low tide—especially minus-tides—reveal nice tide pools, especially on the south end of the beach along the foot of Thomas Point. Beachcombers can find all kinds of interesting rocks, a few shells, including limpets, and many other natural wonders. Dense offshore mussel beds assure a ready supply of the colorful shells, some of which are 8 inches long. Birds abound, and look for tracks left by river otters and raccoons—or maybe get lucky enough to see these animals early in the morning. Photographers will revel in the early morning light and the potential for bedazzling sunset shots, but if you linger after sunset, bring a flashlight and be sure you pay attention to the route on the way down to the beach.

○ China Beach *(continued)*

The two access points leading to trails are located close together along Highway 101, the easier trail leading off North Island Viewpoint at a wide gravel pullout at Highway 101 milepost 347.5, along the southbound lane, 0.25 miles north of Thomas Creek Bridge. Look for the split in the guardrail marking the trailhead (and a small sign). Follow the trail into the forest for about 20 steps to a big Sitka spruce tree on your left, one of its roots forming a ridge across the trail. Look for a small hand-drawn map attached to this tree (it may not be there); a few steps past the tree's thick root, the trail splits, with the obvious path going left and the fainter trail going right. Take this right-hand fork and a few yards down the trail look for a tiny blue Oregon Coast Trail marker on a small tree trunk (there is also such a marker on the left-hand fork). Continue down this trail about 150 yards to an unmarked junction. Again take the right-hand fork (the left fork winds downhill to a small informal viewpoint of part of the beach far below). Hike north for about one-third of a mile, after which the trail begins its decent down to the beach.

Looking south from the north end of China Beach. Photo by John Shewey

The other route leading down to China Beach delivers you to the north end, which is fine at lower tide levels (generally below 4 feet, but much depends on ocean conditions). At high tides, the surf reaches the foot of a narrow rock bluff that cuts off this short stretch of the beach from the much longer main beach to the south. Low tides present no problem, and some hikers enjoy making the loop hike, heading down one trail and up the other, then following the highway back to their vehicle. The north trailhead, also a segment of the Oregon Coast Trail, begins at the south end of a 500-foot-long viewpoint pullout along the southbound lane of Highway 101 at milepost 346.5 (look for small highway signs that announce "Viewpoint Ahead"). Behind the guardrail at the south terminus of this pullout, look for a wooden-post Oregon Coast Trail marker and follow this trail into the woods and then down the steep hillside. This route is shorter, totaling maybe half a mile.

Looking north from the south end of China Beach. Photo by John Shewey

Whaleshead Beach. Photo by John Shewey

Whaleshead Beach

 Location: Samuel H. Boardman State Scenic Corridor, Highway 101 milepost 350, 6.5 miles north of Brookings.

 Access: Steep, rugged gravel road leads to state parks day-use site and short trail to the beach.

Facilities: Picnic tables, restrooms.

 Contact: Samuel H. Boardman State Scenic Corridor, (800) 551-6949, www.oregonstateparks.org.

One of several scenic beaches within the Samuel H. Boardman State Scenic Corridor, Whaleshead Beach—named for a near-shore sea stack—is surprisingly lightly visited. During summer you'll usually find a few people out walking or even picnicking on the mile-long stretch of sand- and fine-pebble-beach. It's a great spot for beachcombing, particularly after winter or spring storms, but also during the height of summer, especially if you get there early in the morning, making yours the first footprints in the sand for the day. At minus tides, the north end offers some nice tide pools, and birdwatchers can often find shorebirds, Heerman's gulls, and brown pelicans here, these latter two species being present during later summer and early autumn.

The state parks day-use site occupies the bottom of a small ravine above the beach, along Whaleshead Creek, and its picnic tables are well sheltered from the wind. From the parking area at the day-use site, a short trail leads to the north end of the beach, leaving a mile-plus-long hike for visitors who want to explore the lesser-known south end, which ends at a small but impassable headland. At very low tides, the rocky surf zone at this south end offers additional tide pools, but it tends to get battered by heavy surf, so be careful. The tide pools at the north end of the beach are better protected. The gravel road down to the day-use site is steep and badly washboarded; rear-wheel-drive cars may have trouble getting back out. An upper parking lot, near the highway, however, allows for an alternative.

Mussels washed up onto Whaleshead Beach. Photo by John Shewey

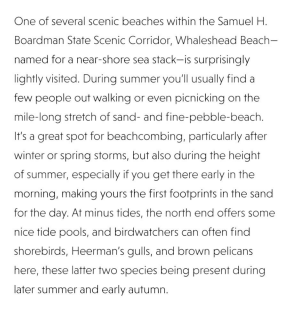

Cape Ferrelo Beach and House Rock Beach

 Location: Highway 101, milepost 352.

 Access: Hike-in only; steep bushwhacker trails.

 Facilities: None.

 Contact: Samuel H. Boardman State Scenic Corridor, (800) 551-6949, www.oregonstateparks.org.

Cape Ferrelo is a broad, rounded, densely vegetated headland a few miles north of Brookings, with signs directing visitors to a state-park viewpoint that provides a scenic view of the rock-studded ocean to the west (and a trail up to the top of the cape). Observant visitors will also notice, barely within view, an intriguing stretch of rocky, gray-sand beach far below, and also a trail (part of the Oregon Coast Trail) leading north from the viewpoint parking area. Exploration-minded brush-busting beachgoers can walk this trail north a short distance and then navigate bushwhacker trails down to this secluded, seldom-trodden beach, which stretches for more than half a mile, its midpoint marked by a giant surf-zone boulder.

Low tide is best and the rocky north and south ends of the beach are approachable only at low tides.

Just to the north, House Rock State Scenic Viewpoint is connected to Cape Ferrelo Viewpoint by trail, and provides a commanding view, often with whales in sight during the migration season for gray whales; for intrepid hikers, a steep, difficult trail leads west down from the viewpoint parking lot to reach a small, rock-and-gravel beach at the mouth of House Rock Creek. This gorgeous, rarely visited cove all but disappears at high tide, but at low tide offers spectacular tide pools and superb scenery. More heavily trodden than the trails leading down to the beach just north from Cape Ferrelo, the trail leads

through coastal forest, open meadows, and sand washes studded with lodgepole pine. At low tide, it's possible to walk south along the narrow beach to the base of Cape Ferrelo, though doing so requires some rock scrambling.

Cape Ferrelo Beach. Photo by John Shewey

○ Lone Ranch Beach

◎ **Location:** 4.5 miles north of downtown Brookings at Highway 101 milepost 352.5.

🚗 **Access:** Short trails lead to the beach from large parking area.

👩👨 **Facilities:** Picnic tables, restrooms.

📞 **Contact:** Samuel H. Boardman State Scenic Corridor, (800) 551-6949, www.oregonstateparks.org.

While Harris Beach just to the south garners all the attention for its scenic splendor, equally beautiful Lone Ranch Beach escapes the notice of most Brookings-area visitors despite easy access and ample signage. Lone Ranch Beach occupies a half-mile-long, sea stack-studded cove framed by a minor headland to the south and the south edge of Cape Ferrelo to the north. The cape protects the north end of the beach, creating excellent opportunity to explore tide pools. During summer, the surf here is frequently calm enough to allow intrepid sea kayakers to launch from the beach. Also during summer, brown pelicans frequent the area and black oystercatchers nest on the rocks here, joined by migratory and wintering shorebirds between late summer and spring. Seals, sea lions, and even gray whales occasionally make appearances.

Stretching between rocky shore at both ends, the beach is composed of fine gray sand, and is a great place for a short morning stroll or for beachcombing at any time of year. A row of picnic tables occupies a low rise on the south end of the beach, providing commanding views of the cove. The south end of Lone Ranch Beach (the parking area is at the north end) is more rugged and wave-hammered—and very scenic any time heavy surf pounds the rocks, throwing white sheets of spray high into the air. Under calmer

South end of Lone Ranch Beach. Photo by John Shewey

conditions and low tides, the south end is great for exploring among the rocks, and a narrow dry-sand (usually) passageway provides egress to another short stretch of beach leading down to Black Point. There is also a tiny secret pocket beach very near here, but the locals are—understandably—protective of it and not appreciative of those who describe its location.

North end of Lone Ranch Beach. Photo by John Shewey

Rainbow Rock Beach. Photo by Lynn Arave

Rainbow Rock Beach

Location: Just north of Brookings, Highway 101 milepost 354.

Access: Unimproved trail leads from unsigned gravel pullout on Highway 101 downhill to the beach.

Facilities: None.

Contact: Brookings–Harbor Chamber of Commerce, (800) 535-9469, www.brookingsharborchamber.com.

Mostly a local's beach, despite its proximity to Highway 101, and a bonus for visitors lodging at Rainbow Rock Retreat (www.rainbowrockretreat.com), Rainbow Rock Beach stretches for almost a mile just north of Harris Beach. Minor headlands at both ends enclose it. Parking is at a wide gravel pullout adjacent to the southbound lane of Highway 101 just south of milepost 354, 0.5 miles south of Rainbow Rock Retreat and 0.7 miles north of the Carpenterville Road turnoff; from here, a bushwhacker trail leads about 100 yards downhill through the brush to the beach. Less than one-half mile north, a wide paved pullout along the highway's southbound lane is signed for "Rainbow Rock Viewpoint," but there is no beach access from this location.

The centerpiece of this beach (located at the north end), Rainbow Rock is formed of colorful, complex, thin, folded layers of chert, and has a narrow tunnel all the way through, generally accessible at low tide. Negative tides are great here, exposing excellent tide pools on the north end of this beach, and until the tide begins to flood, you can walk around the outside of Rainbow Rock and explore the secluded terminal end of the beach. During winter and spring, the tunnel through the rock is easy to walk through, but during summer, when more sand is piled onto the beach, clearance shrinks. Low tides also allow you to scamper past rock outcroppings to explore the south end of the beach.

Poison oak is common on the south coast. Photo by Greg Shine, BLM/Creative Commons

371

Harris Beach State Park

Location: North end of Brookings.

Access: Large state park with easy trails to the beach.

Facilities: Large campground with 35 full-hookup sites, 50 electrical sites with water, 60 tent sites, six yurts (one pet friendly and one with universal access), hiker/biker camp, flush toilets, hot showers, and RV dump station; large day-use parking lot; Junior Ranger programs open to children age 6 through 12 and evening campfire programs for everyone are offered throughout the summer (check with the registration booth for current schedules and information).

Contact: Harris Beach State Park, (541) 469-2021, www.oregonstateparks.org.

An idyllic scene of clean sand beach punctuated with jagged rock outcroppings and a backdrop of dramatic sea stacks welcomes visitors to Harris Beach on the north end of Brookings. Just offshore, massive Bird Island (aka Goat Island) hosts a variety of nesting seabirds, including tufted puffins. Nearer shore, low tide reveals tide pools near several large rocks and boulder gardens visitors can explore until the tide levels rise. The beach comprises two sections, often called the north and south beaches—or more correctly, Harris Beach (adjacent to the day-use parking area) and mile-long South Beach, accessible by hiking down the beach and scrambling through the rocks, or by separate trails from Old Highway 101

leading down to the state park (look for the small parking area just after you turn west off Highway 101). Dividing these two beaches is aptly-named Rock Beach, a narrow band of rock-strewn shoreline with onshore hoodoos, accessed via a steep, scenic, switch-backing trail from the campground.

During summer, Harris Beach is one of the busiest beaches on the south coast, but even then, visitors who venture out on an early morning low tide can hike to the north or south to explore the extensive tide pools and almost always enjoy some measure of solitude. The crowds tend to gather later, and by afternoon,

the sandy sections of Harris Beach, and to a lesser extent, South Beach, can fairly swarm with people. On the other hand, even these easily accessible and gorgeous beaches can be deserted on any given day between September and May. Regardless of crowds, photographers revel in the sunset opportunities, with the many sea stacks, large and small, providing ample fodder for intriguing images—bring a tripod and pick a spot on the beach where you can capture the sun setting behind the rocks. Among the many sea stacks is aptly named Arch Rock, which features a tall, narrow cave cut all the way through. The aforementioned Bird Island hosts an estimated 100,000 nesting seabirds

representing 11 species, including a large population of Leach's storm-petrels.

Harris Beach State Park also includes one of Oregon's designated marine reserves, occupying the broad cove separating Harris Beach from South Beach. The cove features excellent tide pools, especially at minus tides; as a designated reserve, rules here dictate that no organisms may be removed. The Rock Beach Trail across the road from the campground entrance leads down to Arch Rock, which guards the north end of Harris Beach Marine Garden. At the risk of redundancy, it bears repeating that few beachgoers visit the Harris Beach tide pools during early-morning low tides, so if you enjoy solitude, pick a minus tide just after sunrise.

Obvious signs on Highway 101 mark the entrance road down to Harris Beach State Park, located just north of Brookings. The campground can fill completely on prime summer weekends, so reservations are advisable; call (800) 452-5687. With the restaurants and other amenities of Brookings just minutes away, Harris Beach makes a fine base of operations for exploring the far-south coast.

Harris Beach State Park. Photo courtesy of Oregon Coast Visitors Association

Low tide reveals a narrow gravel beach below the bluffs at Chetco Cove. Photo by John Shewey

Chetco Point and Mill Beach

Location: Brookings.

Access: Paved approach trail leads to gravel trails out onto Chetco Point, with short, steep scramble trails down to the beaches; formal access site for Mill Beach sits just above the beach.

Facilities: Outhouse; picnic tables.

Amenities: Brookings offers an array of dining and lodging options, along with all services.

Contact: Brookings-Harbor Chamber of Commerce, (800) 535-9469, www.brookingsharborchamber.com.

The coastline in Brookings, though hidden from Highway 101, is spectacularly scenic, an assemblage of rocky coves and diminutive sand beaches guarded by headlands, islands, and sea stacks. Anchoring the town's hidden oceanfront, Chetco Point juts out beyond the surf zone and provides a sublime panorama.

A well-worn trail threads its way out onto Chetco Point (the city maintains the property as Chetco Point Park), and during mornings and evenings, visitors can expect to share the trail and the headland with locals who enjoy the walk. Chetco Point forms the south border of Macklyn Cove and its scenic little crescent-shaped beach, called Mill Beach. Table Rock occupies the middle of Mill Beach, and its north end is framed by Zwagg Island, truly only an island at high tide, and named for Dutch-born Folker Von Der Zwaag, who settled in Oregon in 1889. According to Oregon Geographic Names by Lewis A. McArthur, Zwagg lived a hermit life on the island with his dog, Sniff.

To the south of Chetco Point, Chetco Cove—actually a double cove, studded with rocks— is rimmed by a narrow, gravelly beachfront, and framed on the south side by Tanbark Point. Picturesque houses line the low bluffs above the coves, but partial access is available via a trail forking south from the Chetco Point Trail, as well as by short, steep informal trails that dive off the edge of the narrow land bridge that connects Chetco Point to the mainland. Likewise, short informal paths drop off the north edge of the land bridge and access a short stretch of rocky beach below, from which you can walk up to Mill Beach. The trail out to Chetco Point totals about one-third of a mile and begins at a gravel

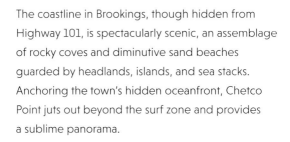

375

○ Chetco Point and Mill Beach *(continued)*

parking lot at the end of Wharf Street in front of the city water-treatment facility. From the poorly marked parking area, walk north past the outhouse and along a paved path, leading around the north side of the treatment plant. A tiny park with picnic tables sits alongside the trail, which swings westerly and drops gently down to Chetco Point. Wharf Street turns south off Highway 101 about 0.2 miles east of Pacific Street (for southbound travelers) and about 0.3 miles west of Oak Street for northbound travelers. Follow Wharf Street 0.5 miles to reach the parking area for Chetco Point.

The public-access point for Mill Beach, a tiny parking area with room for about six vehicles, is quite well hidden: from Highway 101 in Brookings, turn south onto Mill Beach Road (a left turn for southbound travelers) and follow it less than one-half mile to a left turn down the narrow, steep Macklyn Cove Drive; go about 100 yards down to a left turn down to the beach access. Mill Beach, although it tends to attract a few transients (who are routinely asked to leave by the local police because camping on the beach is illegal), occupies a postcard-pretty

cove. During summer, brown pelicans sometimes congregate here, and lucky visitors may get to watch the robust birds plunge-dive for fish in the cove. The beach stretches south down to Chetco Point; to the north, the beach narrows behind Zwagg Island but continues northerly about a quarter mile up to a rocky headland. The entire area offers nice tide pools at minus tides.

Purple sea urchins. Photo by Ed Bierman/Creative Commons

Mill Beach with Chetco Point in the background. Photo by John Shewey

Sporthaven Beach

Location: Brookings-Harbor.

Access: Easy foot access from large parking area adjacent to the boat basin and Chetco River south jetty at the Port of Brookings Harbor.

Facilities: RV Park, restrooms, picnic tables, marina.

Amenities: Restaurants, lodging options, and fresh-seafood markets are located within easy walking distance; charter fishing services on site for bottomfish, salmon, and tuna.

Contact: Brookings-Harbor Chamber of Commerce, (800) 535-9469, www.brookingsharborchamber.com; Port of Brookings Harbor, (541) 469-0672, www.portofbrookingsharbor.com.

A popular tourist beach at the mouth of the Chetco River, Sporthaven Beach is composed primarily of coarse sand and stretches almost a mile southward from the Chetco south jetty. Both a large RV park and a major hotel (Best Western Beachfront) sit literally steps from the beach and copious free parking is available directly above the sand. A few locals enjoy morning or evening walks or jogs along Sporthaven Beach, but mostly it draws tourists in the summer for its easy access and clean beauty. Additionally, though, Sporthaven is a favorite among the small cadre of local surfers, with especially big surf during winter; under ideal conditions the surf here produces big, clean, full-curl breakers. The big surf of winter is generally best for expert-level boarders, but summer can kick up good, though tamer, conditions more appropriate for all experience levels. Most locals paddle out near the jetty to take advantage of the currents there, making the job easier.

A surfer at Sporthaven Beach. Photo courtesy of Brookings Chamber of Commerce

Sporthaven Beach is fairly popular with dog owners, but if you run your dog here, use common courtesy, as this beach can get quite busy. From late summer through spring, shorebirds routinely use Sporthaven Beach, so keep dogs under control so they don't harass the migrating and wintering birds. This beach also offers good fishing for surfperch at times, and anglers also fish from the rocks of the south jetty, which forms the north border of the beach. During the third weekend in July, the Southern Oregon Kite Festival is held at Sporthaven, with most of the official activities and actual kite demos held at Harbor Kite Field along Boat Basin Road a short walk from the beach itself. Restaurants and lodging are also within easy walking distance of Sporthaven Beach.

South end of Sporthaven Beach. Photo courtesy of Oregon Coast Visitors Association

McVay Rock State Recreation Site

 Location: South of Brookings-Harbor.

 Access: Short steep trail from parking area to beach.

Facilities: Outhouse; fenced off-leash dog park.

 Contact: McVay Rock State Recreation Site, (800) 551-6949, www.oregonstateparks.org; Brookings-Harbor Chamber of Commerce, (541) 469-3181, www.brookingsharborchamber.com.

With no highway signage to announce its location, McVay Rock State Recreation Site attracts little attention, even on busy summer days. Go first thing in the morning and you're likely to have this gorgeous, narrow, gravel beach all to yourself for rock-hounding, tidepooling, fishing, or sightseeing. The park here includes a fenced off-leash dog park, making it the perfect place to tire out the pup before you enjoy some time on the beach, upon which dogs must be leashed. The park is day-use only, and parks personnel close the gate around dusk, so don't linger too long after sunset, which can be superbly scenic through offshore rocks here.

McVay Rock Beach holds a natural wonder little known except by locals: a massive redwood stump lodged firmly in the course sand (although a winter storm managed to move the stump inland about 15 feet back in 2007). You can climb up on the stump and still see the tree's growth rings—look carefully and you can easily identify the times this giant lived on easy street (widely spaced rings) and other times when things were bleak indeed (very narrowly spaced rings). Speaking of bleak, the rock for which this park was named no longer exists: an ancient sea stack that sat atop the terrace above the beach, McVay Rock was destroyed by quarrying many decades ago.

The beach is composed entirely of gravel and course sand, making for fun rock collecting, including the occasional agates, although at times, near-shore kelp beds litter the beach with green during rough surf conditions. Because of myriad and varied large rocks embedded in the surf zone, McVay Rock Beach is great for exploring tide pools on minus tides. During periods of calm water, anglers can probe the deeper pockets among the rocks for greenling and perch, and birdwatchers can find a variety of shorebirds here between late summer and late spring. You can hike either direction, but high tides block any progress beyond about a half mile south and just a few hundred yards north; however, if you

start on a falling tide and hit the trouble spots at low water, you can see quite a bit of beachfront in either direction, and can walk all the way to the mouth of the Winchuck River to the south and, on minus-tides, up to Sporthaven Beach to the north (but be quick about it to avoid getting cut off on the return trip).

To find McVay State Recreation Area from the north, follow Highway 101 south through Brookings-Harbor and turn right (west) on Benham Lane; go about 0.5 miles and turn left (south) on Wenbourne, and after 0.2 miles stay left (southbound) on Oceanview Drive and continue 2 miles to the state park on the right. From the south, follow Highway 101 north 1 mile from the California border and turn left (west) on Oceanview Drive; continue northward 1.3 miles to the park entrance.

The beach at McVay Rock State Recreation Site. Photo by John Shewey

Crissey Field Beach

 Location: Crissey Field State Recreation Site (south bank of the Winchuck River) and Winchuck State Recreation Site (north bank of the Winchuck) just north of the California border south of Brookings–Harbor.

Access: Short trails from both recreation sites leading through low coastal dunes and shore pines to the beach.

Facilities: Restrooms, potable water, visitors center.

Contact: Oregon Welcome Center at Crissey Field, (541) 469-4117, www.oregonstateparks.org.

Crissey Field Beach at Crissey Field State Recreation Site stretches half a mile from the California border to the mouth of the little-known Winchuck River. During summer, especially at low tides, the river is little more than a modest creek, its delta on the beach usually easy to ford, but once the autumn rains begin, swollen flows in the Winchuck estuary can become a barrier to walking up the beach from the large Crissey Field State Recreation Site and occasionally even block access to walking down to the beach along the river's north bank from Winchuck State Recreation Site.

Crissey Field Beach is mostly clean sand, but gravel and coarse sand at the north end, where the beach narrows and finally runs up against a small headland 1 mile north from the mouth of the Winchuck. The narrow stretch of beach wrapping around this little headland sits just west of the houses at Fox Drive off Oceanview Drive, but the only public access is via the beach; however, at low tides, intrepid hikers can walk around the headland and continue along another half mile of narrow, scenic beach between the mouth of the Winchuck and McVay State Recreation Site (see previous entry); again though, this is a low-tide-only hike, so a vehicle at both ends or a fairly speedy walk is ideal. You can also hike south from Crissey Field Beach down into California.

In keeping with the banana-belt reputation of the Brookings area, Crissey Field Beach often remains perfectly calm while ferocious winds batter the coast farther north up towards Gold Beach. Under such conditions, this southernmost beach in Oregon is a great place for a picnic on the beach. It's also ideal for beachcombing, kite flying, and surfperch fishing. The upper beach is littered with driftwood of all sizes, ideal for artists who work with such wood to search and sort for inspirational pieces. Each year, inventive visitors erect makeshift wind shelters made from driftwood. During summer, you'll often find kids cooling off by splashing around in the little lagoon formed by the Winchuck River just above the beach (wear shoes, though, to avoid being cut by shells or other debris).

Winchuck State Recreation Site is little more than a large gravel parking lot, a west turn off Highway 101 just past the Winchuck River bridge; from the north, the turnoff is 0.2 miles south of Oceanview Drive

Crissey Field Beach. Photo by John Shewey

○ Crissey Field Beach *(continued)*

(there are no signs). From the west end of the parking lot, a trail leads down to the beach. On the south side of the river, sprawling Crissey Field State Recreation Site, is home to the Oregon Welcome Center, well worth a visit. For a short time in the 1950s and early 1960s, Crissey Field was an airstrip serving the local area; its name comes from the then-landowner, William L. Crissey.

As is often the case with geographical names, this one comes with an interesting and locally significant backstory: the southern Curry County coast is known as the Easter lily capital of the world, and the beautiful white flowers can be seen growing in many fields around the area, their propagation an important local industry. Bill Crissey was one of several pioneers in the southwest Oregon lily bulb industry, having moved to Brookings from Portland in 1928. By the following year, he employed as many as 30 men and women planting white calla lilies and white narcissus. Soon after, Crissey specialized initially in what was called the estate lily, working from bulbs obtained from fellow lily growing pioneer Sidney Croft; according to the *Curry Coastal*

Pilot (May 9, 2001), "Soon the fame of these lilies spread and the growers received so many orders they were unable to fill them."

Crissey's lily farm occupied the land that is now Crissey Field State Recreation Site. The flower-loving Crissey was also the catalyst in the creation of Azalea State Park in Brookings. Prior to moving to Brookings, Crissey, beginning around 1916, had run his "W.L. Crissey Gladiolus Farm" (aka W.L. Crissey Alpine Gardens) located on 40 acres above the Sandy River near Boring, southeast of Portland. The farm became a local attraction, drawing substantial crowds on Sundays. In the Flower Grower, July, 1920, he advertised, "Thousands of bulbs are busy perfecting themselves to delight gardeners all over the United States next summer with 'Torches of Beauty.' My catalog for 1921 will be unusual in several respects...its offerings will include the choicest Gladiolas known..."

Crissey had been working in advertising in Portland, but fell in love with the plot of land, and hustled up the funds to buy his 40 acres. He lived to age 99, born in 1878 and passing away in Clackamas in 1977.

Looking south into California from Crissey Field Beach. Photo by John Shewey

Birding & Blues Festival (Pacific City, late April/early May): Guided field trips, birding hikes, all-day tours, nightly blues concerts, and lectures and presentations. For birders of all experience levels. Information: www.birdingandblues.org

Nehalem Bay Crab Derby (Rockaway Beach, early June): crabbing, tagged crabs for cash and prizes, vendors, activities for children, live music; proceeds benefit local/regional charities. Information: Kelly's Brighton Marina, www.kellysbrightonmarina.com.

Cannon Beach Sandcastle Contest (mid-June): sand sculpture competitions, parade, live music, beach bonfire. Information: Cannon Beach Chamber of Commerce, www.cannonbeach.org.

Rockaway Beach Kite Festival (late May): professional and amateur kite fliers, giant kites, education and information, classes for kids, competitions, live music, vendors, artists. Information: www.rockawaybeach.net/events/kite-festival.

Rockaway Beach Pirate & Costume Festival (Rockaway Beach, late June): Pirate festival and treasure hunt in downtown Rockaway Beach for all ages-- pirate music, roving pirates, festival rides, foods and drinks, vendors selling exotic wares, musical acts, performances, scavenger hunt, and games. Information: www.rockawaybeach.net.

Seaside Beach Run (mid-July): 5K and 10K beach runs, timed and non-timed 5K walks, free Kid's Sand Dash, treasure hunt for children under 12. Information: www.seasidebeachrun.org.

Seaside Beach Volleyball Tournament (second weekend in August): world's largest amateur beach volleyball tournament with competition for all ages and ability levels. Information: www.seasidechamber.com.

Cape Kiwanda Longboard Classic (Pacific City, mid-September): Nearly 200 participants riding 9-foot or longer boards in 20-minute heats in a variety of age groups/divisions; beer gardens and live music. Information: www.capekiwandalongboardclassic.com.

Left: Pacific City Birds & Blues Festival. Photo courtesy of Visit Tillamook Coast Top Right: Rockaway Beach Kite Festival. Photo courtesy of Visit Tillamook Coast
Bottom Right: Cape Kiwanda Longboard Classic. Photo courtesy of Visit Tillamook Coast

Appendix: Oregon Beach Events - Central Coast

Newport Seafood & Wine Festival (Newport, late February): One of the state's biggest and oldest wine and seafood festivals, featuring more than 150 vendors. Information: www.seafoodandwine.com.

Waldport Beachcomber Days (mid-June): live music and other acts, community breakfast, parade, beach bonfire, food booths, vendors, kite flying, sand sculpting, slug races, keg toss, car show, treasure hunt. Information: www.waldport–chamber.com.

Otter Rock n Roll Youth Surf Contest & Beach Cleanup Challenge (Otter Rock, mid-June): youth surfing contest with numerous divisions held on International Surfing Day. Information: www.otterrockandroll.com.

Lincoln City Summer Kite Festival (D River Wayside, late June): kite flying demonstrations, giant kites, free kids kite-making, running of the bols, Kids and Kites Parade on the beach. Information: www.oregoncoast.org/lincoln-city-summer-kite-festival.

DuneFest (Reedsport, late July): competitive moto activities/races, sand drags, freestyle shows, night drive, live music. Information: www.dunefest.com.

Sand Master Jam at Sand Master Park (Florence, mid-July): professional and amateur sandboard competitions, sand sculpting. Information: www.sandmasterpark.com.

Taft Beach Sandcastle Contest (Taft Beach, Lincoln City, mid-August): family-friendly competitive sandcastle building competition with group/family, pairs/couples, adult, and children's divisions (professional sand artists are disqualified from winning). Information: www.oregoncoast.org/sandcastle-contest.

Oregon States Parks Sandcastle Contests (late July at Beachside State Park; mid-August at South Beach): Team and individual competitions, with a variety of prize categories. Information: Oregon State Parks, (541) 270-9794.

Great Albacore Tuna BBQ Challenge (Newport, mid-August): Professional and amateur teams compete for cash and prizes; all-you-can sample tastings of these amazing culinary creations featuring in-season fresh-caught albacore tuna right off the Newport docks. Information: www.tunabbq.com.

Lincoln City Kite Festival. Photo courtesy of Oregon Coast Visitors Association

Lincoln City Fall Kite Festival (D River Wayside, early October): kite flying demonstrations by experts, free kids kitemaking, running of the bols, and some of the most colorful "big" kites in the world. Information: www.oregoncoast.org/lincoln-city-fall-kite-festival.

Lincoln City Chowder & Brewfest (early October): Celebrate the perfect pairing of chowder and craft beer, along with live music and fun games. Presented by Mo's Restaurants. Information: www.oregoncoast.org

Finders Keepers (October through May): Find artisan-crafted glass floats on the beach from mid-October to Memorial Day; nearly 3,000 glass floats are placed along the 7 miles of public beach in Lincoln City, from the Roads End area to Siletz Bay. You find it, you keep it! Information: www.oregoncoast.org

Yachats Village Mushroom Festival (mid-October): Experience delectable wild forest mushroom cuisine, culinary markets, cooking demonstrations, wine and beer tasting, live music, informative mushroom talks, guided walks, workshops, and wild mushrooms displays. Information: www.yachats.org.

Yachats Agate Festival (mid-January): Vendors from throughout the region display and sell rough specimens and finished artistic creations of minerals, gems, crystals, and fossils; family friendly learning opportunities for all ages. www.yachatsagatefestival.com.

Sand Boarder. Photo by Lon Beale/www.sandboard.com

Left: Mo's clam chowder at the Lincoln City Chowder Festival & Brew Fest. Photo courtesy of Lincoln City Visitor and Convention Bureau
Right: Chanterelles are star attractions at the Yachats Village Mushroom Festival. Photo by bjaglin/CreativeCommons

Appendix: Oregon Beach Events - South Coast

Polar Bear Plunge (Sunset Bay State Park, January 1): New Year's dive in to the ocean—the only rule is that you must completely immerse yourself. Information: www.oregonsadventurecoast.com.

Pistol River Wave Bash (Myers Beach/Gold Beach, mid-June): Windsurfing, kite boarding, paddle boarding competitions, all part of the American Windsurfing Tour. Information: www.americanwindsurfingtour.com/pistol-river-wave-bash/.

Southern Oregon Kite Festival (Brookings. Mid-July): professional kite flyers, giant kites, free kid's kite-making, demonstrations, vendors. Information: www.southernoregonkitefestival.com.

Charleston Seafood Festival (second weekend in August): family-friendly; local seafood, beer and wine, crab races and other contests/events, live music. Information: www.oregonsadventurecoast.com.

Wave Young Salmon Barbeque (Bastendorff Beach Park, Charleston, early August): hosted by the Kiwanis Club and featuring their renowned glaze; menu includes barbecued salmon steaks, cole slaw, baked potatoes, rolls, coffee, ice cream. Information: www.facebook.com/bayareakiwanis.

Oregon Shorebird Festival (Oregon Institute of Marine Biology, Charleston, mid-September): Land-based and boating birding tours, presentations, and more. Information: www.fws.gov/refuge/Bandon_Marsh/visit/visitor_activities/shorebird_festival.html

Gold Beach Brew & Art Festival (Gold Beach, mid-September): Sample numerous microbrews, enjoy great food and live music, view classic cars, and check out the work of many artists working in a variety of media. Information: www.goldbeachbrewfest.org.

Cape Arago Whale Watching Week (Cape Arago State Park, December and March): Visit trained "Whale Watching Spoken Here" volunteers at Shore Acres State Park to learn more about migrating Gray whales. Binoculars available. Information: www.oregonstateparks.org (search for "Cape Arago").

Left: Pistol River Wave Bash. Photo by Kevin Pritchard
Top Right: Cape Arago Whale Watchers. Photo by John Shewey Bottom Right: Western sandpiper. Photo by John Shewey

393

○ Key Contacts

North Coast Visitors Bureaus and Chambers of Commerce

Astoria-Warrenton Area Chamber of Commerce, (503) 325-6311, www.travelastoria.com and www.oldoregon.com

Seaside Chamber of Commerce, (503) 738-6391, www.seasidechamber.com

Seaside Visitors Bureau, (888) 306-2326, www.seasideor.com

Cannon Beach Chamber of Commerce, (503) 436-2623, www.cannonbeach.org

Visit Tillamook Coast, (503) 842-2672, www.tillamookcoast.com

Nehalem Bay Area Chamber of Commerce, (503) 368-5100

Rockaway Beach Chamber of Commerce, (503) 335-8108, www.rockawaybeach.net

Visit Garibaldi (City of Garibaldi), www.visitgaribaldi.com

Tillamook Area Chamber of Commerce, (503) 842-7525, www.tillamookchamber.org

Pacific City–Nestucca Valley Chamber of Commerce, (888) 549-2632, www.pcnvchamber.org

Central Coast Visitors Bureaus and Chambers of Commerce

Lincoln City Chamber of Commerce, (541) 994-3070, www.lcchamber.com

Depoe Bay Chamber of Commerce, (877) 485-8348, www.depoebaychamber.org

Greater Newport Chamber of Commerce, (541) 265-8801, www.newportchamber.org

Waldport Chamber of Commerce, (541) 563-2133, www.waldport-chamber.com

Yachats Area Chamber of Commerce & Visitors Center, (541) 547-3530, www.yachats.org

Florence Area Chamber of Commerce & Visitor Center, (541) 997-3128, www.florencechamber.com

South Coast Visitors Bureaus and Chambers of Commerce

Reedsport–Winchester Bay Chamber of Commerce, (541) 271-3495, www.reedsportcc.org

Bay Area Chamber of Commerce (Coos Bay/North Bend/Charleston), (541) 266-0868, www.coosbaynorthbendcharlestonchamber.com

Coos Bay–North Bend Visitor & Convention Bureau, (541) 269-0215, www.oregonsadventurecoast.com

Bandon Chamber of Commerce, (541) 347-9616, www.bandon.com

Port Orford Chamber of Commerce, (541) 366-8319, www.portorfordchamber.com

Gold Beach Chamber of Commerce, (541) 247-0923, www.goldbeachchamber.com

Gold Beach Visitors Center, (800) 525-2334, www.goldbeach.org

Brookings-Harbor Chamber of Commerce, (800) 535-9469, www.brookingsharborchamber.com

Brookings-Harbor Visitors Center, (541) 469-3181

General Information

Oregon State Parks, (503) 872-5646, www.oregonstateparks.org

Travel Oregon (Oregon Tourism Commission), (800) 547-7842, www.traveloregon.com

Oregon Coast Visitors Association, (541) 574-2679, www.visittheoregoncoast.com

Bureau of Land Management, Coos Bay District, (541) 756-0100, www.blm.gov/or/districts/coosbay

Oregon Department of Fish and Wildlife, www.dfw.state.or.us

Astoria office, (503) 325-2462

Newport office, (541) 867-4741

Charleston office, (541) 888-5515

Brookings office, (541) 412-7364

Siuslaw National Forest, (541) 750-7000, www.fs.usda.gov/siuslaw

SOLVE (beach cleanup events), (503) 844-9571, www.solveoregon.org

Acknowledgements

Numerous photographers, friends, and agencies contributed immeasurably to this work, many providing captivating images, others offering valuable insights and information. Among them, I offer special thanks to Lynn Arave, Jim Bauer, Lon Beale, Pat Benjamins/P&L Stables, Tim Blount, Nan Devlin (Visit Tillamook Coast), Karen Hayungs, Steven J. Henrickson, Eric Johnson (Lincoln City Visitor & Convention Bureau), Michael King, Liz Kiren, Parker Knight, John Koss, Claudia Kuenkel, Mason Marsh, David McClurg, Steve Morey (www.theoutershores.com), Richard O'Neill, Dan Portman, Kevin Pritchard, Ian Sane, Reed Shipley, Barbara Sletmoe, Troy Smith, John Sparks, Pat Steeb, Steve Tolleson, Mike Yost (Newport Chamber of Commerce), Brookings Chamber of Commerce, City of Newport, Oregon Coast Visitors Association, Bureau of Land Management, U.S. Fish and Wildlife Service, U.S. Forest Service, Oregon Department of Fish and Wildlife, Oregon State Parks. In addition, I offer profound thanks to the many photographers who make their work available for commercial purposes through CreativeCommons; among them are individuals with several photos in this book: Doug Kerr, Jerry Kirkhart, Paige Hamm, Eli Duke, and Nate Angell, along with Bureau of Land Management photographers Pam Rivers, Tara Silber, and Bob Wick, and U.S. Fish and Wildlife Service photographer Roy Lowe. —John Shewey

Creative Commons Images